Google™ Web Toolkit
Solutions

Google™ Web Toolkit Solutions

More Cool & Useful Stuff

David Geary
with Rob Gordon

PRENTICE
HALL

Upper Saddle River, NJ • Boston • Indianapolis • San Francisco

New York • Toronto • Montreal • London • Munich • Paris • Madrid

Cape Town • Sydney • Tokyo • Singapore • Mexico City

Many of the designations used by manufacturers and sellers to distinguish their products are claimed as trademarks. Where those designations appear in this book, and the publisher was aware of a trademark claim, the designations have been printed with initial capital letters or in all capitals.

The authors and publisher have taken care in the preparation of this book, but make no expressed or implied warranty of any kind and assume no responsibility for errors or omissions. No liability is assumed for incidental or consequential damages in connection with or arising out of the use of the information or programs contained herein.

The publisher offers excellent discounts on this book when ordered in quantity for bulk purchases or special sales, which may include electronic versions and/or custom covers and content particular to your business, training goals, marketing focus, and branding interests. For more information, please contact:

> U.S. Corporate and Government Sales
> (800) 382-3419
> corpsales@pearsontechgroup.com

For sales outside the United States, please contact:

> International Sales
> international@pearsoned.com

 This Book Is Safari Enabled

The Safari® Enabled icon on the cover of your favorite technology book means the book is available through Safari Bookshelf. When you buy this book, you get free access to the online edition for 45 days.

Safari Bookshelf is an electronic reference library that lets you easily search thousands of technical books, find code samples, download solutions, and access technical information whenever and wherever you need it.

To gain 45-day Safari Enabled access to this book:

- Go to http://www.prenhallprofessional.com/safarienabled
- Complete the brief registration form
- Enter the coupon code 7WD3-FRHC-8IH2-41C8-LBR2

If you have difficulty registering on Safari Bookshelf or accessing the online edition, please e-mail customer-service@safaribooksonline.com.

Visit us on the Web: www.prenhallprofessional.com

Library of Congress Cataloging-in-Publication Data:

Geary, David M.

  Google Web toolkit solutions : more cool & useful stuff / David Geary with Rob Gordon.

    p. cm.

  ISBN 0-13-234481-5 (pbk. : alk. paper) 1. Ajax (Web site development technology) 2. Java (Computer program language) 3. Google. I. Gordon, Rob. II. Title.

  TK5105.8885.A52G43 2007

  006.7′6—dc22

                    2007021607

Pearson Education, Inc
Rights and Contracts Department
501 Boylston Street, Suite 900
Boston, MA 02116
Fax (617) 671 3447

ISBN-13: 978-0-13-234481-4
ISBN-10: 0-13-234481-5
Text printed in the United States on recycled paper at RR Donnelley in Crawfordsville, Indiana
First printing November 2007

Acquisitions Editor	**Proofreader**
Greg Doench	Water Crest Publishing
Development Editors	**Editorial Assistant**
Sheri Cain	Michelle Housley
Chris Zahn	**Interior Designer**
Managing Editor	Louisa Adair
Gina Kanouse	**Cover Designer**
Senior Project Editor	Chuti Prasertsith
Kristy Hart	**Senior Compositor**
Indexer	Gloria Schurick
Heather McNeill	

Contents

Foreword

The success of Ajax is a curious one. It's hard to point to a particular release, product, or article that signaled the arrival of what we now call Ajax. It seemed to have just happened. Even the article by Jesse James Garret which gave us the name Ajax, laid no claim to its invention, but instead pointed to it as a curious phenomenon worthy of a second look. And now that we're all so aware of its presence, we can't really come to any agreement on exactly what it is "Ajax" means. Listen to 20 experts speak on the subject and you'll hear no less than 22 different definitions. And if I had to summarize their opinions, I would be forced to conclude that Ajax is simultaneously the best and worst thing to happen in software in the last 15 years. Yet despite the fact that we don't know where it came from or what it is or whether it's good or not, everyone in the software industry seems eager to launch their next product with a sleek new Ajax interface. From the technologist's perspective, it doesn't seem to make sense. Browsers are limited in their capabilities, difficult to develop with, and plagued with inconsistencies. They rightly point out that from their perspectives, it looks like a pretty bad proposition.

But the beautiful thing about Ajax is that it is not being driven by the technologist alone. There is another force working to temper to the technologist's obsession with architectural beauty—it's users' ever-increasing expectation that software should simplify, not complicate, their lives. So while the technologist bemoans the browser as a crufty place to develop software, the user praises it for familiarity and comfort. It reduces all the complexities of Internet connectivity down to a few key concepts: address, link, forward, back, and search. This is the language of the Web and users are happy with this restrictive view of technology. And why shouldn't they be? In addition to being familiar to them, the added constraints have forced software developers to think more carefully about what users want. The overwhelming theme in successful Ajax development is to do what makes sense for the user, despite the technology available to you. And while this is clearly a very healthy approach that leads to innovation in application development, the price we must pay as software developers is paid in increased pain and frustration.

Increasingly as I hear about new projects there is a common chorus of "and, of course, the UI is going to be very Ajaxy." Generally, I can gauge how much progress they've made by the level of affection they still feel for the project. Those who are just beginning are thrilled with the prospect of being able to work in an area that is getting so much attention. They'll talk about the process of selecting a framework and maybe some rough descriptions of the early UI mockups. At this point, they've built a few small examples without a great deal of fuss. It is very easy to conclude at this point that the frustrations of working in a browser are exaggerated and contented by the technological conquest, they decide to treat themselves to one of those fashionable espresso drinks. A few months later, when I run into them, they're starting to be a bit more evasive about the project. They'll inevitably tell me how a few tasks that initially seemed so easy proved to be a bit more challenging. "We were planning to have this update in real time, but it just took way too long to load." I can start to detect that their faith weakening and I try to offer them words of support, but I know the test of endurance is just beginning. This is when I usually advise that they give up the espresso drinks in favor of tea. Tea provides a more sustaining and gentle dose of caffeine; coffee will betray you in your time of need. Putting the finishing touches on a good Ajax application is, most definitely, a time of need. Often though they remain optimistic that their nearing the end of the real challenges they usually laugh off the suggestion.

The real meltdown starts when projects start to answer the question: What do our users think? Most people wisely answer this question with user testing or early beta releases. Others, perhaps the same crowd that doesn't wash fruit before eating it, charge ahead with a full release confident they've anticipated the exact needs of their users. It is these people that I pity most. At this point, both sets of developers realize a few things. First, some of the decisions they made to avoid harder problems were actually bad decisions for users. Secondly, they realize that there is no testing like actual use. Now these realizations are not unique to UI's built-in Ajax. I don't know of a single successful project that has avoided this particular stop along the way. What is unique to Ajax applications is that it now becomes increasingly hard to resolve these issues because there are so many elements that seem to conspire against you.

This is usually where the browsers behavioral differences start to show up. Users are reporting that on one browser, their menus are showing up in the wrong location. On another browser the text is wrapping. On yet another browser, it all works great except after about 15 minutes of use the whole thing begins to flicker annoyingly when anything changes. Second, you find that use patterns are not exactly what you had expected and parts of the UI must be changed—which would be fine, except the flexible expressiveness of Javascript that had once been so charming now seems downright offensive and rude. I have tried on numerous occasions to seamlessly refactor large JavaScript code bases and have never been pleased with the results. On top of all of these complications, one fact remains: your application must be good for users. So beyond the immediate frustrations I'm describing, the primary goal of maximizing user experience still remains. And when you do launch your application, this is the only thing anyone will ever see. Did you make an application that serves the needs of your users?

This is Google Web Toolkit's mission in a nutshell; make it much easier for developers to confidently answer "Yes" to that question. We grew tired of attacking the headaches of Ajax development in Sisyphean manner tirelessly shoving the browsers around without ever really gaining any momentum or mechanical advantage. That approach inevitably leads to a situation where you eventually know what is good for the user, but can never quite reach it because you're effectively building a house without the luxury of a hammer. GWT makes the most of existing tools. There are some good hammers in software engineering, so it was a little bewildering to us why none could be used effectively in Ajax development. We're pretty adamant that the way to ensure that web applications continue to improve is to leverage the good engineering tools and practices that already exist. So rather than bemoaning the status quo, GWT allows you to write your Ajax code in Java, leveraging concepts and patterns that have become very familiar to UI developers; develop using proven development environments that include good code completion and refactoring tools like Eclipse; debug your apps by running them in a real browser, using a solid debugger; then use a compiler to translate all that Java code to tiny, high-performance JavaScript that automatically works around most browser quirks without so much as a nod from the developer. And of course, make it possible to slip seamlessly into JavaScript when the need arises to do things we never even anticipated. GWT is not about trends and language wars, it's about pragmatism and sound solutions.

This is why it pleases me greatly to see that David Geary's GWT Solutions holds true to its name and focuses on concrete and practical solutions. This is very much in keeping with the spirit of GWT. It is not enough to talk about design patterns and elegance of code without following through with why such things are relevant to your users. David does a very nice job here of giving us something that goes beyond the contrived example. Each of the solutions work well on two levels. First they take us through the process of building good user interfaces in GWT making apparent the common patterns and even calling attention to many of the likely pitfalls. But secondly, each of the solutions is actually reusable in the form that he presents it. I will not be surprised to see many of his examples showing up in future GWT applications. I think readers will agree with the effectiveness of this approach. In fact, to hold the solutions to the same crucial metric that I apply to GWT itself: Will *Google Web Toolkit Solutions* aid you in creating applications that serve the needs of your users? I would have answer, Yes.

Kelly Norton, Google

Preface

There are what, six million Java developers? And the majority of those have used a desktop application framework such as Swing. I speak about Google Web Toolkit (GWT) regularly on the No Fluff Just Stuff (nofluffjuststuff.com) tour, at Java Users Groups, and at other conferences, and one of the first things I do is ask how many of the attendees have used either the Abstract Window Toolkit (AWT), Swing, or SWT. The response is always about 95 percent.

What do AWT, Swing, and SWT have to do with Google Web Toolkit? In many respects, GWT is Swing for web applications that do not require an enabling technology like Web Start. GWT lets you develop applications that run in a browser using familiar idioms from AWT, Swing, and SWT. After asking attendees if they've used Swing, AWT, or SWT, the next thing I tell them is, "For those of you who raised your hands, intuitively you already know how to use GWT." Of course, they must learn a new framework and API (and for that, they undoubtedly will need a good book), but the point is that instinctively, they already know how to implement Ajax-enabled applications that run in a browser. If you've used AWT, Swing, or SWT, and I tell you that you typically write event handlers by implementing event handler interfaces in anonymous inner classes with GWT, you know exactly what I mean. And if I tell you that GWT provides adapter classes with no-op implementations of those interfaces so you can selectively override only the methods that you are interested in, you should feel like you've finally arrived home after a long and arduous journey coaxing simple Ajax functionality out of JavaScript, HTML, CSS, and XMLHttpRequest objects. The fact that GWT is so immediately accessible to so many developers is one of its greatest selling points.

When Rob and I realized what GWT was and what it could do, we were very excited about its potential. In fact, we were so excited that we decided to write this book. I've written seven Java books over the past ten years, and it seems that no matter how many books I write, it's still a great deal of work to write another one, so I don't commit to a book unless I believe the topic has the potential to be the "next big thing." GWT was compelling enough for me to put my money on, and to spend six months of my life to get this book in your hands.

But GWT is not just about building Ajax-enabled web applications. It's about building *desktop-like applications* that run in a browser. In this book, Rob and I show you how to implement an application that lets you open multiple windows inside your browser, where each window contains a map of an address you supply to the Yahoo! Maps web service. You can drag the windows around inside the browser, resize the windows, and drag the maps around inside their windows. Not only that, but you can zoom in and out of the maps by manipulating a GWT widget that floats above the map inside the window. You can also initiate animated scrolling, very similar to Apple's animated scrolling of contact lists on the iPhone, by quickly dragging a map. When you drag the map for less than half a second, the application initiates animated scrolling of the map in the direction of the drag and at a speed relative to the amount of pixels the drag covered. That sort of functionality is simply not possible in other web application frameworks such as Struts—and yes, even Ruby on Rails—without writing a good deal of JavaScript code and integrating it into the framework.

So, GWT differentiates itself from other web application frameworks by providing support for desktop-like applications that run in a browser. It's a mistake to think of GWT as simply a web application framework with Ajax baked in. GWT, like Flash or Flex, empowers developers to implement all of the rich features you would find in a desktop application.

This book is not an introduction to GWT. If you are not familiar with GWT, we cover some basics in the first solution, but from then on out, we leave the basics behind and dive into the good stuff. We assume that you can get the basics from the web, or from other books that cover such banal ground. We want to show you the cool stuff and teach you how to kick ass with GWT. So turn that page, and let's commence with the asskicking!

Acknowledgments

Writing a book is never a solitary pursuit, and this book is no different. Many people had a hand in taking this book from conception to bookstore shelves.

First, we would like to thank Kelly Norton from Google. Kelly is a Google engineer who works on Google Web Toolkit (GWT), and his contribution to this book cannot be understated. Kelly gave us excellent review comments and insights that only a GWT engineer could have provided. He was instrumental in helping us modify our raw code samples into refined examples that illustrate best practices and take advantage of GWT nuances. In fact, many of the tips in this book are directly attributable to Kelly's comments.

We would also like to thank our other reviewers, who provided valuable feedback ranging from comments on subject matter that gave us more thorough coverage to coding suggestions that helped to increase the quality of the book's code: Henry Crutcher, Ido Green, Thad Humphries, Jeff Kurtz, Shailesh Mangal, Ted Neward, Sang Shin, and Dick Wall. We also received great comments from Robert Kuhar and the other folks at the WingDings Book Study Group.

We are also very grateful to Anthony Francavilla and Dan Moore. Anthony is CTO of Colorado Homefinder, which maintains a real estate website (www.cohomefinder.com). That website is a Struts application, implemented by Dan, with embedded GWT widgets. Anthony and Dan were gracious enough to give us the code for their mortgage calculator, which we use in the last solution of this book on integrating the GWT with legacy code.

Once again, Mary Lou Nohr was our technical editor, and as always, she not only polished our writing, but also taught us how to be better writers the next time around. It's because of Mary Lou that we now know things like: "Compound subjects modified by 'each,' 'every,' or 'many a' require a singular verb. When each follows a plural subject, the verb is plural." Thanks, Mary Lou.

Finally, we'd like to thank the folks at Prentice Hall who were instrumental in making this book a reality. Greg Doench, our Signing Editor, orchestrated the many moving pieces necessary to bring everything together; Christopher J. Zahn, Ph.D, our Development Editor, who helped us with the book layout; and Kristy Hart, Senior Project Editor, who took the book through production.

About the Authors

David Geary is the author of eight books on Java technology, including the best-selling *Graphic Java 2 Series*, *Advanced JavaServer Pages*, and *Core JavaServer Faces* (all from Prentice-Hall). David was a member of Sun's Expert Groups for the JavaServer Pages Standard Template Library (JSTL), and JavaServer Faces (JSF) 1.0. He also was the second Apache Struts committer and the inventor of the Struts Template Library, the precursor to the popular Tiles open-source framework for composing web pages from JSP fragments. David wrote questions for Sun's Web Developer Certification Exam and is the president of Clarity Training Inc., a training and consulting company focusing on server-side Java technology.

Rob Gordon is an independent consultant specializing in the design and implementation of enterprise systems. He is a former Sun developer and author of *Essential JNI* and coauthor of *Essential JMF*.

GWT Fundamentals and Beyond

Over the past few years, Java-based web application frameworks have been evolving, starting with the first generation of frameworks that included the venerable Apache Struts.

Then came a wave of second-generation frameworks, such as Tapestry and JavaServer Faces, that delivered welcome improvements such as the ability to wire input fields directly to JavaBeans component properties.[1] But the defining feature of those second-generation frameworks was their support for *components*. With components, developers could create their own components and drop them into their web pages for instant gratification.

Now comes the third wave of frameworks, led by Google Web Toolkit (GWT). Like second-generation frameworks, GWT offers components, known in GWT as widgets. But unlike second-generation frameworks, GWT is not an evolution but truly a revolution *because it totally breaks the mold for web applications.*

Unlike the frameworks that came before it, GWT is not based on classic, form-based applications, although you can certainly create those old-school applications with GWT if you choose. Instead, GWT is the first mainstream, Java-based web application framework that lets you build *desktop-like applications in a browser.* Say goodbye to web applications that are composed of archaic web pages, and say hello to applications that live in a single browser window, similar to desktop applications you may have developed with the AWT, Swing, or the SWT.

In This Book

In this book, we show you how to implement features that you may have thought would never be possible in the confines of your run-of-the-mill browser, such as the features shown in Figure 1.1: moveable, resizable windows inside your browser; scrolling viewports that support user gestures to animate scrolling, very similar to the animated scrolling found in Apple's iPhone; a Rolodex that lets you edit entries in a pop-up panel; and a drag-and-drop framework.

[1.] See http://struts.apache.org for more information about Struts and http://java.sun.com/javaee/javaserverfaces for more information about JavaServer Faces.

Our goal, however, is not to simply show you cool and useful stuff but to show you *how to implement* cool and useful stuff. For example, by showing you how to implement drag and drop, we uncover a wealth of useful GWT techniques—such as capturing events, inhibiting browser reactions to mouse events, and temporarily changing a widget's cursor—that you will undoubtedly find useful in your own applications in many contexts other than drag and drop.

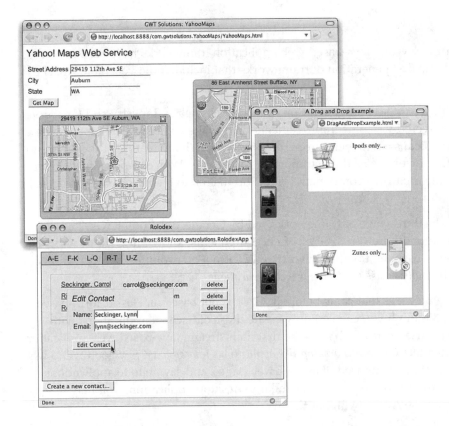

Figure 1.1   Some cool and useful stuff

This book is an unapologetic advanced treatment of GWT that shows you many useful techniques through the construction of cool and useful features.

We do not show you how to install GWT, we do not cover basics such as the differences between horizontal and vertical panels, and we *absolutely refuse to drag you through a mundane Hello World example*. If you desire those things, consult a different book or find those topics on the Web. When you are done, come back and step into the fast lane with us.

Having said that, we realize that not all our readers are well versed in GWT fundamentals, so this solution, with the aid of a robust login application, will quickly bring you up to speed on the basic tenets of GWT. Like all our solutions in this book, this one begins by listing *stuff you're going to learn* in this solution.

Is GWT Better Than Ruby on Rails?

Ruby on Rails, a web application framework implemented in the Ruby language, burst on the scene in 2005. Rails is an incredibly productive framework with Ajax goodness baked in. It also is an end-to-end solution that automatically stitches your views to a backend database. Fundamentally, however, Rails is, in many respects, a classic, form-based web application framework that employs an analog to JavaServer Pages (JSPs)—rhtml files—to create web pages.

GWT, on the other hand, other than its support for RPCs, is essentially a client-side-only framework. Unlike Rails, GWT is not a classic web application framework; instead, GWT lets you implement desktop-like applications in a browser.

So, to answer the question: If you are building classic, database-backed, form-based applications, then all other things being equal, Rails may a better choice than GWT because of its database integration. But if you want to break out of classic web applications and implement desktop-like applications that run in a browser, then GWT is tough to beat.

Stuff You're Going to Learn

This solution explores the following aspects of GWT:

If you've used GWT, you may be familiar with some of the techniques listed previously, such as composing user interfaces with GWT panels. On the other hand, you may not know that GWT, like AWT, is really a peer-based system. In this solution, we discuss the ramifications of that design and some other topics that aren't exactly fundamental, such as integrating the browser's Back button and packaging custom widgets in a reusable GWT module.

As with all the solutions in this book, feel free to pick and choose the stuff you're interested in and peruse at your leisure, or if you prefer, start at the beginning and read straight through the solution. Either way, when you are done, you will be a better GWT developer.

Introduction to GWT Widgets

Like the Abstract Window Toolkit (AWT) and Swing, GWT is based on *widgets*. To create a user interface, you instantiate widgets, add them to panels, and then add your panels to the application's root panel, which is a top-level container that contains all of the widgets in a particular view. GWT contains many widgets whose classes are described by an inheritance hierarchy. An illustration of some of those widgets is shown in Figure 1.2.

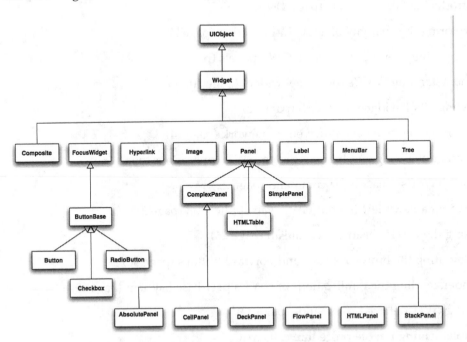

Figure 1.2   A severely truncated view of GWT widget hierarchy

GWT, out of the box, provides many more widgets than we show in Figure 1.2. Some of the commonly used widgets are listed in Table 1.1.

Table 1.1   Commonly Used GWT Widgets (all classes are from
com.google.gwt.user.client.ui)

Widget Class	Implemented Interfaces	Description
AbsolutePanel	EventListener, HasWidgets	A panel that lets you place widgets a pixel locations.
Button	EventListener, HasFocus, HasHTML, HasText, SourcesClickEvents, SourcesFocusEvents, SourcesKeyboardEvents	A button that the user can click.
CheckBox	EventListener, HasFocus, HasHTML, HasName, SourcesClickEvents, SourcesFocusEvents, SourcesKeyboardEvents	A checkbox that can be checked by users. Multiple checkboxes can be checked at the same time.
Composite	EventListener	An opaque wrapper for a set of widgets.
FlexTable	EventListener, HasWidgets, SourcesTableEvents	A flexible table that can add or remove rows, columns, and cells at runtime.
Grid	EventListener, HasWidgets, SourcesTableEvents	A table that arranges its widgets in a grid.
HorizontalPanel	EventListener, HasAlignment, HasHorizontalAlignment, HasVerticalAlignment, HasWidget, IndexedPanel	A panel that arranges its widgets horizontally.
Hyperlink	EventListener, HasHTML, HasText, SourcesClickEvents	A link that can be hooked into GWT's history mechanism.
Image	EventListener, SourcesClickEvents, SourcesLoadEvents, SourcesMouseEvents	An image that can fire load events when it loads its corresponding image file.
Label	EventListener, HasHorizontalAlignment, HasText, HasWordWrap, SourcesClickEvents, SourcesMouseEvents	Text that supports word wrap and horizontal alignment.
ListBox	EventListener, HasFocus, HasName, SourcesChangeEvents, SourcesClickEvents, SourcesFocusEvents, SourcesKeyboardEvents	A list of choices that the user can select. Can be either a list box or a drop-down list.

continues

Table 1.1   Commonly Used GWT Widgets (all classes are from
com.google.gwt.user.client.ui)   *continued*

Widget Class	Implemented Interfaces	Description
PopupPanel	EventListener, EventPreview, HasWidgets, SourcesPopupEvents	A panel that pops up when it's shown.
RadioButton	EventListener, EventPreview, HasWidgets, SourcesPopupEvents	A radio button the user can select. Radio buttons are mutually exclusive.
RootPanel	EventListener, HasWidgets	The root panel for an application that contains all other widgets.
ScrollPanel	EventListener, HasWidgets, SourcesScrollEvents	A panel that automatically adds scrollbars to itself on demand.
TabBar	EventListener, ClickListener, SourcesTabEvents	A horizontal bar that contains selectable widgets.
TextArea	EventListener, HasFocus, HasName, HasText, SourcesChangeEvents, SourcesClickEvents, SourcesFocusEvents, SourcesKeyboardEvents	A multiline text widget.
TextBox	EventListener, HasFocus, HasName, HasText, SourcesChangeEvents, SourcesClickEvents, SourcesFocusEvents, SourcesKeyboardEvents	A single-line text widget.

As evidenced by Table 1.2, GWT's widgets are based on a number of interfaces. All the widgets listed in Table 1.2 implement the EventListener interface, which allows widgets to receive low-level browser events, such as onfocus, onblur, mouse clicks, keyboard events, and so on. See the Javadocs for GWT's event class for a complete list of events. Widgets can receive one or more types of events from GWT by calling the widget's sinkEvents method. See "Sinking Events" (page 215) for more information on sinking events.

The rest of the interfaces listed in Table 1.1 have descriptive names that require little discussion; for example, buttons and labels have text, so they both implement the HasText interface. The HasName interface is implemented by widgets whose name and value may be transmitted by GWT in an HTML form request. See "Apache Commons fileUpload" (page 297) for more information about submitting HTML form requests with GWT.

Most widgets also source some type of event. Sourcing an event means that you can register listeners with the widget to receive notification of a particular type of event. For example, you can register a click listener with a button, so buttons implement the `SourcesClickEvents` interface. See "Event-Driven Programming with GWT" on page 14 for more information about sourcing, and handling, events.

Anatomy of a GWT Application

Fundamentally, GWT applications all have a directory structure similar to the one shown in Figure 1.3, which shows the files and directories for the Login Start application, which we discuss in "User Interfaces Composed with GWT Panels" on page 8.

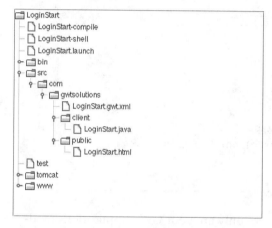

Figure 1.3   The files and directories for the login application

GWT applications start out with a single HTML page and a single Java class. Over time, your applications will undoubtedly add more Java classes, but you will rarely, if ever, add another HTML page. GWT applications run in a single HTML page that's connected by a `meta` tag to your Java class. For example, Listing 1.1 shows the HTML page for the Login Start application.

Listing 1.1   LoginStart.html

```
1.<html>
2.    <head>
3.        <title>GWT Solutions: LoginStart</title>
4.
5.        <script language='javascript'
6.          src='com.gwtsolutions.LoginStart.nocache.js'></script>
7.    </head>
8.
9.    <body></body>
10.</html>
```

When the preceding HTML page is loaded in a browser, GWT invokes the Java class specified by the meta tag to populate the HTML page. That Java class defines the application module's *entry point*, which is analogous to a classic Java application's main class.

Also, notice that the HTML page includes the GWT JavaScript file, gwt.js.

Those two ingredients—the meta tag and the gwt.js JavaScript file—transform an otherwise ordinary HTML page into a GWT application.

Besides an HTML page, GWT applications also have an XML configuration file—this is a Java-based web application, after all. That configuration file defines the application's module. Listing 1.2 lists the configuration file for the Login Start application.

Listing 1.2   LoginStart.gwt.xml

```
1.<module>
2.
3.<!— Inherit the core Web Toolkit stuff.            —>
4.<inherits name='com.google.gwt.user.User'/>
5.
6.<!— Specify the app entry point class.             —>
7.<entry-point class='com.gwtsolutions.client.LoginStart'/>
8.
9.</module>
```

Modules are an interesting GWT concept. Not only are your GWT applications modules, but they can contain other modules, which are useful for encapsulating reusable code. In "Custom Widget Packaging in GWT Modules" on page 43, we discuss encapsulating custom widgets in a module. On line 4 of preceding listing, we include the user module, which give us basic GWT capabilities.

 You Can Plug GWT Widgets into Any HTML Page
One of the most powerful aspects of GWT is that you can use a meta tag and include GWT's JavaScript from gwt.js, in *any* HTML page—even HTML pages that reside in a web application that uses another web application framework, such as Struts, JavaServer Faces, or Tapestry. That means you can incorporate GWT widgets into your legacy applications, something that we discuss in detail in Solution 12.

User Interfaces Composed with GWT Panels

This solution illustrates the techniques listed previously in "Stuff You're Going to Learn" with a login application. Ultimately, our login application makes a remote procedure call (RPC) to validate a name and password on the server, makes use of

Script.aculo.us special effects to display a pulsating error message when validation fails, and handles the browser's Back and Forward buttons, among other things.

Like a map on which sheets of acetate containing additional map information are overlaid, our login application starts simply. We then selectively add features and show you how to incorporate them in your own applications.

Figure 1.4 shows our login application in its infancy; in fact, it can hardly be called a login application at all at this point, because it merely displays the login view's widgets.

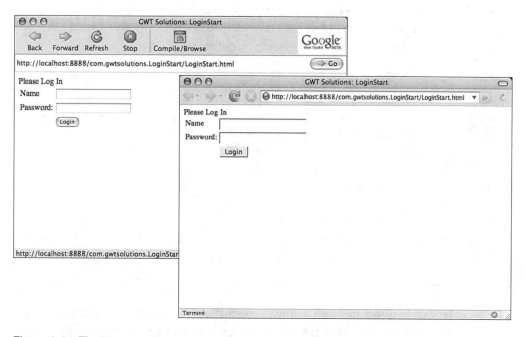

Figure 1.4   The basic login application in both hosted (left) and web (right) modes

The fledgling login application shown in Figure 1.4 is listed in Listing 1.3.

Listing 1.3   com.gwtsolutions.client.LoginStart.java

```
1.package com.gwtsolutions.client;
2.
3.import com.google.gwt.core.client.EntryPoint;
4.import com.google.gwt.user.client.ui.Button;
5.import com.google.gwt.user.client.ui.Grid;
6.import com.google.gwt.user.client.ui.Label;
7.import com.google.gwt.user.client.ui.PasswordTextBox;
8.import com.google.gwt.user.client.ui.RootPanel;
9.import com.google.gwt.user.client.ui.TextBox;
```

continues

Listing 1.3   com.gwtsolutions.client.LoginStart.java   *continued*

```
10.
11.public class LoginStart implements EntryPoint {
12.   public void onModuleLoad() {
13.      final Label loginPrompt = new Label("Please Log In");
14.      final Grid grid = new Grid(3, 2);
15.      final Label namePrompt = new Label("Name");
16.      final TextBox nameTextbox = new TextBox();
17.      final Label passwordPrompt = new Label("Password");
18.      final PasswordTextBox passwordTextbox =
19.          new PasswordTextBox();
20.      final Button button = new Button("Login");
21.
22.      grid.setWidget(0, 0, namePrompt);
23.      grid.setWidget(0, 1, nameTextbox);
24.
25.      grid.setWidget(1, 0, passwordPrompt);
26.      grid.setWidget(1, 1, passwordTextbox);
27.
28.      grid.setWidget(2, 1, button);
29.
30.      RootPanel.get().add(loginPrompt);
31.      RootPanel.get().add(grid);
32.   }
33.}
```

The preceding code illustrates how you can create a user interface with a grid containing three rows and two columns, populated with labels, text boxes, and a button. We add a label to the application's root panel and add the grid below that label. Users can enter information into the fields and click the button, but at this point clicking the button is not a very satisfying experience. We wire some event handling to the button in "Event-Driven Programming with GWT" on page 14.

Before we move on to styling widgets with CSS, it's worthwhile to briefly discuss GWT's root panel.

The Root Panel

Every GWT application has a root panel. That panel resides at the top of your application's widget containment hierarchy; for example, in the preceding example, the root panel contained a label and a grid. The grid contained the labels, textfields, and button. Ultimately, every widget was contained in the root panel.

In the preceding example, we added widgets directly to the root panel, which means that ultimately, GWT adds those widgets' DOM elements to the HTML body element of the web page in which the application resides. If you are developing a desktop-like application that runs in a browser, adding widgets directly to the root panel is the accepted practice.

On the other hand, if you have a traditional web application, perhaps implemented with a web application framework such as Struts, JavaServer Faces, or Tapestry, you can insert GWT widgets in existing HTML or JSP pages by placing those widgets in *slots*. Slots are simply named HTML elements, such as DIVs or table data elements embedded in an existing web page. In fact, because the ability to add GWT widgets to existing web applications is such an important feature of GWT, we devote an entire solution to that topic. See Solution 12 for more details.

The user.client.ui API

com.google.gwt.user.client.ui.RootPanel

- get()

  Returns a reference to an application's root panel. Applications typically have only one root panel, in which the application runs.

- add(Widget w)

  Adds a widget to the root panel. Widgets are added to the root panel from top to bottom when more than one widget is added to the root panel.

com.google.gwt.user.client.ui.Grid

- setWidget(int row, int column, Widget w)

  Adds a widget to a grid at a specific row and column location.

  Be sure to instantiate your grid with enough rows and columns; if you specify a row or column that's out of bounds, GWT throws an exception.

You Are Not Limited to a Single Root Panel

Although most GWT applications have a single root panel, in practice, you are not limited to one root panel per application. For example, if you are adding GWT widgets to an existing web application, you could have several root panels, each of which is placed in a slot—where a slot is an HTML element such as a DIV or table data element—and each root panel would anchor its own containment hierarchy of widgets.

Widget Styling with CSS Styles

Our first order of business is to make our application look better. The next iteration of our login application is shown in Figure 1.5.

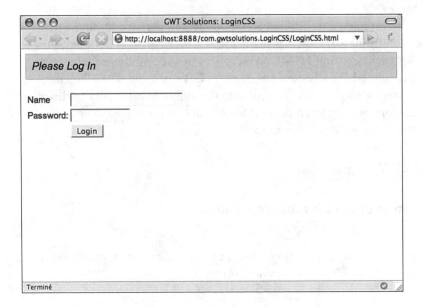

Figure 1.5   The login application with CSS styles

We achieve a more pleasing look with cascading stylesheets (CSS). Listing 1.4 shows the modifications we made to the original login application shown in Listing 1.3.

Listing 1.4   com.gwtsolutions.client.LoginCSS.java

```
1.package com.gwtsolutions.client;
2....
3.public class LoginCSS implements EntryPoint {
4.  public void onModuleLoad() {
5.    ...
6.    loginPrompt.addStyleName("loginPrompt");
7.    nameTextbox.addStyleName("nameField");
8.    passwordTextbox.addStyleName("passwordField");
9.    ...
10.  }
11.}
```

All GWT widgets can be associated with a set of CSS styles. You specify that set by calling the widget's addStyleName method, which adds the specified style to the set of styles that are applied to the widget. As you might suspect, widgets have a corresponding `removeStyleName` method that lets you selectively remove styles. We make good use of those methods in a couple of other solutions where we temporarily change a widget's cursor during an operation; for example, when we drag widgets.

We must define CSS styles before we associate them with a widget. Listing 1.5 shows the stylesheet for our application.

Listing 1.5   css/styles.css

```
1.body,td,a,div,.p{font-family:arial,sans-serif}
2.div,td{color:#000000}
3.a:link,.w,.w a:link{color:#0000cc}
4.a:visited{color:#551a8b}
5.a:active{color:#ff0000}
6.
7..loginPrompt {
8.   background: #dddddd;
9.   font-style: italic;
10.   margin-bottom: 20px;
11.   padding: 10px;
12.   font-size: 1.25em;
13.    border: thin solid #aaaaaa;
14.}
15.
16.
17..nameField {
18.    width: 15em;
19.}
20.
21..passwordField {
22.    width: 8em;
23.}
24.
```

There's nothing special about this stylesheet, which resides in a `css` directory contained in our application's `public` directory.

One more thing: We need to link the stylesheet into our application. We could do that in our application's HTML file with a `link` element, which is the norm for old-school web applications, but a more reusable solution is to include them in our application's module configuration file, which is listed in Listing 1.6.

Listing 1.6   com.gwtsolutions.client.LoginCSS.gwt.xml

```
1.<module>
2.
3.<!— Inherit the core Web Toolkit stuff.              —>
4.<inherits name='com.google.gwt.user.User'/>
5.
6.  <!— Link in the application's stylesheet            —>
7.  <stylesheet src="css/styles.css"/>
8.
9.<!— Specify the app entry point class.               —>
10.<entry-point class='com.gwtsolutions.client.LoginCSS'/>
11.
12.</module>
```

We discuss modules in more detail on page 182.

com.google.gwt.user.client.ui.UIObject

- addStyleName(String style)

  Adds a CSS style to the set of styles applied to a single GWT widget.

 You Can Set Styles in Addition to Adding Them

GWT widgets have default CSS styles. If you define those styles, GWT automatically applies them to all widgets of the corresponding type. For example, if you define a style gwt-Label, GWT automatically applies that style to all GWT labels. Default styles let you define skins for your applications.

You create default styles by invoking a widget's setStyleName method. Whereas addStyleName() adds a particular style to a widget, setStyleName() sets the default style name for a type of widget. The setStyleName method is most useful when you are developing custom widgets. See "Adding a default CSS Style Name for a Custom Widget" (page 112) for more information on custom widgets and the setStyleName method.

Event-Driven Programming with GWT

Desktop applications are typically implemented with event-driven programming. With event-driven programming, you instantiate your widgets and then attach listeners to them that react to widget events. Figure 1.6 shows our login application modified to show a window alert when a user clicks the Login button. Later on, in "Remote Procedure Call Implementation" on page 34, we show you how to implement an RPC in the button's click listener.

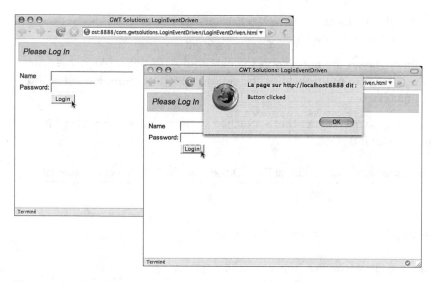

Figure 1.6   The login application with a button click listener

Listing 1.7 shows the additions we made to our login application to react to a button click.

Listing 1.7   com.gwtsolutions.client.LoginEventDriven.java

```
1.package com.gwtsolutions.client;
2....
3.import com.google.gwt.user.client.ui.ClickListener;
4....
5.public class LoginEventDriven implements EntryPoint {
6.   public void onModuleLoad() {
7.     ...
8.     Button button = new Button("Login");
9.     ...
10.
11.     button.addClickListener(new ClickListener() {
12.       public void onClick(Widget sender) {
13.         Window.alert("Button clicked");
14.       }
15.     });
16.     ...
17.   }
18.}
```

The preceding code uses an *anonymous inner class* to react to the button click. Because anonymous inner classes are succinct and because you can see what a listener does in

the same place you attach a listener to a widget, anonymous inner classes are pre-
ferred for attaching listeners to a widget.

But anonymous inner classes are not always the best choice; for example, if you want
to attach the same listener to multiple widgets, you do not want to implement identical anonymous inner classes.

Listing 1.8 shows a keyboard listener that's attached to the name and password text
boxes in our simple user interface.

Listing 1.8   com.gwtsolutions.client.LoginEventDriven.java (with External Listener Class)

```
1. package com.gwtsolutions.client;
2. ...
3. import com.google.gwt.user.client.ui.ClickListener;
4. ...
5. public class LoginEventDriven implements EntryPoint {
6.    Button button = new Button("Login");
7.
8.    public void onModuleLoad() {
9.       ...
10.      final TextBox nameTextbox = new TextBox();
11.      final PasswordTextBox passwordTextbox =
12.          new PasswordTextBox();
13.      ...
14.      SubmitListener sl = new SubmitListener();
15.      passwordTextbox.addKeyboardListener(sl);
16.      nameTextbox.addKeyboardListener(sl);
17.      ...
18.   }
19.
20.   private class SubmitListener extends KeyboardListenerAdapter {
21.      public void onKeyPress(Widget sender, char key, int mods) {
22.         if (KeyboardListener.KEY_ENTER == key)
23.            button.click();
24.      }
25.   }
26. }
```

In the preceding code, we implement a keyboard listener that clicks the Login button
when the user types the Enter key in either the name or password text boxes. We
implement a single instance of that listener on line 14 and attach it to both text boxes.

GWT provides a number of event listeners, listed in Table 1. 2.

Table 1.2   GWT Listener Interfaces (all interfaces are from
`com.google.gwt.user.client.ui`)

Listener Interface	Source Interface	Widgets That Fire Events
ChangeListener	SourcesChangeEvents	ListBox, PasswordTextBox, TextArea, TextBox, TextBoxBase
ClickListener	SourcesClickEvents	Button, ButtonBase, CheckBox, FocusPanel, Focuswidget, HTML, Hyperlink, Image, Label, ListBox, PasswordTextBox, RadioButton, TextArea, TextBox, TextBoxBase
FocusListener	SourcesFocusEvents	Button, ButtonBase, CheckBox, FocusPanel, FocusWidget, ListBox, PasswordTextBox, RadioButton, TextArea, TextBox, TextBoxBase, Tree
KeyboardListener	SourcesKeyboardEvents	Button, ButtonBase, CheckBox, FocusPanel, FocusWidget, ListBox, PasswordTextBox, RadioButton, TextArea, TextBox, TextBoxBase, Tree
Loadlistener	SourcesLoadEvents	Image
MouseListener	SourcesMouseEvents	FocusPanel, HTML, Image, Label
PopupListener	SourcesPopupEvents	DialogBox, PopupPanel
ScrollListener	SourcesScrollEvents	ScrollPanel
TabListener	SourcesTabEvents	TabBar, TabPanel
TableListener	SourcesTableEvents	FlexTable, Grid, HTMLTable
TreeListener	SourcesTreeEvents	Tree

For every event listener, GWT provides an event source; for example, there is a
`SourcesChangeEvents` interface that widgets implement when they wish to support
change listeners.

com.google.gwt.user.client.Window

- alert(String message)

  Shows a JavaScript alert with the specified message.

com.google.gwt.user.client.ui.ButtonBase

- addClickListener(ClickListener listener)

Adds a click listener to a button. All types of buttons in the GWT support click listeners.

com.google.gwt.user.client.ui.ClickListener

- onClick(Widget sender)

Handles a click on a widget. The widget passed to the method is the widget that sent the event.

Objects Accessed in Anonymous Inner Classes Must Be Final

Whenever you access an object in an anonymous inner class, that object must be declared as final.

The Login Application Has No Forms!

You may have noticed that in Listing 1.8, we do something you might take for granted in a classic web application: We programmatically click the Login button when the user presses the Enter key in a field. Why didn't GWT do that automatically for us?

Remember that our login application does not have an HTML form. As we show you in "A New 'View' in Your GWT Web Application" on page 23, GWT applications are not composed of web pages; everything runs in a single HTML page, known as the root panel of the application. Therefore, since we don't have a form, we don't get the typical submit-form-on-Enter-in-textfield behavior for HTML forms.

Can't live without HTML forms? No problem: GWT has a `FormPanel` class, which we explore in Solution 9. You may need an HTML form once in a while, for performing a file upload, for example, but for the most part, you'll be glad to break out of the form-based paradigm that HTML forces on you in classic web applications.

Internationalization and Localization

Because it compiles Java to JavaScript, GWT severely restricts the Java libraries you can use on the client. Because of that restriction, internationalization and localization is implemented differently in GWT than it is in standard Java applications.

GWT internationalization requires four steps:

- Inherit the GWT's i18n module in your application's module configuration file.

- Define a properties file with key/value pairs, as in standard Java internationalization.

- Define a Java interface whose methods all return String and have the same name as the keys in your properties file.

- Create an instance of the interface with GWT.create() and pull values out of your resource bundle by invoking methods corresponding to keys in your properties file.

Implementing the Four Steps for GWT Internationalization

The configuration file for our login application's module is listed in Listing 1.9.

Listing 1.9   src/com/gwtsolutions/LoginHistory.gwt.xml

```
1.<module>
2.
3.    <!— Inherit the core Web Toolkit stuff. —>
4.    <inherits name='com.google.gwt.user.User'/>
5.
6.    <!— Inherit internationalization support. —>
7.    <inherits name='com.google.gwt.i18n.I18N'/>
8.
9.    <!— Link in the application's stylesheet. —>
10.   <stylesheet src="css/styles.css"/>
11.
12.    <!— Specify the app entry point class. —>
13.    <entry-point class='com.gwtsolutions.client.LoginHistory'/>
14.
15.</module>
```

The properties file used in our login application is listed in Listing 1.10.

Listing 1.10   com.gwtsolutions.client.LoginConstant.properties

```
1.loginPrompt=Please log in
2.namePrompt=Name
3.passwordPrompt=Password
4.loginButtonText=Log in
5.errorMsg=Invalid name/pwd combination. Please try again.
6.welcomeMsg=Welcome to the GWT!
7.logoutLinkText=Logout...
```

The Java interface corresponding to the properties file listed in Listing 1.10 is listed in Listing 1.11.

Listing 1.11   com.gwtsolutions.client.LoginConstants.java

```
1.package com.gwtsolutions.client;
2.
3.import com.google.gwt.i18n.client.Constants;
4.
5.public interface LoginConstants extends Constants {
6.    String loginPrompt();
7.    String namePrompt();
8.    String passwordPrompt();
9.    String loginButtonText();
10.   String errorMsg();
11.   String welcomeMsg();
12.   String logoutLinkText();
13.}
```

Finally, Listing 1.12 shows how we access values in our properties file.

Listing 1.12   com.gwtsolutions.LoginI18N

```
1.package com.gwtsolutions.client;
2....
3.public class LoginI18N implements EntryPoint {
4.    private static final LoginConstants constants =
5.        (LoginConstants) GWT.create(LoginConstants.class);
6.
7.    public void onModuleLoad() {
8.        final Label loginPrompt =
9.            new Label(constants.loginPrompt());
10.       final Grid grid = new Grid(3, 2);
11.       final Label namePrompt = new Label(constants.namePrompt());
12.       final TextBox nameTextbox = new TextBox();
13.       final Label passwordPrompt =
14.           new Label(constants.passwordPrompt());
15.       final PasswordTextBox passwordTextbox =
16.           new PasswordTextBox();
17.       final Button button =
18.           new Button(constants.loginButtonText());
19.       ...
20.    }
21. }
```

Interestingly enough, we never actually implement our interface. GWT does that for us, on the fly, when we call GWT.create().

GWT's Reduced Support for Java on the Client Isn't a Huge Drawback

GWT severely restricts the Java libraries available to you on the client. You get selected classes from java.lang and java.util, and not a whole lot more. Initially, that seems like a showstopper.

But realize two things. First, you really don't need all the Java capabilities on the client to build your user interface. Second, if you need the full power of Java technology for some reason, you can make an RPC to the server, where all of Java is available to you.

com.google.gwt.core.client.GWT

- create(Class class)

  Is passed a class literal, specified with NameOfClassORInterface.class. Given that class literal, GWT.create() returns an object that implements that class.

  GWT.create() is used for accessing constants objects and for remote procedure calls. See "Remote Procedure Call Implementation" on page 34 for more information on using GWT.create() for RPCs.

Do Not Pass GWT.create() a Class Object Instead of a Class Literal

Make sure that you pass a class *literal* to GWT.create() when you are creating your constants object. If you pass a class object instead, your application may work in hosted mode, but when you move your application to an external server, your application will quit working. See Solution 11 for more information on deploying your GWT applications to an external server.

GWT's Internationalization Provides Compile-Time Type Checking

Localizing strings with GWT's internationalization provides compile-time type checking; for example, in Listing 1.12, if we had tried to access an invalid key from our resource bundle—for example, constants.nonExistentKey()—you would get a compile error. In fact, if you are using a capable IDE, such as Eclipse, NetBeans, or IDEA, such invalid keys would be flagged immediately after you typed the invalid key.

Not only do you get compile-time type checking, but GWT's localization is more efficient than Java's localization because GWT does not have to look up values in resource bundles at runtime.

Using GWT's i18nCreator Command

GWT comes with scripts to create a project and an application. It also comes with a script to create your properties file and Java interface for internationalization.

Figure 1.7 shows how we used the i18nCreator command to create our properties file and Java interface.

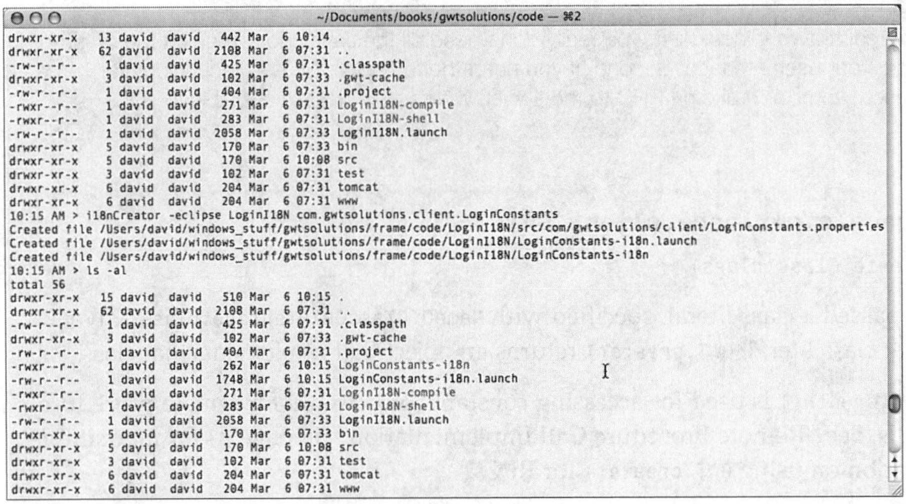

```
● ● ○                          ~/Documents/books/gwtsolutions/code — ⌘2
drwxr-xr-x  13 david  david   442 Mar  6 10:14 .
drwxr-xr-x  62 david  david  2108 Mar  6 07:31 ..
-rw-r--r--   1 david  david   425 Mar  6 07:31 .classpath
drwxr-xr-x   3 david  david   102 Mar  6 07:33 .gwt-cache
-rw-r--r--   1 david  david   404 Mar  6 07:31 .project
-rwxr--r--   1 david  david   271 Mar  6 07:31 LoginI18N-compile
-rwxr--r--   1 david  david   283 Mar  6 07:31 LoginI18N-shell
-rw-r--r--   1 david  david  2058 Mar  6 07:33 LoginI18N.launch
drwxr-xr-x   5 david  david   170 Mar  6 07:33 bin
drwxr-xr-x   5 david  david   170 Mar  6 10:08 src
drwxr-xr-x   3 david  david   102 Mar  6 07:31 test
drwxr-xr-x   6 david  david   204 Mar  6 07:31 tomcat
drwxr-xr-x   6 david  david   204 Mar  6 07:31 www
10:15 AM > i18nCreator -eclipse LoginI18N com.gwtsolutions.client.LoginConstants
Created file /Users/david/windows_stuff/gwtsolutions/frame/code/LoginI18N/src/com/gwtsolutions/client/LoginConstants.properties
Created file /Users/david/windows_stuff/gwtsolutions/frame/code/LoginI18N/LoginConstants-i18n.launch
Created file /Users/david/windows_stuff/gwtsolutions/frame/code/LoginI18N/LoginConstants-i18n
10:15 AM > ls -al
total 56
drwxr-xr-x  15 david  david   510 Mar  6 10:15 .
drwxr-xr-x  62 david  david  2108 Mar  6 07:31 ..
-rw-r--r--   1 david  david   425 Mar  6 07:31 .classpath
drwxr-xr-x   3 david  david   102 Mar  6 07:33 .gwt-cache
-rw-r--r--   1 david  david   404 Mar  6 07:31 .project
-rwxr--r--   1 david  david   262 Mar  6 10:15 LoginConstants-i18n
-rw-r--r--   1 david  david  1748 Mar  6 10:15 LoginConstants-i18n.launch
-rwxr--r--   1 david  david   271 Mar  6 07:31 LoginI18N-compile
-rwxr--r--   1 david  david   283 Mar  6 07:31 LoginI18N-shell
-rw-r--r--   1 david  david  2058 Mar  6 07:33 LoginI18N.launch
drwxr-xr-x   5 david  david   170 Mar  6 07:33 bin
drwxr-xr-x   5 david  david   170 Mar  6 10:08 src
drwxr-xr-x   3 david  david   102 Mar  6 07:31 test
drwxr-xr-x   6 david  david   204 Mar  6 07:31 tomcat
drwxr-xr-x   6 david  david   204 Mar  6 07:31 www
```

Figure 1.7   Using the i18nCreator command

In addition to creating your properties file and Java interface, the i18nCreator command also creates another command, [Interface name]-i18n, that you can use to update your Java interface when you change your properties file. Figure 1.8 shows the use of the LoginConstants-i18n script for our login application. After we ran i18nCreator to create our properties file, Java interface, and LoginConstants-i18n command, we added key/value pairs to our properties file and ran LoginConstants-i18n, which updated our Java interface with method declarations that matched the keys in our properties file.

```
000                    ~/Documents/books/gwtsolutions/code/LoginI18N — ⌘2
10:16 AM > cat src/com/gwtsolutions/client/LoginConstants.properties
loginPrompt=Please log in
namePrompt=Name
passwordPrompt=Password
loginButtonText=Log in
errorMsg=Invalid name/pwd combination. Please try again.
welcomeMsg=Welcome to the GWT!
logoutLinkText=Logout...10:16 AM >
10:16 AM > LoginConstants-i18n
10:17 AM > ls -al src/com/gwtsolutions/client/LoginConstants.java
-rw-r--r--   1 david  david  1353 Mar  6 10:17 src/com/gwtsolutions/client/LoginConstants.java
10:17 AM > cat src/com/gwtsolutions/client/LoginConstants.java
package com.gwtsolutions.client;


/**
 * Interface to represent the constants contained in resource  bundle:     I
 *      '/Users/david/windows_stuff/gwtsolutions/frame/code/LoginI18N/src/com/gwtsolutions/client/LoginConstants.properties'.
 */
public interface LoginConstants extends com.google.gwt.i18n.client.Constants {

  /**
   * Translated "Logout...".
   *
   * @return translated "Logout..."
   * @gwt.key logoutLinkText
   */
  String logoutLinkText();

  /**
   * Translated "Name".
   *
   * @return translated "Name"
   * @gwt.key namePrompt
   */
  String namePrompt();
```

Figure 1.8   Using the script generated by the i18nCreator command

The i18nCreator command makes it easy to keep your Java interface in sync with your properties file.

 You Can Create Messages in Addition to Constants

With standard Java internationalization, you can use a message format object to inject values into a string; for example, you can have this string in a properties file: {0} is not a valid username. Then you can inject a value into the {0} in that string to customize the message for a particular input field in your user interface.

GWT also supports messages; instead of extending Constants in your Java interface, as we did in Listing 1.11 on page 20, you can extend Messages. The i18nCreator command comes with built-in support for messages in addition to constants. See the GWT online documentation for more information.

A New "View" in Your GWT Web Application

If your background is strictly web development, you may wonder how you load a new page, or view, in your GWT application; for example, how do you navigate from the login view to a welcome view? The answer is that, with GWT, you don't. Instead, you clear out the root panel and repopulate it when you want to present a new set of widgets to the user. Figure 1.9 shows how the login application clears out the root panel and repopulates it with a welcome message for a successful login.

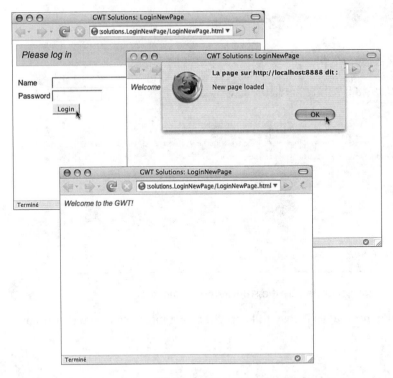

Figure 1.9   Repopulating GWT's root panel

Listing 1.13 shows the additions we made to our login application to display the welcome label after the user clicks the Login button.

Listing 1.13   com.gwtsolutions.client.LoginNewPage

```
1.package com.gwtsolutions.client;
2....
3.public class LoginNewPage implements EntryPoint {
4.   ...
5.   public void onModuleLoad() {
6.     loadLoginView();
7.   }
8.
9.   private void loadLoginView() {
10.    ...
11.    final Button button = new Button("Login");
12.
13.    button.addClickListener(new ClickListener() {
14.      public void onClick(Widget sender) {
15.        loadWelcomeView();
16.      }
```

```
17.      });
18.
19.      button.addClickListener(new ClickListener() {
20.        public void onClick(Widget sender) {
21.          Window.alert("New page loaded");
22.        }
23.      });
24.      ...
25.    }
26.
27.    private void loadWelcomeView() {
28.      final Label welcomeMsg = new Label(constants.welcomeMsg());
29.      welcomeMsg.addStyleName("welcomeMsg");
30.
31.      RootPanel.get().clear();
32.      RootPanel.get().add(welcomeMsg);
33.    }
34.}
```

In the preceding code, we left the Login button's original click listener intact and added another click listener that calls loadWelcomeView(). We left the original click listener to illustrate that you can attach multiple listeners of the same type to a single widget.

When you attach multiple listeners to a single widget, GWT calls those listeners in the order you added them to the widget. That's why the alert came up over the welcome view in Figure 1.9. If you switch the order that listeners are added to the Login button in Listing 1.13, the alert comes up over the login view before the welcome view is displayed.

The loadWelcomeView method clears the root panel and adds our welcome message to the root panel.

You might notice that we didn't include a way to log out of the application. We implement logout in the next section when we look at GWT's history mechanism.

com.google.gwt.user.client.ui.RootPanel

- clear()

  Removes all widgets from the root panel. This method is useful when you want to simulate loading a new web page.

GWT's History Mechanism

With GWT history mechanism, you can hook into the browser's Back and Forward buttons. We discuss that use of the history mechanism in "Integrating the Browser's Back Button" on page 30, but first let's see how we can use GWT history to log out of our application.

Figure 1.10 shows a modified login application that adds a Logout link to the welcome view.

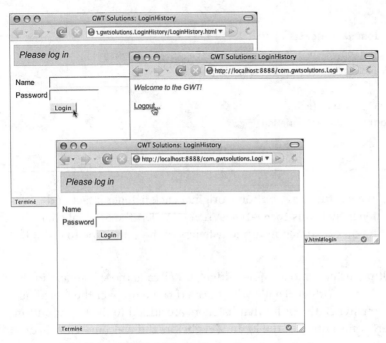

Figure 1.10   Using GWT's history mechanism to log out

The first order of business when using GWT's history mechanism is to add an HTML iframe to our application's HTML file, as shown in Listing 1.14.

Listing 1.14   src/com/gwtsolutions/public/LoginHistory.html

```
1. <html>
2.   <head>
3.     <title>GWT Solutions: LoginHistory</title>
4.     <meta name='gwt:module'
5.         content='com.gwtsolutions.LoginHistory'>
6.   </head>
7.
8.   <body>
9.     <script language="javascript" src="gwt.js"></script>
```

```
10.
11.      <!— OPTIONAL: include this if you want history support —>
12.      <iframe id="__gwt_historyFrame"
13.             style="width:0;height:0;border:0"></iframe>
14.   </body>
15.</html>
```

The iframe in the preceding listing is automatically included by GWT when the applicationCreator command is run.

Adding the History Class and History Listeners

Once our iframe is in place, we make some changes to our application, shown Listing 1.15.

Listing 1.15   com.gwtsolutions.client.LoginHistory

```
1.package com.gwtsolutions.client;
2....
3.import com.google.gwt.user.client.ui.Hyperlink;
4.import com.google.gwt.user.client.History;
5.import com.google.gwt.user.client.HistoryListener;
6.
7.public class LoginHistory implements EntryPoint,
8.    HistoryListener {
9.   ...
10.   private static final String LOGIN_STATE = "login";
11.   private static final String WELCOME_STATE = "welcome";
12.
13.   public void onModuleLoad() {
14.     setupHistory();
15.   }
16.   private void setupHistory() {
17.     History.addHistoryListener(this);
18.     History.onHistoryChanged(LOGIN_STATE);
19.   }
20.   public void onHistoryChanged(String historyToken) {
21.     if (LOGIN_STATE.equals(historyToken)) {
22.       loadLoginView();
23.     }
24.     else
25.       if (WELCOME_STATE.equals(historyToken)) {
26.         loadWelcomeView();
```

continues

Listing 1.15   com.gwtsolutions.client.LoginHistory   *continued*

```
27.        }
28.    }
29.
30.    private void loadLoginView() {
31.        ...
32.        final Button button = new Button("Login");
33.        ...
34.        RootPanel.get().clear();
35.        ...
36.        button.addClickListener(new ClickListener() {
37.            public void onClick(Widget sender) {
38.                History.onHistoryChanged(WELCOME_STATE);
39.            }
40.        });
41.        ...
42.    }
43.
44.    private void loadWelcomeView() {
45.        final Label welcomeMsg = new Label(constants.welcomeMsg());
46.
47.        welcomeMsg.addStyleName("welcomeMsg");
48.
49.        RootPanel.get().clear();
50.        RootPanel.get().add(welcomeMsg);
51.        RootPanel.get()
52.            .add(
53.                new Hyperlink(constants.logoutLinkText(),
54.                    LOGIN_STATE));
55.    }
56.}
```

There are two key players in GWT's history mechanism: the History class and history listeners. The concept is pretty simple: You implement the HistoryListener interface and register with the History class to receive history change notifications. When you are notified of those changes, GWT passes you a string representing the new history token and you modify your user interface to reflect that token.

In the preceding code, our application implements the HistoryListener interface by implementing the only method defined by that interface: onHistoryChanged() on line 20 of Listing 1.15.

When the application starts, we add the application to the `History` class's list of history listeners on line 17, and on line 18 we initialize the history state by calling `History.onHistoryChanged()`, passing it the initial state, or token, for our application—`LOGIN_STATE`. When we call `History.onHistoryChanged()` on line 18, GWT calls our listener's `onHistoryChanged` method, which starts on line 20. In that method, we react to the `LOGIN_STATE` history token by loading the widgets shown in the top picture in Figure 1.10 on page 26.

Subsequently, when the user clicks the Login button, we call `History.onHistoryChanged()`, but this time we pass the `WELCOME_STATE` token. Once again, GWT invokes our history listener's `onHistoryChanged` method starting on line 20, but this time it passes the `WELCOME_STATE` token. We react to that token by clearing out the root panel and repopulating it with the widgets you see in the middle picture in Figure 1.10.

Notice the link in the middle picture in Figure 1.10. That's the `Hyperlink` widget that we instantiated on line 53 in the preceding code. Now notice the second argument to the `Hyperlink` constructor: `LOGIN_STATE`. When the user clicks that hyperlink, GWT invokes our application's `onHistoryChanged` method and passes it the `LOGIN_STATE` token. We react to that token by reloading the widgets shown in the top picture in Figure 1.10.

---

com.google.gwt.user.client.History

- `addHistoryListener(HistoryListener historyListener)`

  Is a `static` method that adds a history listener to GWT's history mechanism. Calls to `History.onHistoryChanged()` and `History.newItem()` (both are `static` methods) result in a call to all history listeners.

- `onHistoryChanged(String historyToken)`

  Adds a new history token to GWT's history and calls all history listeners registered with the `History` class.

---

com.google.gwt.user.client.HistoryListener

- `onHistoryChanged(String historyToken)`

  Is called by GWT when the user clicks the browser's Back or Forward button or when the application programmatically calls `History.newItem()`.

Integrating the Browser's Back Button

As we showed in the preceding section, you can hook into GWT's history mechanism to react to state changes in your application. But GWT's history mechanism adds one more vital feature: the capability to hook into the browser's Back and Forward buttons.

With one small change to the application listed in Listing 1.15, we can get history change notifications from the browser itself when users click the Back or Forward button, or alternatively, if they use keyboard shortcuts to do the same thing.

Listing 1.16 shows our updated application.

Listing 1.16   com.gwtsolutions.client.LoginHistory

```
1.package com.gwtsolutions.client;
2....
3.public class LoginHistory implements EntryPoint,
4.     HistoryListener {
5.   ...
6.   private void loadLoginView() {
7.     ...
8.     final Button button = new Button("Login");
9.     ...
10.    RootPanel.get().clear();
11.    ...
12.    button.addClickListener(new ClickListener() {
13.      public void onClick(Widget sender) {
14.        History.newItem(WELCOME_STATE);
15.      }
16.    });
17.    ...
18.  }
19.}
```

On line 14 of the preceding listing, we changed our call to `History.onHistoryChanged()` to `History.newItem()`. The `newItem` method is just like `onHistoryChanged` except that it hooks into the browser's history mechanism. With that one change, we can now use the browser's Back and Forward buttons to move between the two views in our application, as shown in Figure 1.11 (notice the cursor over the browser's Back and Forward buttons).

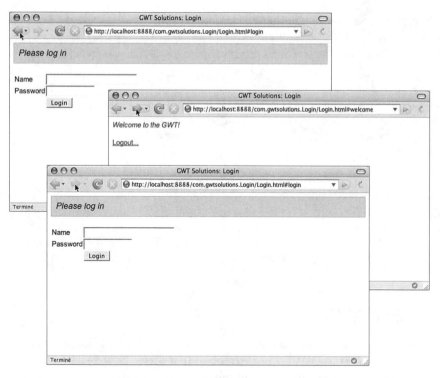

Figure 1.11   Controlling the browser's back and forward buttons

com.google.gwt.user.client.History

* newItem(String historyToken)

Hooks into the browser's history. That means users can subsequently click the browser's Back and Forward buttons to navigate after calling this method.

ℹ️ The Browser's Back Button

Users can wreak havoc in web applications when they use the browser's Back and Forward buttons instead of sticking to the web application's mechanisms for changing state. Over the years, web application developers have found it difficult to deal with the Back and Forward buttons. GWT solves the problem nicely with a natural solution that integrates those buttons into your application.

GWT's History Mechanism Accounts for Bookmarks, Too

Notice the address bars in the screenshots in Figure 1.11. When you use `History.newItem` to set the history token, GWT appends the history token to the URL for the page you are on.

For instance, in the preceding example, when you are on the login page, the URL is http://localhost:8888/com.gwtsolutions.Login/Login.html#login, and when you are on the welcome page, the URL is http://localhost:8888/com.gwtsolutions.Login/Login.html#welcome. By adding history tokens to URLs, GWT supports bookmarks in addition to the Back and Forward buttons.

History and Login Views

In the preceding example, we showed you how to use GWT's history mechanism to hook into the browser's history mechanism. However, that example was purely for illustrative purposes. In a real application, you probably wouldn't want a user to use the Back and Forward buttons to move between a login page and the first page of the application.

GWT's Peers: DOM Elements

Java's first user interface framework was the Abstract Window Toolkit,[2] known as the AWT. Java folklore has it that the AWT was developed in a scant six weeks by a handful of developers at Sun Microsystems. Developing a user interface toolkit in so few man-hours was possible because the AWT was a *peer-based* system, meaning that widgets were wired to operating-system-specific controls. Because of that peer-based implementation, Sun's developers could take advantage of already existing functionality to quickly implement a user interface toolkit.

GWT is also a peer-based system, except that its peers are Document Object Model (DOM) elements. It's important to understand that the GWT widgets ultimately represent DOM elements, as we see repeatedly throughout this book.

Use of Deferred Commands to Give Widgets Keyboard Focus

When you instantiate a GWT widget, such as a `Button` or `TextBox`, the widget's DOM element is not attached to the DOM tree until you add your widget to another widget.

During the time your widget exists but its DOM element is not attached to the DOM tree, certain widget method calls do not work. For example, if you try to give focus to a `TextBox` by calling its `setFocus` method before the text box's DOM element has been created, the call to `setFocus` does not stick.

[2.] See Geary, *Graphic Java AWT*, Sun Microsystems Press, 2001.

To work around this widget/DOM element mismatch, you can use *deferred commands*. You create a deferred command, and the GWT defers its execution until it has handled all events on the current event stack. Figure 1.12 shows our login application as it initially appears. Notice that the Name text box initially has focus.

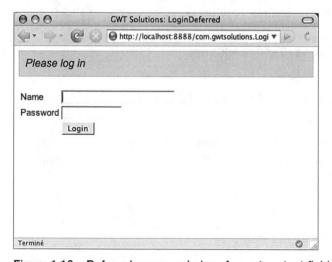

Figure 1.12   Deferred command gives focus to a text field when the application starts

Listing 1.17 shows how we give focus to the Name text box with a deferred command.

Listing 1.17   com.gwtsolutions.client.LoginDeferred

```
1.package com.gwtsolutions.client;
2....
3.import com.google.gwt.user.client.Command;
4.import com.google.gwt.user.client.DeferredCommand;
5....
6.public class LoginDeferred implements EntryPoint,
7.    HistoryListener {
8.    ...
9.  private void loadLoginView() {
10.     ...
11.     final TextBox nameTextbox = new TextBox();
12.     ...
13.     DeferredCommand.addCommand(new Command() {
14.       public void execute() {
15.         nameTextbox.setFocus(true);
16.       }
17.     });
18.  }
19.  ...
20.}
```

If you remove the deferred command from the preceding listing and just call `nameTexbox.setFocus(true)` directly, the `Name` text box will not have focus when the application starts because, at the time the call was made to `setFocus`, the text box's underlying DOM element was not attached to the DOM tree. Wrapping that `setFocus` call in a deferred command defers execution of the `setFocus` method until the text box's DOM element has been added to the DOM tree, and therefore the call to `setFocus` sticks.

com.google.gwt.user.client.DeferredCommand

- add(Command command)

  Is a `static` method that is called to add a command to GWT's list of deferred commands.

  GWT executes deferred commands after all events on the current event stack have been handled. This method is useful for deferring calls to widgets until they are visible.

com.google.gwt.user.client.Command

- execute()

  Is called by GWT when the command is executed.

Active Events Can Interfere with Calls Made in an Event Handler

In the preceding example, we used a deferred command to give focus to a widget whose DOM element had not yet been added to the DOM tree.

Another place where you will need deferred commands is in some event handlers. For example, if you try to give a widget focus inside a click listener, that mouse click will interfere with the call to `setFocus`. You call `setFocus(true)` in the click listener, but GWT is not done handling that mouse click, and therefore invalidates your call to `setFocus()`. The solution, once again, is to place the call to `setFocus()` in a deferred command so that the `setFocus` call is made after GWT has completely handled the mouse click.

Remote Procedure Call Implementation

In "Is GWT Better Than Ruby on Rails?" on page 3, we said that GWT is primarily a client-side application framework. Unlike Struts, JavaServer Faces, Tapestry, or Rails, GWT doesn't provide event handling on the server; instead, nearly all events are handled on the client in the browser.

But in a nontrivial web application, you will undoubtedly have to do some work on the server. For example, you might want to access a database, upload files, or as we do in our login application, validate some data.

Fortunately, GWT affords excellent support for making remote procedure calls (RPCs) from the client to the server. The GWT takes care of marshalling data and passing it over the wire from client to server, and vice versa.

Implementing an RPC with the GWT is a five-step process:

- Create a remote service interface.

- Create a corresponding asynchronous interface.

- Build a remote servlet that implements the remote service interface.

- Declare the remote service in the application's configuration file.

- Instantiate an instance of the asynchronous interface and use it to make an RPC call.

Figure 1.13 shows our login application making an RPC to validate the name and password that the user entered. The top two pictures in Figure 1.13 show the result of an invalid name/password combination, and the bottom two pictures illustrate a valid name/password combination.

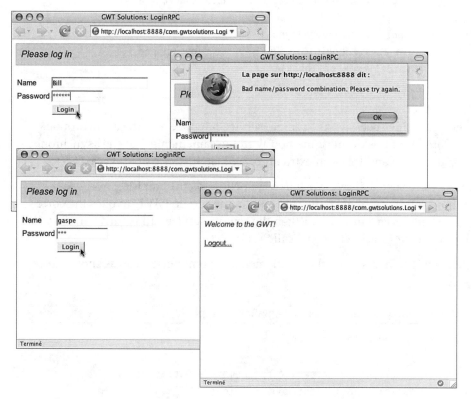

Figure 1.13   Invoking an RPC call

First, we define a remote service interface in Listing 1.18.

Listing 1.18   com.gwtsolutions.client.LoginService

```
1.package com.gwtsolutions.client;
2.
3.import com.google.gwt.user.client.rpc.RemoteService;
4.
5.public interface LoginService extends RemoteService {
6.   public boolean isValidLogin(String username, String pwd);
7.}
```

Next, we define a corresponding asynchronous interface in Listing 1.19.

Listing 1.19   com.gwtsolutions.client.LoginServiceAsync

```
1.package com.gwtsolutions.client;
2.
3.import com.google.gwt.user.client.rpc.AsyncCallback;
4.
5.public interface LoginServiceAsync {
6.   public void isValidLogin(String username, String pwd,
7.        AsyncCallback callback);
8.}
```

Notice the similarities between the remote service interface and the asynchronous interface. Both interfaces define a method with the same name, but the asynchronous method returns void and takes an extra argument, an instance of AsyncCallback.

The two interfaces listed above work in conjunction to effect an RPC. You use the asynchronous interface to make the call, and on the server, GWT invokes the corresponding remote service interface. When the remote service call is finished, the GWT calls a method in your asynchronous callback object.

Finally, we implement a servlet that implements the remote service, as shown in Listing 1.20.

Listing 1.20   com.gwtsolutions.server.LoginServiceImpl

```
1.package com.gwtsolutions.server;
2.
3.import com.google.gwt.user.server.rpc.RemoteServiceServlet;
4.import com.gwtsolutions.client.LoginService;
5.
6.public class LoginServiceImpl extends RemoteServiceServlet
7.                    implements LoginService {
```

```
8.   private static final long serialVersionUID = 1L;
9.   private static final String VALID_USERNAME = "Gaspe";
10.  private static final String VALID_PWD = "gwt";
11.
12.  public LoginServiceImpl() { // must have
13.  }
14.
15.  public boolean isValidLogin(String name, String pwd) {
16.     return VALID_USERNAME.equals(name)
17.                && VALID_PWD.equals(pwd);
18.  }
19.}
```

Our servlet is pretty simple. The isValidLogin method checks against a single valid name/password combination and returns true if the name and password it is passed are valid; otherwise, it returns false.

Listing 1.20 is the implementation of our RPC on the server. Listing 1.21 shows how we use that RPC on the client.

Listing 1.21   com.gwtsolutions.client.LoginRPC

```
1.package com.gwtsolutions.client;
2....
3.import com.google.gwt.user.client.rpc.AsyncCallback;
4.import com.google.gwt.user.client.rpc.ServiceDefTarget;
5.
6.public class LoginRPC implements EntryPoint,
7.   HistoryListener {
8.   ...
9.   private void loadLoginView() {
10.     ...
11.     final Button button = new Button("Login");
12.
13.     button.addClickListener(new ClickListener() {
14.       public void onClick(Widget sender) {
15.         LoginServiceAsync ls =
16.             (LoginServiceAsync) GWT.create(LoginService.class);
17.         ServiceDefTarget target = (ServiceDefTarget) ls;
18.         target.setServiceEntryPoint(GWT.getModuleBaseURL()
19.             + "/loginService");
20.
21.         ls.isValidLogin(nameTextbox.getText(), passwordTextbox
22.             .getText(), new AsyncCallback() {
```

continues

Listing 1.21   com.gwtsolutions.client.LoginRPC   *continued*

```
23.            public void onSuccess(Object result) {
24.                if (true == ((Boolean) result).booleanValue()) {
25.                    History.newItem(WELCOME_STATE);
26.                }
27.                else {
28.                    Window.alert("Bad name/password combination. " +
29.                        "Please try again.");
30.                }
31.            }
32.            public void onFailure(Throwable caught) {
33.                Window.alert("rpc call failed: "
34.                    + caught.getMessage());
35.            }
36.        });
37.    }
38.  });
39.
40.    ...
41.  }
42.}
```

As we did for internationalization in "Internationalization and Localization" on page 18, we call GWT.create(), only this time we pass it the class literal for our *remote service interface*. Given that class literal, GWT returns an object that implements our *asynchronous* interface. The object that GWT returns from GWT.create() also implements GWT's ServiceDefTarget interface. That interface defines one method—setServiceEntryPoint()—which defines the mapping to our remote servlet. We call that method on line 18.

Once we've told our remote service the name of our servlet mapping, we call the RPC on line 21. We invoke the asynchronous interface's isValidLogin method, passing the name, password, and an implementation of AsyncCallback. That callback has two methods—onSuccess() and onFailure()—that GWT calls in response to the RPC. If the call succeeds, GWT calls onSuccess(); if it fails, GWT calls onFailure().

Notice that GWT passes the onSuccess method of our asynchronous callback the result of the RPC, which is either true or false, depending on the validity of the name/password combination the RPC was passed. We react to that result either by loading the welcome view or by displaying an alert, as shown in Figure 1.13 on page 35.

The only thing left to do is to map the service entry point, specified on line 18 in the preceding listing, to our remote servlet class. We do that in our application's module configuration file, which is listed in Listing 1.22.

Listing 1.22   src/com/gwtsolutions/LoginRPC.gwt.xml

```
1.<module>
2.
3.    <!— Inherit the core Web Toolkit stuff. —>
4.    <inherits name='com.google.gwt.user.User'/>
5.
6.    <!— Inherit internationalization support. —>
7.    <inherits name='com.google.gwt.i18n.I18N'/>
8.
9.    <!— Link in the application's stylesheet —>
10.   <stylesheet src="css/styles.css"/>
11.
12.   <!— Specify the mapping to the remote service servlet —>
13.   <servlet path="/loginService"
14.           class="com.gwtsolutions.server.LoginServiceImpl"/>
15.
16.   <!— Specify the app entry point class. —>
17.   <entry-point class='com.gwtsolutions.client.LoginRPC'/>
18.
19.</module>
```

---

com.google.gwt.user.client.rpc.ServiceDefTaget

● setServiceEntryPoint(String entryPoint)

Sets the entry point for a remote procedure call. The entry point is the mapping to a remote servlet. That mapping is specified in a module configuration file for applications running in hosted mode, and is specified in a deployment descriptor for applications deployed to an external server.

com.google.gwt.user.client.rpc.AsyncCallback

● onSuccess(Object result)

Is called by GWT in response to a successful RPC. The result object is the result of the RPC.

That result can be a primitive type (like int) or a corresponding object wrapper (like Integer), a String or Date, or a serializable user-defined type. You can also pass arrays of any of the preceding types. Note that serializable user-defined types are GWT serializable, meaning they implement GWT's isSerializable interface.

Solution 1: GWT Fundamentals and Beyond

- onFailure(Throwable throwable)

  Is called by GWT in response to a failed RPC.

  Remote procedure calls can fail for many reasons; for example, network problems. When an RPC fails, GWT passes the onFailure method a throwable that contains information about why the RPC failed.

You Must Implement a No-Argument Constructor in Your Remote Servlet

Even if it does nothing, as is the case in Listing 1.20 on page 36, you must implement a no-argument constructor in your remote servlet. If you neglect to implement a no-argument constructor, GWT throws an exception when you make your remote procedure call.

GWT Does Not Support Synchronous RPCs

If you've implemented Ajax by hand, using the XMLHttpRequest object, you know that you can implement either an asynchronous request or a synchronous request. In practice, you should never implement *synchronous Ajax requests because synchronous requests lock up the browser during the Ajax call*. Because of that drawback to synchronous Ajax calls, GWT does not support synchronous remote procedure calls.

Custom Widget Use

In Listing 1.21 on page 37, we displayed a window alert in response to a bad name/password combination. In this section, we use a custom widget to embed an error message in the application's root panel, as shown in Figure 1.14.

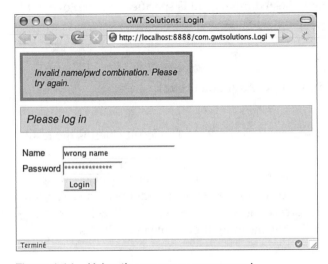

Figure 1.14   Using the message component

The error message shown in Figure 1.14 is encapsulated in a custom widget. That widget is part of the GWT Solutions widget library that we implemented for this book. See "Custom Widget Packaging in GWT Modules" on page 43 for more details about that library.

Although Figure 1.14 doesn't show it, the message component has a special twist: It pulsates to get the user's attention. We discuss that component in detail in "A Low-Level Custom Widget" (page 95), but if you're curious, we show the pulsating effect in "A Low-Level Custom Widget," (page 95). For now, our goal is simply to show you how to use a custom widget, meaning a widget that does not come with GWT.

Listing 1.23 shows how the login application uses the message component.

Listing 1.23   com.gwtsolutions.client.Login.java

```
1.package com.gwtsolutions.client;
2.
3....
4.import com.gwtsolutions.components.client.ui.Message;
5.
6.public class Login implements EntryPoint, HistoryListener {
7.   ...
8.   private final Message message =
9.      new Message(constants.errorMsg(), Message.PULSATE, 0.75);
10.  ...
11.  private void loadLoginView() {
12.     ...
13.    button.addClickListener(new ClickListener() {
14.      public void onClick(Widget sender) {
15.         ...
16.        ls.isValidLogin(nameTextbox.getText(), passwordTextbox
17.            .getText(), new AsyncCallback() {
18.          public void onSuccess(Object result) {
19.            if (true == ((Boolean) result).booleanValue()) {
20.              History.onHistoryChanged(WELCOME_STATE);
21.            }
22.            else {
23.              message.setVisible(true);
24.            }
25.          }
26.          public void onFailure(Throwable caught) {
27.            Window.alert("rpc call failed: "
28.                + caught.getMessage());
29.          }
30.        });
```

continues

Listing 1.23   com.gwtsolutions.client.Login.java   *continued*

```
31.        }
32.    });
33.    ...
34.    message.setVisible(false);
35.    ...
36.  }
37.  ...
38.}
```

On line 4, we import the widget, and on line 8, we instantiate an instance of the widget. On line 34, we initially set the widget's visibility to `false`, and subsequently, in response to a `false` result from our RPC, we set the widget's visibility to `true` on line 23. The component itself takes care of the pulsating effect.

We package the GWT Solutions widgets in a JAR file that you can incorporate into your application. For the import on line 4 to work, we must have that JAR file on our classpath. In Figure 1.15, we add the `Components` JAR file to our login application in Eclipse.

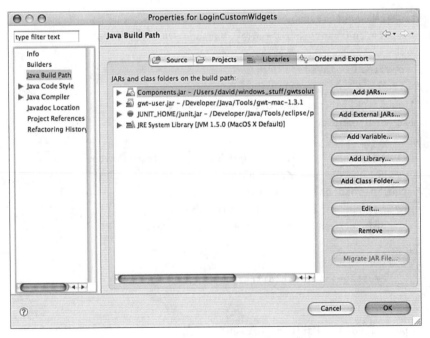

Figure 1.15   Adding the Components JAR to your build path

Our GWT Solutions widgets are packaged in a GWT module, so in addition to adding the widgets JAR file to our application's build path, we also need to inherit that module in our application's module configuration file, which is listed in Listing 1.24.

Listing 1.24   com/gwtsolutions/public/Login.gwt.xml

```
1.<module>
2.
3.    <!— Inherit the core Web Toolkit stuff. —>
4.    <inherits name='com.google.gwt.user.User'/>
5.    <inherits name="com.google.gwt.i18n.I18N"/>
6.    <inherits name='com.gwtsolutions.components.Components'/>
7.
8.    <stylesheet src="css/styles.css"/>
9.
10.    <!— Specify the app entry point class. —>
11.    <entry-point class='com.gwtsolutions.client.Login'/>
12.    <servlet path="/loginService"
13.            class="com.gwtsolutions.server.LoginServiceImpl"/>
14.</module>
```

---

com.google.gwt.user.client.ui.UIObject

- setVisible(boolean visible)

Sets a widget's visibility. If you pass true to this method, GWT makes your widget visible, provided that its corresponding DOM element is currently attached to the DOM tree. If you pass false to this method, GWT hides the widget.

Custom Widget Packaging in GWT Modules

This book comes with a fair number of custom widgets that we developed while we were writing the book. To emphasize that GWT widgets are comparable to components in other web application frameworks like JavaServer Faces and Tapestry, we put our widgets in a module named Components. Figure 1.16 shows a high-level view of the directory structure for our module, in addition to a couple of key files.

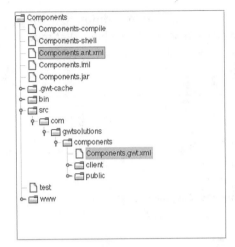

Figure 1.16   The Components module's files and directories

You've probably used GWT's `projectCreator` script to create an Eclipse project for your GWT applications, but you can also use `projectCreator` with the `-ant` option. That option creates an Ant build file, which in turn creates a JAR file to package your project as a JAR file that you can distribute. The `-ant` option is just the ticket to package our custom widgets and share them with you. It's also your ticket to package your own custom widgets and share them with whomever you desire.

The Ant build file created with `projectCreator` with the `-ant` option is listed in Listing 1.25.

Listing 1.25   Components.ant.xml

```
1.<?xml version="1.0" encoding="utf-8" ?>
2.<project name="Components" default="package" basedir=".">
3.
4.   <description>
5.     Components build file.  This is used to package up
6.     your project as a jar if you want to distribute it.
7.     This isn't needed for normal operation.
8.   </description>
9.
10.   <!— set classpath —>
11.   <path id="project.class.path">
12.      <pathelement path="${java.class.path}/"/>
13.      <pathelement
14.path="/Developer/Java/Tools/gwt-mac-1.3.1/gwt-user.jar"/>
15.      <!— Additional dependencies (such as junit) go here —>
16.   </path>
```

```
17.
18.  <target name="compile" description="Compile src to bin">
19.    <mkdir dir="bin"/>
20.    <javac srcdir="src:test" destdir="bin" includes="**"
21.              debug="on"
22.        debuglevel="lines,vars,source"
23.            source="1.4">
24.      <classpath refid="project.class.path"/>
25.    </javac>
26.  </target>
27.
28.  <target name="package" depends="compile"
29.    description="Package up the project as a jar">
30.      <jar destfile="Components.jar">
31.        <fileset dir="bin">
32.          <include name="**/*.class"/>
33.        </fileset>
34.        <!— Get everything; source, modules, html files —>
35.        <fileset dir="src">
36.          <include name="**"/>
37.        </fileset>
38.        <fileset dir="test">
39.          <include name="**"/>
40.        </fileset>
41.      </jar>
42.  </target>
43.
44.  <target name="clean">
45.    <!— Delete the bin directory tree —>
46.    <delete file="Components.jar"/>
47.    <delete>
48.      <fileset dir="bin" includes="**/*.class"/>
49.    </delete>
50.  </target>
51.
52.  <target name="all" depends="package"/>
53.
54.</project>
```

When we make changes to our module, we run Ant, like this:

```
ant -buildfile Components.ant.xml clean package
```

That Ant command creates a new JAR file containing all of our widgets.

The projectCreator command, as usual, also creates a module configuration file. The configuration file for our Components module is listed in Listing 1.26.

Listing 1.26   com/gwtsolutions/components/Components.gwt.xml

```
1.<module>
2.
3.  <!— Inherit the core Web Toolkit stuff.                —>
4.  <inherits name='com.google.gwt.user.User'/>
5.  <inherits name='com.google.gwt.xml.XML' />
6.  <inherits name='com.google.gwt.i18n.I18N' />
7.  <inherits name='com.google.gwt.http.HTTP' />
8.  <inherits name='com.google.gwt.json.JSON' />
9.
10.  <script src="javascript/prototype.js">
11.     if ($wnd.$) {
12.        return true;
13.     }
14.     else {
15.        return false;
16.     }
17.  </script>
18.
19.  <script src="javascript/effects.js">
20.     if ($wnd.Effect) {
21.        return true;
22.     }
23.     else {
24.        return false;
25.     }
26.  </script>
27.
28.</module>
```

If you've implemented any GWT applications on your own, then you've seen a module configuration file or two before. If that's the case, look at the previous listing and see if anything that's normally present in a GWT application is missing from the configuration file. Go ahead, we'll give you a minute.

There's no entry point specified in our configuration file because our module is not an application; instead, it's a collection of custom GWT widgets that you use in *your* application. Because our module does not represent an application, it has no entry

point. For the same reason, it also doesn't have a Java class that implements
`EntryPoint`.

By virtue of "Custom Widget Use" on page 40, you already know how to use our custom widgets by adding our JAR file to your classpath and by inheriting our module in your application module's configuration file. Now you know how we packaged our module for distribution, and consequently you know how to package your own custom widgets for distribution.

☆ **GWT 1.4 Will Not Require Ready Scripts for Loading JavaScript**

In Listing 1.26, we implemented what's known as ready scripts, meaning `<script>` elements that returned `true` when the JavaScript was fully loaded and returned `false` otherwise. As we went to press, the current version of the GWT was 1.3.3, but in version 1.4, you will no longer need ready scripts, so instead of this...

```
<script src="javascript/prototype.js'>
    if ($wnd.$) {
        return true;
    }
    else {
        return false;
    }
</script>
```

...you will be able to just do this instead:

```
<script src="javascript/prototype.js"/>
```

The Complete Login Application

For completeness, we list the finished login application in Listing 1.27.

Listing 1.27   com.gwtsolutions.client.Login

```
1.    package com.gwtsolutions.client;
2.
3.    import com.google.gwt.core.client.EntryPoint;
4.    import com.google.gwt.core.client.GWT;
5.    import com.google.gwt.user.client.History;
6.    import com.google.gwt.user.client.HistoryListener;
7.    import com.google.gwt.user.client.Window;
8.    import com.google.gwt.user.client.rpc.AsyncCallback;
9.    import com.google.gwt.user.client.rpc.ServiceDefTarget;
10.   import com.google.gwt.user.client.ui.Button;
11.   import com.google.gwt.user.client.ui.ClickListener;
12.   import com.google.gwt.user.client.ui.Grid;
13.   import com.google.gwt.user.client.ui.Hyperlink;
```

continues

Listing 1.27   com.gwtsolutions.client.Login   *continued*

```
14.   import com.google.gwt.user.client.ui.KeyboardListener;
15.   import com.google.gwt.user.client.ui.KeyboardListenerAdapter;
16.   import com.google.gwt.user.client.ui.Label;
17.   import com.google.gwt.user.client.ui.PasswordTextBox;
18.   import com.google.gwt.user.client.ui.RootPanel;
19.   import com.google.gwt.user.client.ui.TextBox;
20.   import com.google.gwt.user.client.ui.Widget;
21.   import com.gwtsolutions.components.client.ui.Message;
22.
23.   public class Login implements EntryPoint, HistoryListener {
24.     private static final String LOGIN_STATE = "login";
25.     private static final String WELCOME_STATE = "welcome";
26.
27.     // The error message, which is initially invisible,
28.     // at the top of the page
29.     private final Message message =
30.         new Message(constants.errorMsg(), Message.SHAKE, 10);
31.
32.     // The Please log in prompt
33.     final Label loginPrompt =
34.       new Label(constants.loginPrompt());
35.
36.     // Labels and textboxes
37.     final Label namePrompt = new Label(constants.namePrompt());
38.     final TextBox nameTextbox = new TextBox();
39.     final Label passwordPrompt =
40.         new Label(constants.passwordPrompt());
41.     final PasswordTextBox passwordTextbox =
42.         new PasswordTextBox();
43.
44.     // Login button
45.     final Button button = new Button("Login");
46.
47.     // I18N
48.     private static final LoginConstants constants =
49.         (LoginConstants) GWT.create(LoginConstants.class);
50.
51.     public void onModuleLoad() {
52.       setupHistory();
53.     }
54.     private void setupHistory() {
```

```
55.        // Add ourself to the history listener's list of listeners,
56.        // and call History.onHistoryChanged, which calls this
57.        // listener's onHistoryChanged method (below)
58.        History.addHistoryListener(this);
59.        History.onHistoryChanged(LOGIN_STATE);
60.    }
61.    public void onHistoryChanged(String historyToken) {
62.        // Load the view that corresponds to the history token
63.        if (LOGIN_STATE.equals(historyToken)) {
64.          loadLoginView();
65.        }
66.        else if (WELCOME_STATE.equals(historyToken)) {
67.          loadWelcomeView();
68.        }
69.    }
70.    private void loadLoginView() {
71.        // Load the login view by clearing the root panel and
72.        // repopulating it with a grid of components
73.        RootPanel.get().clear();
74.
75.        final Grid grid = new Grid(3, 2);
76.
77.        button.addClickListener(new ClickListener() {
78.          public void onClick(Widget sender) {
79.            // Get a reference to the asynchronous login service
80.            LoginServiceAsync ls =
81.                (LoginServiceAsync) GWT.create(LoginService.class);
82.
83.            // Set the login service's entry point
84.            ServiceDefTarget target = (ServiceDefTarget) ls;
85.            target.setServiceEntryPoint(GWT.getModuleBaseURL()
86.                + "/loginService");
87.
88.            // Disable the button to prevent the user from trying
89.            // to login before this login request is processed
90.            button.setEnabled(false);
91.
92.            String name = nameTextbox.getText();
93.            String pwd = passwordTextbox.getText();
94.
95.            // Call the RPC
96.            ls.isValidLogin(name, pwd, new AsyncCallback() {
```

continues

Listing 1.27   com.gwtsolutions.client.Login *continued*

```
97.              public void onSuccess(Object result) {
98.                // If RPC returns true, login was successful
99.                if (true == ((Boolean) result).booleanValue()) {
100.                 // Load the welcome state and hook into the
101.                 // browser's history. You could call
102.                 // History.onHistoryChanged(WELCOME_STATE)
103.                 // instead, which would also load the welcome
104.                 // state, but would not hook into the browser's
105.                 // history.
106.                 History.newItem(WELCOME_STATE);
107.               }
108.               else {
109.                 // Show the error message for a bad login
110.                 message.setVisible(true);
111.               }
112.               // Request is over, so enable the button
113.               button.setEnabled(true);
114.             }
115.              public void onFailure(Throwable caught) {
116.                Window.alert("rpc call failed: "
117.                    + caught.getMessage());
118.
119.                // Request is over, so enable the button
120.                button.setEnabled(true);
121.             }
122.           });
123.         }
124.     });
125.
126.     // SubmitListener is a private class that clicks the
127.     // Login button on an ENTER key in the corresponding
128.     // text box
129.     SubmitListener sl = new SubmitListener();
130.     passwordTextbox.addKeyboardListener(sl);
131.     nameTextbox.addKeyboardListener(sl);
132.
133.     loginPrompt.addStyleName("loginPrompt");
134.     nameTextbox.addStyleName("nameField");
135.     passwordTextbox.addStyleName("passwordField");
136.
137.     // Hide the error message initially
```

```
138.        message.setVisible(false);
139.
140.     // Populate the grid...
141.        grid.setWidget(0, 0, namePrompt);
142.        grid.setWidget(0, 1, nameTextbox);
143.
144.        grid.setWidget(1, 0, passwordPrompt);
145.        grid.setWidget(1, 1, passwordTextbox);
146.
147.        grid.setWidget(2, 1, button);
148.
149.     // Populate the root panel
150.        RootPanel.get().add(message);
151.        RootPanel.get().add(loginPrompt);
152.        RootPanel.get().add(grid);
153.
154.     // Give the name textbox focus. Prior to GWT 1.4, this
155.     // call had to be executed in a deferred command.
156.        nameTextbox.setFocus(true);
157.   }
158.   private void loadWelcomeView() {
159.        final Label welcomeMsg = new Label(constants.welcomeMsg());
160.
161.        welcomeMsg.addStyleName("welcomeMsg");
162.
163.     // Clear the root panel, and load the message and link
164.        RootPanel.get().clear();
165.        RootPanel.get().add(welcomeMsg);
166.        RootPanel.get()
167.           .add(
168.              new Hyperlink(constants.logoutLinkText(),
169.                  LOGIN_STATE));
170.   }
171.   private class SubmitListener extends KeyboardListenerAdapter {
172.     // Click the Login button when GWT detects an ENTER in
173.     // the listener's associated textbox
174.      public void onKeyPress(Widget sender, char key, int mods) {
175.        if (KeyboardListener.KEY_ENTER == key)
176.           button.click();
177.      }
178.   }
179. }
```

Stuff We Covered in This Solution

In this solution, we explored many GWT fundamentals, including event-driven programming, internationalization, and widget styling with CSS. Additionally, we covered some not-so-fundamental topics such as using deferred commands to defer calls on widgets until their DOM elements are displayed; handling the browser's Back and Forward buttons; and packaging custom widgets in a reusable module.

We used a simple, but fairly robust login application to illustrate GWT techniques. We come back to the login application briefly in Solution 2 when we discuss integrating JavaScript programs into GWT applications, and also again in Solution 3 when we discuss implementing custom GWT widgets.

For the rest of this book, we build on this fundamental base to explore many interesting corners of GWT, including scrolling viewports and drag and drop. Not only do we show you how to implement those features, but along the way we point out GWT techniques that you will find useful in the context of your own web applications.

As you can tell from this solution, you can easily implement Ajax effects with GWT. In fact, implementing Ajax is so easy and natural with GWT that you may not have noticed that we used Ajax in this solution. But when the login application's Login button is clicked, we use an RPC to validate name and password on the server, and then we update part of the DOM tree by making our error message visible for an invalid login. When we make that error message visible, the GWT does not repaint the entire application, so we have updated just a portion of the browser's DOM tree. Updating part of the DOM tree in response to information from the server is what Ajax is all about.

Notice that even though we used Ajax in this solution, we did not write a single line of JavaScript code. That's also what GWT is about: giving you the ability to implement Ajax without writing any JavaScript code. On the other hand, you might want to take advantage of the many cool JavaScript programs already developed apart from GWT, so GWT lets you integrate JavaScript programs into your GWT applications. JavaScript integration into GWT applications is the topic of the next solution.

JavaScript Integration

GWT exists so that you can easily implement rich-client applications that run in a browser with minimal knowledge of JavaScript. In fact, GWT is so effective in that regard that you can create Ajax-enabled applications without writing one line of JavaScript code, or for that matter, even knowing what Ajax stands for.

That said, however, a whole world of JavaScript goodness exists outside GWT. Ever since Jesse James Garrett[1] first coined the term Ajax, folks have been plugging away to create a universe of cool JavaScript stuff that you may very well pine for. The big guns, such as Prototype, Script.aculo.us, Rico, and Dojo, are all JavaScript frameworks that offer amenities such as special effects, Ajaxian controls, drag and drop, and behaviors. Additionally, countless JavaScript utilities, such as calendars and the like, are available on the Web. Eventually, you, your boss, or your clients, will want to mix some of that third-party JavaScript into your GWT applications. That's what this solution is all about.

Stuff You're Going to Learn

This solution explores the following aspects of GWT:

- Integrating popular JavaScript libraries in an application (page 54)

- Utilizing third-party, ad hoc JavaScript code from the Internet (page 64)

- Integrating Script.aculo.us effectively on multiple platforms (page 60)

- Accessing the `window` and `document` JavaScript objects (page 60)

- Avoiding pitfalls you may encounter when incorporating JavaScript programs (page 62)

- Importing JavaScript code from your GWT configuration file (page 63)

[1.] See http://www.adaptivepath.com/publications/essays/archives/000385.php.

Fundamentally, incorporating third-party JavaScript programs into your GWT applications is a fairly simple task. GWT ingeniously uses native Java methods to incorporate JavaScript code, but that's just the mechanics. In this solution, we show you how to implement those native methods, but we take things a step further by pointing out some best practices that you should adhere to and several pitfalls that you're likely to encounter along the way.

The Script.aculo.us JavaScript Library Integration

You may have heard of the Prototype JavaScript library, which is a spinoff from Ruby on Rails. Prototype is a collection of low-level add-ons to JavaScript that add some cool stuff from Ruby (or Smalltalk if you prefer), besides making Ajax easy to implement in JavaScript. With GWT, you don't really have much need for any of that stuff because GWT already gives you the ability to implement Ajax, without even realizing what you're doing. So why do we mention Prototype?

Prototype is the basis for a number of high-level JavaScript toolkits, such as Script.aculo.us and Rico. Script.aculo.us, in particular, contributes special effects and a set of convenient JavaScript controls, such as pulsating DIVs and lists with draggable items. For example, check out the pulsating error message shown in Figure 2.1.

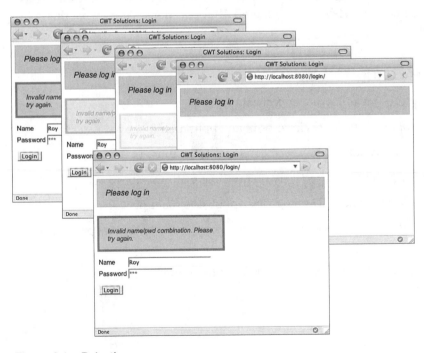

Figure 2.1   Pulsating error message

Admittedly, the pulsating effect loses something in the translation to the printed page, but it will definitely get your user's attention when they supply an incorrect username and password.

In addition to Pulsate, Script.aculo.us gives you a set of effects, such as the following:

- BlindDown/BlindUp
- Grow/Shrink
- Appear/Fade
- Highlight/Shake

For the login application we discussed in Solution #1, we use the Pulsate effect for our error message, but you can easily replace it with other Script.aculo.us effects, such as an error message that grows out of the page or shakes back and forth. Figure 2.2 shows the files and directories contained in our login application.

Figure 2.2   The login application's files and directories

In keeping with the other examples in this book, the login application is a full-fledged application, replete with an RPC that validates username and password and a welcome view that you can customize.

If your users need to log in to your application(s), feel free to take the login application and customize it as you wish. In Solution #1, we discussed various aspects of the login application, such as its use of remote procedure calls and internationalization.

We put the Prototype JavaScript file, which is `prototype.js`, and the Script.aculo.us effects file, which is `effects.js`, in our application's `public` directory. We show you two ways to incorporate those files into the application in "Importing a JavaScript File in Your HTML File" on page 61 and "Importing a JavaScript File in Your GWT Configuration File" on page 63.

In Solution #1, we also discussed the login application's use of a custom widget that wraps Script.aculo.us effects. Here, we take a step back and discuss a version of the login application that integrates Script.aculo.us effects directly, without using a custom widget. Later, in Solution #3, we discuss the implementation of the message component.

Listing 2.1 shows a version of the login application—`LoginNoComponent.java`—that directly incorporates the Script.aculo.us pulsate effect.

Listing 2.1   com.gwtsolutions.client.LoginNoComponent.java (truncated)

```
1.package com.gwtsolutions.client;
2....
3.public class LoginNoComponent implements EntryPoint,
4.    HistoryListener {
5.  ...
6.  private static final LoginConstants constants =
7.      (LoginConstants) GWT
8.          .create(LoginConstants.class);
9.
10.  public void onModuleLoad() {
11.    ...
12.  }
13.  ...
14.  private void loadLoginView() {
15.    ...
16.    final Label errorMessage = new Label();
17.    ...
18.    errorMessage.setText(constants.errorMsg());
19.    errorMessage.setVisible(false);
20.
21.    button.addClickListener(new ClickListener() {
22.      public void onClick(Widget sender) {
23.        LoginServiceAsync ls =
```

```
24.                (LoginServiceAsync) GWT.create(LoginService.class);
25.            ServiceDefTarget target = (ServiceDefTarget) ls;
26.            target.setServiceEntryPoint(GWT.getModuleBaseURL()
27.                + "/loginService");
28.
29.            button.setEnabled(false);
30.            ls.isValidLogin(nameTextbox.getText(), passwordTextbox
31.                .getText(), new AsyncCallback() {
32.              public void onSuccess(Object result) {
33.                if (true == ((Boolean) result).booleanValue()) {
34.                  History.newItem(WELCOME_STATE);
35.                }
36.                else {
37.                  errorMessage.setVisible(true);
38.                  applyEffect("Pulsate", errorMessage.getElement());
39.                }
40.                button.setEnabled(true);
41.              }
42.              public void onFailure(Throwable caught) {
43.                Window.alert("rpc call failed: "
44.                    + caught.getMessage());
45.                button.setEnabled(true);
46.              }
47.            });
48.        }
49.      });
50.      ...
51.  }
52.  private void loadWelcomeView() {
53.      ...
54.  }
55.  ...
56.  private native void applyEffect(
57.      String effect, Element element) /*-{
58.    var ne = $wnd._nativeExtensions;
59.    $wnd._nativeExtensions = false;
60.    $wnd.Effect[effect](element);
61.    $wnd._nativeExtensions = ne;
62.  }-*/;
63.}
```

The interesting parts of the preceding class, from our immediate perspective, are line 19, where we initially set the visibility of our error message `Label` to `false`, line 38, where we apply the effect, and line 56, where we start listing the `applyEffect` native method.

When the login view is first displayed, the error message is not visible: thus the call to `errorMessage.setVisible(false)` on line 19. On line 30, we invoke the RPC when the user clicks the Log In button to validate the username and password. If the RPC is successful but the result is not `true`, we know that the user entered an invalid username/password combination, so we call the native method `applyEffect`, passing the name of the effect—`Pulsate`—and the DOM element with which to apply the effect. Notice that we obtain the DOM element for the `errorMessage` widget merely by calling `errorMessage.getElement()`. As you gain more experience with GWT, you will undoubtedly run into other occasions for which you need to access a widget's DOM element, and the `getElement` method is just the ticket.

The `applyEffect` method at the end of the previous listing is where we incorporate the JavaScript to apply the effect. That method is a native method with a commented body. To the Java compiler, that method looks like this:

```
private native void applyEffect(String effect, Element);
```

The GWT compiler, on the other hand, processes the JavaScript code inside the comments. The result is that you can call `applyEffect` as you would call any Java method, and GWT executes the corresponding JavaScript code.

In the JavaScript code contained in the `applyEffect` method, we access an object named `Effect` that is attached to the JavaScript Window object. That `Effect` object is created by Script.aculo.us when you load the Script.aculo.us effects library.

Notice the syntax for native methods that implement JavaScript. The comment must be started with this sequence of characters: `/*-{` and ended with this sequence: `}-*/`. If you violate that convention, for example, by forgetting the dashes, like this...

```
// This method will not work
private native void applyEffect(String effect, Element element) /*{

    ...

}*/;
```

...your application will not load. If you are using Eclipse, you will see the error message shown in Figure 2.3, which is not very helpful. If you are using Intellij's IDEA, on the other hand, you will get a very explicit and helpful error message as shown in Figure 2.4.

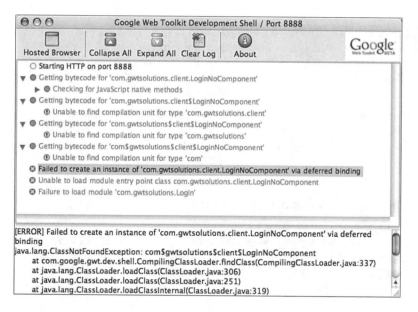

Figure 2.3   Eclipse error message

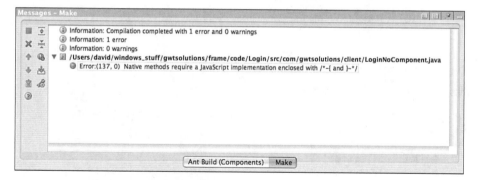

Figure 2.4   IDEA error message

> ### ☆ Disable Components During RPC Calls
>
> You may have noticed that on line 29 of Listing 2.1, we disabled the Log In button, and then we subsequently enabled it on lines 40 and 45 after a successful or failed RPC, respectively.
>
> It's often lost on developers when they are implementing applications that are developed on a fast local server, but the fact is that if users access your application from remote locations, RPCs can take significantly longer than when they are tested by developers on a local server.

continues

Users often become impatient when a request takes time, and they may try to resubmit the request again while the initial request is executing, which means they will invoke another, identical request after the initial request completes, and then they will have to wait twice as long. And, of course, during the second RPC, they may try to resubmit the request yet again, and suddenly, the user is in a precarious position.

Because of latency introduced by remote access, and because of user's impatience, you should get in the habit of disabling widgets that invoke RPCs while the RPC is executing, as we did for the `Log In` button in the preceding example.

Go Through These JavaScript Objects

For JavaScript code that you implement in native methods, you must access the Java-Script `window` object through $wnd and the `document` object through $doc. If you fail to do so for the `applyEffect()` method from the preceding example, you will get the following exception (look in the Development Shell window for that exception):

```
[ERROR] Uncaught exception escaped

com.google.gwt.core.client.JavaScriptException: JavaScript TypeError
exception: 'Effect' is undefined
```

(The exception stacktrace is truncated here for brevity.)

Integrating Script.aculo.us on the Mac

In the preceding code listing, we did this:

```
private native void applyEffect(String effect, Element element) /*-{
    var ne = $wnd._nativeExtensions;
    $wnd._nativeExtensions = false;
    $wnd.Effect[effect](element);
    $wnd._nativeExtensions = ne;
}-*/;
```

Because of an issue with Safari and iframes (the Google browser uses Safari on the Mac), you must sidestep native extensions, in effect, forcing Prototype to hand-copy the appropriate properties directly to the DOM element. On Windows, that workaround is not necessary, and you can get by with this:

```
private native void applyEffect(String effect, Element element) /*-{
    $wnd.Effect[effect](element);
}-*/;
```

It's a good idea to implement effects as we did in the first code fragment listed above so that your code is portable. Side-stepping native extensions works on all platforms.

Okay, so that's how you implement and use native methods containing JavaScript. Now let's see how you import JavaScript files into your GWT application.

com.google.gwt.user.client.ui.UIObject

- Element getElement()

Returns a Java object that represents a DOM element. The UIObject class is the superclass of the Widget class. When you pass an Element Java object to a native method that implements JavaScript, GWT transforms that Java object into a bona fide DOM element that you can access in the JavaScript code in your native method.

com.google.gwt.user.client.ui.FocusWidget

- void setEnabled(boolean enabled)

Sets the enabled state to either enabled (for a true argument) or disabled (for a false argument). It is often a good idea to disable components, such as buttons, that trigger RPCs so users cannot reissue an RPC while it is in progress.

Importing a JavaScript File in Your HTML File

You can import JavaScript into your GWT application in two ways: either in your HTML file or in your GWT configuration file. The latter is preferable, but we show you both ways. Listing 2.2 shows how you import the Script.aculo.us effects library in your HTML file.

Listing 2.2   Login.html

```
1.<html>
2.   <head>
3.      <title>GWT Solutions: Login (A Low-level Custom Widget)
4.      </title>
5.
6.      <meta name='gwt:module'
7.            content='com.gwtsolutions.Login'>
8.
9.      <script language="javascript" src="prototype.js"></script>
10.     <script language="javascript" src="effects.js"></script>
11.   </head>
12.
13.   <body>
14.      <script language="javascript" src="gwt.js"></script>
15.
16.      <!— OPTIONAL: include this if you want history support —>
```

continues

Listing 2.2   Login.html *continued*

```
17.    <iframe id="__gwt_historyFrame"
18.            style="width:0;height:0;border:0"></iframe>
19.  </body>
20.</html>
21.
```

This is pretty standard fare, using the script element to load a JavaScript file. Notice that we first load the Prototype library, which is required for Script.aculo.us, before loading the Script.aculo.us effects library.

 Give <script> Elements an Empty Body

If you use a <script> element to include JavaScript in your application's HTML file, DON'T DO THIS:

```
<script src="js/prototype.js" type="text/javascript"/>
```

Instead, DO THIS:

```
<script src="js/prototype.js" type="text/javascript"></script>
```

You must have an empty body for the <script> element or your JavaScript will not be processed. Worse yet, if you don't provide an empty body in the Yahoo! trips application, GWT does not call your application's `onModuleLoad` method, meaning the application won't work at all. That can lead to a lengthy and difficult debugging session.

 Don't Load Script.aculo.us with the Load Option

If you've used Script.aculo.us outside GWT before, you may be accustomed to doing this...

```
<script language="javascript" src="prototype.js"></script>
<script language="javascript" src="scriptaculous.js?load="effects,
controls"></script>
```

...which loads the effects.js and controls.js Script.aculo.us libraries. *That technique does not work with GWT;* you must do this:

```
<script language="javascript" src="prototype.js"></script>
<script language="javascript" src="effects.js"></script>
<script language="javascript" src="controls.js"></script>
```

You must load each Script.aculo.us library individually.

Importing JavaScript code in your HTML file is fine unless you are implementing a module that others will use. In that case, it's better to import JavaScript code in your GWT configuration file.

Importing a JavaScript File in Your GWT Configuration File

If you implement a reusable GWT module, you will want to encapsulate JavaScript importation in your GWT configuration file so that users of your module don't have to import your required JavaScript code in their HTML file. Listing 2.3 shows how you import Script.aculo.us in a GWT config file.

Listing 2.3   Login.gwt.xml

```
1.<module>
2.
3.    <!— Inherit the core Web Toolkit stuff —>
4.    <inherits name='com.google.gwt.user.User'/>
5.
6.    <!— Inherit internationalizatin support —>
7.    <inherits name="com.google.gwt.i18n.I18N"/>
8.
9.    <!— Include the application's stylesheet —>
10.   <stylesheet src="css/styles.css"/>
11.
12.   <!— Specify the app entry point class. —>
13.   <entry-point class='com.gwtsolutions.client.Login'/>
14.
15.   <!— Specify the servlet mapping for the RPC —>
16.   <servlet path="/loginService"
17.           class="com.gwtsolutions.server.LoginServiceImpl"/>
18.
19.   <!— Load JavaScript —>
20.   <script src="javascript/prototype.js">
21.     if ($wnd.$) {
22.       return true;
23.     }
24.     else {
25.       return false;
26.     }
27.   </script>
28.
29.   <script src="javascript/effects.js">
30.     if ($wnd.Effect) {
31.       return true;
32.     }
33.     else {
34.       return false;
```

continues

Listing 2.3   Login.gwt.xml *continued*

```
35.    }
36.    </script>
37.</module>
```

In the preceding configuration file, we monitor the loading of the Prototype and Script.aculo.us effects library, returning true when those libraries are fully loaded. To determine when the libraries are loaded, we check for the existence of two objects that we know are created by Prototype and Script.aculo.us: the $ function and the Effects object, respectively. GWT repeatedly invokes the config file's script elements until they return true, to ensure that the libraries are properly loaded.

 Import JavaScript Code in Your Module's Configuration File

You can choose how you import JavaScript code. You can either include it with a script element in your HTML page or you can include it in your GWT configuration file. The former is more familiar, but the latter lets you develop modules that others can use without having to manually include the JavaScript code that the module requires.

Now that we know how to load and use a JavaScript library, let's take a look at one more example that incorporates an ad hoc JavaScript from the Web.

A JavaScript Calendar Integration

As we mentioned, a great deal of JavaScript code is freely available on the Web. Figure 2.5 shows Matt Kruse's website. Matt implemented a pretty cool JavaScript pop-up calendar, and all he asks in return for its use is to mention his website. So we've gone one step better by including a screenshot of it.

We took Matt's calendar and incorporated it into a GWT application, as you can see from Figure 2.6. From top to bottom in Figure 2.6, we click the Pick a date link, which pops up the calendar, and then we select a date from the calendar, which hides the calendar and populates the selected date in the text box.

Figure 2.5   Matt Kruse's website

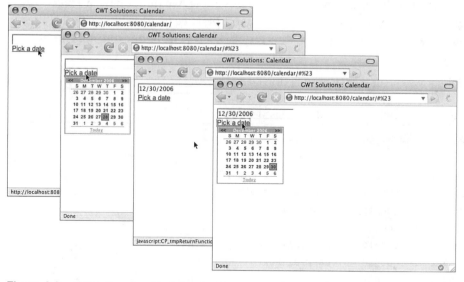

Figure 2.6   Using the JavaScript calendar

The calendar application's associated files and directories are shown in Figure 2.7.

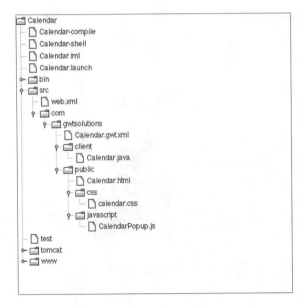

```
Calendar
  Calendar-compile
  Calendar-shell
  Calendar.iml
  Calendar.launch
  bin
  src
    web.xml
    com
      gwtsolutions
        Calendar.gwt.xml
        client
          Calendar.java
        public
          Calendar.html
          css
            calendar.css
          javascript
            CalendarPopup.js
  test
  tomcat
  www
```

Figure 2.7   The calendar application's files and directories

In the calendar application, we've placed the necessary JavaScript file in a `javascript` directory in the public directory. To keep things simple, we didn't have a `javascript` directory for the login application, but it's a good practice to add subdirectories such as `css` and `javascript` to your public directory to keep your public directory from becoming too cluttered.

Listing 2.4 shows the `Calendar` application class.

Listing 2.4   com.gwtsolutions.client.Calendar.java

```
1.  package com.gwtsolutions.client;
2.
3.  import com.google.gwt.core.client.EntryPoint;
4.  import com.google.gwt.user.client.DOM;
5.  import com.google.gwt.user.client.Element;
6.  import com.google.gwt.user.client.ui.ClickListener;
7.  import com.google.gwt.user.client.ui.Hyperlink;
8.  import com.google.gwt.user.client.ui.RootPanel;
9.  import com.google.gwt.user.client.ui.SimplePanel;
10. import com.google.gwt.user.client.ui.TextBox;
11. import com.google.gwt.user.client.ui.VerticalPanel;
12. import com.google.gwt.user.client.ui.Widget;
13.
14. public class Calendar implements EntryPoint {
15.   private static final String CALENDAR_ANCHOR ="calendarAnchor";
```

```
16.    private static final String CALENDAR_DIV = "calendarDiv";
17.
18.    public void onModuleLoad() {
19.      final TextBox dateTextBox = new TextBox();
20.
21.      // Pass an empty string to the Hyperlink's constructor
22.      // for links that don't participate in the GWT's
23.      // history mechanism
24.      final Hyperlink link = new Hyperlink("Pick a date", "");
25.      final SimplePanel panel = new SimplePanel();
26.
27.      // Set ids for the link and panel
28.      DOM.setElementProperty(link.getElement(), "id",
29.          CALENDAR_ANCHOR);
30.
31.      DOM.setElementProperty(panel.getElement(), "id",
32.          CALENDAR_DIV);
33.
34.      // Popup the calendar when the user clicks the link
35.      link.addClickListener(new ClickListener() {
36.        public void onClick(Widget widget) {
37.          popupCalendar(dateTextBox.getElement(),
38.              CALENDAR_ANCHOR, CALENDAR_DIV);
39.        }
40.      });
41.
42.      VerticalPanel verticalPanel = new VerticalPanel();
43.      verticalPanel.add(dateTextBox);
44.      verticalPanel.add(link);
45.      verticalPanel.add(panel);
46.
47.      RootPanel.get().add(verticalPanel);
48.    }
49
50.    private static native boolean popupCalendar(
51.        Element textboxElement, String calendarAnchor,
52.        String calendarDiv) /*-{
53.      var cal = new $wnd.CalendarPopup(calendarDiv);
54.      cal.setCssPrefix("gwtSolutions");
55.      cal.select(textboxElement, calendarAnchor, 'MM/dd/yyyy');
56.      return true;
57.    }-*/;
58. }
```

Once again, we've implemented a native method that encapsulates the JavaScript code to pop up Matt's calendar. Notice that we use GWT's $wnd object, as required by GWT, to access the CalendarPopup object attached to the JavaScript Window object.

The popupCalendar method invokes the CalendarPopup.select JavaScript function, which is passed an input DOM element into which the calendar places the selected date and the ID of a DOM element that represents the link used to activate the calendar.

Listing 2.5 lists the configuration file for the calendar application.

Listing 2.5   Calendar.gwt.xml

```
1.<module>
2.
3.<!— Inherit the core Web Toolkit stuff.                    —>
4.<inherits name='com.google.gwt.user.User'/>
5.
6.<!— Specify the app entry point class.                     —>
7.<entry-point class='com.gwtsolutions.client.Calendar'/>
8.
9.   <stylesheet src="css/calendar.css"/>
10.
11.   <script src="javascript/CalendarPopup.js">
12.      if ($wnd) {
13.         return true;
14.      }
15.      else {
16.         return false;
17.      }
18.   </script>
19.
20.</module>
```

In this case, we could have just as easily imported the required JavaScript file in our application's HTML file because we're not implementing a reusable module. But in general, it's a good idea to adhere to the best practice of including JavaScript in our configuration file, even though in this case there's really no advantage to doing so.

The UIObject class is the superclass of the Widget class. This method returns a Java object that represents a DOM element. When you pass an Element Java object to a native method that implements JavaScript code, GWT transforms that Java object into a bona fide DOM element that you can access in the JavaScript code in your native method.

com.google.gwt.user.client.ui.DOM

- void setElementProperty (Element element, String property, String value)

Sets the value of a given DOM element's property.

You Can Use Hyperlinks Without Hooking into GWT's History Mechanism

In "GWT's History Mechanism" (page 26), we showed you how to use a hyperlink to hook into GWT's history mechanism; all you do is create a `Hyperlink` with the `Hyperlink(String text, String historyToken)` constructor and specify the history token that you want to associate with the link.

One thing that's not documented in GWT javadocs is how you use a hyperlink without hooking into GWT's history mechanism. Sometimes, as in the preceding example, you don't want a link to participate in the history mechanism. For those situations, just pass an empty string for the history token to the `Hyperlink` constructor.

Always Include the History iframe When You Use Hyperlinks

In the preceding Tip, we showed you how to use a hyperlink without hooking into the history mechanism, but the use of such a hyperlink still fires up GWT's history mechanism, which results in warnings when you run your application.

Regardless of whether you actually hook into GWT's history mechanism, you should always include the history iframe in your application's HTML page, like this:

```
<iframe id="__gwt_historyFrame"
style="width:0;height:0;border:0"></iframe>
```

Stuff We Covered in This Solution

Incorporating JavaScript—whether it's an industrial-strength framework like Prototype or Script.aculo.us, ad hoc JavaScript code downloaded from the Web, or even a few lines of JavaScript code that you may need to make ends meet—is pretty easy to do with GWT, although there are a few pitfalls that we've taken the time to point out in this solution.

You can certainly get by without much, if any, third-party JavaScript code in your GWT applications, but you can also really jazz up your applications by mixing in a bit of JavaScript for things like special effects and custom controls. Now that you know how to incorporate JavaScript into your GWT applications, you can add a little spit and polish to an already rich-client user interface.

In the next solution—Custom Widgets—we show you how to wrap third-party JavaScript in custom GWT widgets, which is a much more reusable solution than ad hoc JavaScript additions to your application, as we illustrated in this solution.

Solution 3

Custom Widget Implementation

GWT has a very well-thought-out and complete set of widgets right out of the box. But, of course, it doesn't have everything you could possibly think of, and at some point, you're going to need a widget or two that GWT does not provide. That's where we come in.

There are three types of custom GWT widgets:

- *Composite* widgets—Composed of one or more existing widgets. For example, an autocomplete text box might be composed of a text box, list box, and a pop-up panel. Composite widgets extend GWT's Composite class.

- *Intermediate* widgets—Extensions of existing widget classes. For example, a simple window widget might be an extension of the PopupPanel class. Intermediate widgets extend subclasses of GWT's Widget class.

- *Low-level* widgets—Composed of DOM elements. For example, a message component might be composed of a DIV. Low-level widgets extend GWT's Widget class.

In this solution, we explore the composite autocomplete text box widget and low-level message widget referenced above.

In Solution 7, we discuss an intermediate custom widget, the SimpleWindow class, that extends PopupPanel. We decided to put simple window in a solution of its own because it's more complex than the two widgets discussed in this solution and it illustrates numerous GWT techniques besides custom widget implementation.

Stuff You're Going To Learn

This solution explores the following aspects of GWT:

- Building composite custom widgets (page 72)

- Implementing form completion (page 72)

- Implementing pass-through methods in a composite to make a subset of the wrapped widget's methods available to users of the composite (page 88)

- Firing change events from custom widgets (page 90)

- Implementing custom widgets that can be submitted in an HTML form (page 91)

- Implementing the `HasText` and `HasName` interfaces (page 90)

- Integrating JavaScript code into custom widgets (page 74)

- Incorporating animations into custom widgets (page 73 and page 91)

- Creating low-level custom widgets (page 95)

- Being aware of the differences between composite and low-level custom widgets, and knowing when you should prefer one or the other (page 95)

- Using the `DOM` class in low-level custom widgets (page 99)

- Setting default CSS styles for custom widgets (page 99)

- Parameterizing Script.aculo.us effects in a custom widget (page 99)

Composite Custom Widgets

For our composite custom widget, we implement an autocomplete text box that's composed of three existing widgets: a text box, a pop-up panel, and a list box. Figure 3.1 shows our autocomplete application in action.

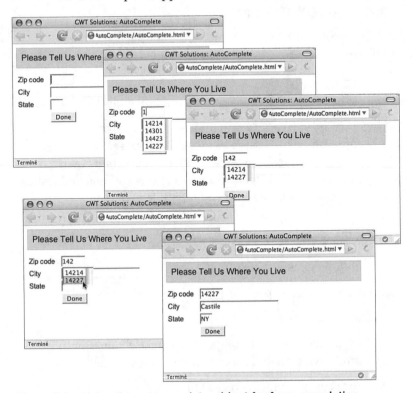

Figure 3.1   Using the autocomplete widget for form completion

The example application shown in Figure 3.1 uses classic form completion: You select a zip code and the application populates the city and state fields to match.

The autocomplete widget implements standard behavior. As a user types characters in the autocomplete widget's text box, the widget checks for matches against a list of strings that the developer provides. If there are matches for what's currently displayed in the text box, a pop-up window with a list box containing the matches appears below the text box, and as the user continues typing, the set of matches is narrowed or expanded accordingly.

At any point while typing in the text box, the user can press the down arrow key, which selects the first entry in the pop-up's list box and populates the text box with that entry. The user can subsequently use the up or down arrow key to navigate the strings in the list box and can select an item by pressing any key other than the up or down arrows. As the user selects items from the list box with the up or down arrow keys, the autocomplete widget populates the text box with the selected item. The user can also click an item in the list box to select it.

When the pop-up containing the list box first appears, we use a Script.aculo.us special effect, known as *blind down*, to make the pop-up visible, as shown in Figure 3.2.

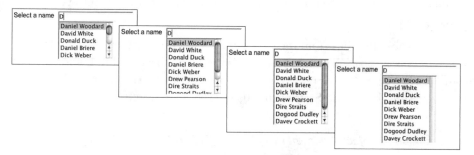

Figure 3.2   Animating the autocomplete text box's drop-down list

As we illustrated in Solution 2, integrating Script.aculo.us effects into your GWT application is straightforward. Here, we've taken that a step further by integrating an effect into a custom widget.

The autocomplete application's associated files and directories are shown in Figure 3.3.

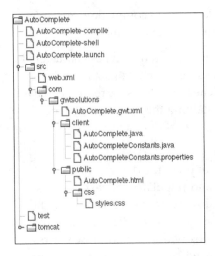

Figure 3.3   The autocomplete application's files and directories

If you look closely at Figure 3.3, you'll notice that there's an autocomplete application, but no widget. That's because we've encapsulated each of our custom widgets in a GWT module of its own so that you can easily incorporate our widgets into your own applications.

In Figure 3.4, we show the files from the Components module that are relevant to the autocomplete text box: `AutoCompleteTextBox.java`, which is discussed in Listing 3.2 on page 80; and `prototype.js` and `effects.js`, which are the JavaScript files for the Prototype JavaScript library and Script.aculo.us effects, respectively.

 Encapsulation Is Object-Oriented Programming's Fundamental Tenet

In Solution 2, we showed you how to incorporate JavaScript directly into your GWT applications. In this solution, we show you how to encapsulate JavaScript into GWT custom widgets. Encapsulating functionality in custom widgets instead of implementing them in applications is a better choice because it's more reusable. If you incorporate JavaScript directly into your application, then only your application can use that JavaScript, but if you incorporate it into a custom widget, then other developers can take advantage of that JavaScript.

New in GWT 1.4: The SuggestBox Widget

As we went to press, GWT 1.4 was released, complete with a SuggestBox widget that is functionally similar to the AutoCompleteTextBox custom widget discussed in this section. You should use the SuggestBox widget in your applications.

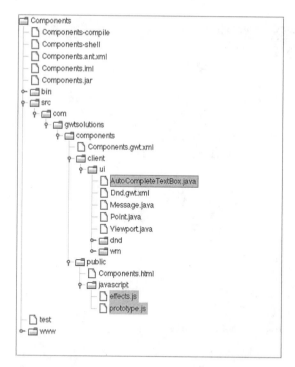

Figure 3.4   The Components module's files and directories

Listing 3.1 shows the AutoComplete application class.

| Listing 3.1   com.gwtsolutions.client.AutoComplete.java |

```
1.   package com.gwtsolutions.client;
2.
3.   import com.google.gwt.core.client.EntryPoint;
4.   import com.google.gwt.core.client.GWT;
5.   import com.google.gwt.user.client.ui.Button;
6.   import com.google.gwt.user.client.ui.ChangeListener;
7.   import com.google.gwt.user.client.ui.Grid;
8.   import com.google.gwt.user.client.ui.HasText;
9.   import com.google.gwt.user.client.ui.Label;
10.  import com.google.gwt.user.client.ui.RootPanel;
11.  import com.google.gwt.user.client.ui.TextBox;
12.  import com.google.gwt.user.client.ui.Widget;
13.  import com.gwtsolutions.components.client.ui.AutoCompleteTextBox;
14.
15.  public class AutoComplete implements EntryPoint {
16.    private static final String[] zipCodes =
17.    {
18.        "80001", "80132", "81623", "81650",
```

continues

Listing 3.1   com.gwtsolutions.client.AutoComplete.java   *continued*

```
19.         "14214", "14301", "14423", "14227"
20.     };
21.
22.     private static final String[] cities =
23.     {
24.         "Arvada", "Monument", "Carbondale", "Rifle",
25.         "Buffalo", "Niagra Falls", "Caledonia", "Castile"
26.     };
27.
28.     public void onModuleLoad() {
29.       AutoCompleteConstants constants =
30.         (AutoCompleteConstants)GWT.create
31.           (AutoCompleteConstants.class);
32.
33.       final AutoCompleteTextBox zipTextBox =
34.           new AutoCompleteTextBox() {
35.             public String[] getCompletionCandidates() {
36.               return zipCodes;
37.             }
38.           };
39.
40.       Label heading = new Label(constants.heading());
41.       Label zipLabel = new Label(constants.zipPrompt());
42.       Label cityLabel = new Label(constants.cityPrompt());
43.       Label stateLabel = new Label(constants.statePrompt());
44.       heading.setStyleName("heading");
45.
46.       final TextBox cityTextBox = new TextBox();
47.       final TextBox stateTextBox = new TextBox();
48.       stateTextBox.setVisibleLength(2);
49.
50.       Grid grid = new Grid(4, 2);
51.       grid.setWidget(0, 0, zipLabel);
52.       grid.setWidget(0, 1, zipTextBox);
53.       grid.setWidget(1, 0, cityLabel);
54.       grid.setWidget(1, 1, cityTextBox);
55.       grid.setWidget(2, 0, stateLabel);
56.       grid.setWidget(2, 1, stateTextBox);
57.       grid.setWidget(3, 1, new Button("Done"));
58.
59.       RootPanel.get().add(heading);
60.       RootPanel.get().add(grid);
```

```
61.
62.        zipTextBox.setTitle(constants.zipTooltip());
63.
64.        zipTextBox.addChangeListener(new ChangeListener() {
65.            // This change listener monitors changes to the
66.            // autocomplete widget's textbox, and reacts by
67.            // filling in the city and state textboxes
68.            public void onChange(Widget sender) {
69.                HasText ht = (HasText) sender;
70.                String zip = ht.getText();
71.                for (int i=0; i < zipCodes.length; ++i) {
72.                    if (zipCodes[i].equals(zip)) {
73.                        cityTextBox.setText(cities[i]);
74.                        if (zip.startsWith("8"))
75.                            stateTextBox.setText("CO");
76.                        else
77.                            stateTextBox.setText("NY");
78.                    }
79.                }
80.            }
81.        });
82.
83.        zipTextBox.setVisibleLength(5);
84.        zipTextBox.setFocus(true);
85.    }
86. }
```

The autocomplete widget is implemented as an abstract class with one abstract method: public String[] getCompletionCandidates(), which returns the complete set of candidate strings for autocompletion. Matching those strings against the text that currently resides in the autocomplete widget's text box is done in the autocomplete widget itself. In the preceding application, we implement the getCompletionCandidates method on line 35 to return the list of zip codes.

After we instantiate the autocomplete widget on line 33, we construct the application's simple user interface, adding labels and text boxes to a grid panel, similar to the application listed in Solution 1.

Finally, we add a change listener to the autocomplete widget on line 64. Whenever the user makes a selection from the autocomplete's list box to populate the autocomplete's text box, the autocomplete widget fires a change event to all change listeners that have registered with the listener. The application's change listener reacts to that change by populating the city and state fields that match the selected zip code.

Notice that on line 62 of the previous listing, we call `autoCompleteTextBox.setTitle()`, which doesn't really set a title, but rather sets a tooltip for the widget. That `setTitle` method is inherited from the `UIObject` class (`UIObject` is the `Widget` class's superclass). Figure 3.5 shows the tooltip in Firefox.

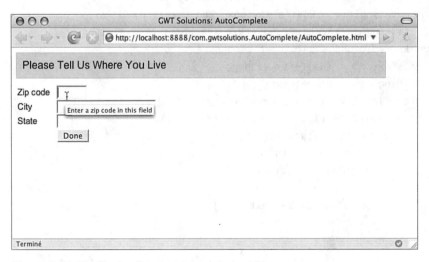

Figure 3.5   Tooltip for the autocomplete text box

com.google.gwt.user.client.ui.UIObject

• void setTitle(String tooltip)

Sets the tooltip that's displayed when the mouse cursor hovers over the associated widget.

com.google.gwt.user.client.ui.TextBox

• void setVisibleLength(int length)

Sets the size of the text box so that it displays `length` visible characters. You can get the number of visible characters with the corresponding `getVisibleLength` method. You can also set the maximum number of characters that can be typed into a text box with `setMaximumLength()`. The maximum number of characters is unrelated to the number of visible characters.

com.google.gwt.user.client.ui.ChangeListener

- void onChange(Widget sender)

Invoked by GWT when a widget's state changes.

This method is supported by widgets that fire change events by implementing the SourcesChangeEvents interface; those widgets include list boxes and text boxes. See Table 1.2 (page 17) for a complete list of widgets that implement the ChangeListener interface.

com.google.gwt.user.client.ui.HasText

- void setText(String text)

Sets a widget's text. The HasText interface is supported by numerous GWT widgets, which, not surprisingly, display text, including buttons, hyperlinks, labels, menu items, text boxes and text areas, and tree items.

- String getText()

Returns a widget's text.

Form Completion with Ajax

In the preceding example, we implemented form completion, whereby a user types a value in one field and the application responds by automatically filling in related fields.

When the application places values in the city and state fields in response to a zip code, it does not redraw the entire page; instead, it updates only a portion of the browser's document object model (DOM).

Updating a portion of the DOM in response to user input is the essence of Ajax, although for our application to truly claim Ajaxian credentials, some would argue that we must update the DOM in response to a call to the server. Either way, the effect is the same.

Now that we've seen an application that uses the autocomplete widget, let's look at Listing 3.2, which shows the code for the AutoCompleteTextBox widget.

Listing 3.2   com.gwtsolutions.components.client.ui.AutoCompleteTextBox.java

```java
1. package com.gwtsolutions.components.client.ui;
2.
3. import java.util.ArrayList;
4. import java.util.Iterator;
5.  import java.util.List;
6.
7. import com.google.gwt.user.client.DOM;
8. import com.google.gwt.user.client.Element;
9. import com.google.gwt.user.client.Event;
10.import com.google.gwt.user.client.ui.ChangeListener;
11.import com.google.gwt.user.client.ui.ChangeListenerCollection;
12.import com.google.gwt.user.client.ui.ClickListener;
13.import com.google.gwt.user.client.ui.Composite;
14.import com.google.gwt.user.client.ui.HasName;
15.import com.google.gwt.user.client.ui.HasText;
16.import com.google.gwt.user.client.ui.KeyboardListener;
17.import com.google.gwt.user.client.ui.KeyboardListenerAdapter;
18.import com.google.gwt.user.client.ui.ListBox;
19.import com.google.gwt.user.client.ui.PopupPanel;
20.import com.google.gwt.user.client.ui.SourcesChangeEvents;
21.import com.google.gwt.user.client.ui.TextBox;
22.import com.google.gwt.user.client.ui.Widget;
23.
24.abstract public class AutoCompleteTextBox extends Composite
25.    implements HasName, HasText, SourcesChangeEvents {
26.
27.   // THE THREE WIDGETS THAT REPRESENT THIS COMPOSITE
28.   private final TextBox textBox = new TextBox();
29.   private final PopupPanel popup = new PopupPanel(true);
30.   private final ListBox listBox = new ListBox() {
31.     // This extension of ListBox is necessary to work around
32.     // a bug in Safari: When you press a key in a Safari
33.     // listBox, Safari generates a click event. 8-(
34.     // To work around that bug, we disable click events
35.     // unless they are preceded by a mouse down event.
36.     //
37.     // Thanks to Kelly Norton from Google for providing
38.     // this workaround, in addition to many other comments
39.     // he made to GWT Solutions.
```

```
40.     public boolean allowClickEvent = false;
41.
42.     public void onBrowserEvent(Event event) {
43.       switch (DOM.eventGetType(event)) {
44.         case Event.ONMOUSEDOWN:
45.           // After this mouse down event, set a flag
46.           // indicating that it's okay to handle the
47.           // ensuing onClick event, if it occurs
48.           allowClickEvent = true;
49.           break;
50.         case Event.ONCLICK:
51.           // If a mouse down event did not precede this
52.           // onClick event, do not give the superclass
53.           // a chance to handle the onClick event
54.           if (!allowClickEvent) {
55.             return;
56.           }
57.           // Reset the flag for handling onClick events
58.           // to false
59.           allowClickEvent = false;
60.       }
61.       // Let the superclass handle the event
62.       super.onBrowserEvent(event);
63.     }
64.   };
65.
66.   // PRIVATE VARIABLES
67.   private final ArrayList matches = new ArrayList();
68.   private String lastTextBoxText = null;
69.   private ChangeListenerCollection listeners;
70.
71.   // This is the lone abstract methods that subclasses
72.   // must implement to be concrete classes.
73.   public abstract String[] getCompletionCandidates();
74.
75.   public AutoCompleteTextBox() {
76.     initWidget(textBox);        // set the composite's widget
77.     popup.add(listBox);         // add the list box to the popup
78.     listBox.setVisible(false);  // hide the list box
79.
80.     // Sink mouse events and onClick events for the listBox.
```

continues

```
81.      // This is part of the workaround for the Safari bug
82.      // mentioned above in the ListBox extension. This call
83.      // to sinkEvents means GWT will call the listBox's
84.      // onBrowserEvent method whenever a mouse event occurs
85.      // in the listBox.
86.      listBox.sinkEvents(Event.MOUSEEVENTS);
87.
88.      // EVENT HANDLERS
89.
90.      // Keyboard handler for the textBox
91.      textBox.addKeyboardListener(new KeyboardListenerAdapter() {
92.        public void onKeyUp(Widget sender,
93.            final char keyCode, int modifiers) {
94.          // If the listBox is not visible, or it is visible
95.          // and the key pressed was not the down key,
96.          // (re)populate the completion items
97.          if (! listBox.isVisible()
98.              ¦¦ listBox.isVisible() && keyCode != KEY_DOWN) {
99.            populateCompletionItems(textBox.getText());
100.         }
101.         // If listBox is visible and key is down arrow, give
102.         // listBox focus, select the first item in the listBox,
103.         // and copy that item to the textBox
104.         else if (listBox.isVisible() && keyCode == KEY_DOWN) {
105.           listBox.setFocus(true);
106.           listBox.setSelectedIndex(0);
107.           copyListBoxSelectedItemToTextBox();
108.         }
109.       }
110.     });
111.
112.     // Keyboard handler for the listBox
113.     listBox.addKeyboardListener(new KeyboardListenerAdapter() {
114.       public void onKeyUp(Widget sender,
115.           final char keyCode, int modifiers) {
116.         if (keyCode == KEY_DOWN ¦¦ keyCode == KEY_UP) {
117.           copyListBoxSelectedItemToTextBox();
118.         }
119.         else {
120.           // Any key other than up or down arrow finishes
121.           // autocompletion
```

```
122.              complete();
123.          }
124.       }
125.    });
126.
127.    // Click listener for the listBox
128.    listBox.addClickListener(new ClickListener() {
129.       public void onClick(Widget widget) {
130.          copyListBoxSelectedItemToTextBox();
131.          complete();
132.       }
133.    });
134. }
135.
136. // CHANGE LISTENER SUPPORT
137.
138. // Add a change listener to this autocomplete widget.
139. // This method lazily instantiates a change listener
140. // collection and adds that listener, if it's non-null,
141. // to the collection.
142. public void addChangeListener(ChangeListener listener) {
143.    if (listener == null)
144.       return;
145.
146.    if (listeners == null) {
147.       listeners = new ChangeListenerCollection();
148.    }
149.    listeners.add(listener);
150. }
151.
152. // Removes the specified change listener, assuming the
153. // listener and the listener collection are non-null
154. public void removeChangeListener(ChangeListener listener) {
155.    if (listeners == null ¦¦ listener == null) {
156.       return;
157.    }
158.    listeners.remove(listener);
159. }
160.
161. // TEXTBOX PASS-THROUGH METHODS
162.
163. public void setFocus(boolean b) {
164.    textBox.setFocus(b);
```

continues

Listing 3.2   com.gwtsolutions.components.client.ui.AutoCompleteTextBox.java   *continued*

```
165.    }
166.
167.    public void addKeyboardListener(KeyboardListener kl) {
168.       textBox.addKeyboardListener(kl);
169.    }
170.
171.    public void removeKeyboardListener(KeyboardListener kl) {
172.       textBox.removeKeyboardListener(kl);
173.    }
174.
175.    public void setVisibleLength(int length) {
176.       textBox.setVisibleLength(length);
177.    }
178.
179.    public int getVisibleLength() {
180.       return textBox.getVisibleLength();
181.    }
182.
183.      public void setText(String text) {
184.       textBox.setText(text);
185.    }
186.
187.    public String getText() {
188.       return textBox.getText();
189.    }
190.
191.    public void setName(String name) {
192.       textBox.setName(name);
193.    }
194.
195.    public String getName() {
196.       return textBox.getName();
197.    }
198.
199.    // COMPLETION METHODS
200.
201.    protected void complete() {
202.       // React to a selection from the list box by hiding the
203.       // popup and listBox, giving the textBox focus, and firing
204.       // a change event to registered change listeners
205.       popup.hide();
206.       listBox.setVisible(false);
```

```
207.     textBox.setFocus(true);
208.
209.     if (listeners != null) {
210.        listeners.fireChange(this);
211.     }
212.   }
213.
214.   private void copyListBoxSelectedItemToTextBox() {
215.     String selectedItem =
216.        listBox.getItemText(listBox.getSelectedIndex());
217.     textBox.setText(selectedItem);
218.     lastTextBoxText = selectedItem;
219.   }
220.
221.   private List getCompletionItems(String s) {
222.     // If the string passed to this method is inconsequential,
223.     // do nothing
224.     if (s == null || s.equals(""))
225.        return null;
226.
227.     // Clear out the matches
228.     matches.clear();
229.
230.     // Get completion candiates from subclasses
231.     String[] candidates = getCompletionCandidates();
232.
233.     if (candidates != null) {
234.        // Add completion candidates that match the string
235.        // passed to this method to the matches list
236.        for (int i = 0; i < candidates.length; ++i) {
237.          if (candidates[i].startsWith(s)
238.              && candidates[i].length() > s.length())
239.            matches.add(candidates[i]);
240.        }
241.     }
242.     // If there were matches, return them; otherwise,
243.     // return null
244.     return matches.size() > 0 ? matches : null;
245.   }
246.
247.   // PRIVATE HELPER METHODS
248.
249.   // This method sets, or resets, the completion items
```

continues

Listing 3.2   com.gwtsolutions.components.client.ui.AutoCompleteTextBox.java   *continued*

```
250.   // displayed in the listBox, but only if the text in the
251.   // textBox has changed since the last keyboard event
252.   // in the textBox
253.   private void populateCompletionItems(String s) {
254.     if ( ! textBoxTextChanged())
255.       return;
256.
257.     // Clear the items in the listBox
258.     listBox.clear();
259.
260.     // Get completion items that match the string passed
261.     // to this method
262.     List items = getCompletionItems(s);
263.
264.     if (items != null) { // If we found matching items...
265.       // ...add them to the listBox
266.       Iterator it = items.iterator();
267.       while (it.hasNext())
268.         listBox.addItem((String) it.next());
269.
270.       // Set the listBox's visible item count to match
271.       // the number of matching completion items
272.       listBox.setVisibleItemCount(items.size());
273.
274.       if (!listBox.isVisible()) {
275.         positionPopup();
276.         popup.show();
277.
278.         // If the listBox is not visible, make it
279.         // visible with a Script.aculo.us BlindDown effect
280.         applyEffect("BlindDown", listBox
281.             .getElement());
282.       }
283.     }
284.     else {
285.       // If there were no completion items,
286.       // hide the popup and the listBox. We
287.       // explicitly hide the listBox so the next
288.       // time it is shown, Script.aculo.us will
289.       // apply the Blind Down effect (Script.aculo.us
290.       // in-effects only work on DOM elements that
291.       // are not visible at the time the effect
```

```
292.        // is applied)
293.        popup.hide();
294.        listBox.setVisible(false);
295.    }
296. }
297.
298. // This method returns true if the textBox's text has
299. // changed since the last time we detected a change to
300. // the textBox's text
301. private boolean textBoxTextChanged() {
302.    String s = textBox.getText();
303.    boolean changed = true;
304.
305.    if (lastTextBoxText != null)
306.        if (s.equals(lastTextBoxText))
307.            changed = false;
308.
309.    // Save the text currently in the textBox so we
310.    // can check for changes the next time around
311.    lastTextBoxText = s;
312.
313.    return changed;
314. }
315.
316. // Position the popup directly under the textBox. It's
317. // tempting to use a boolean flag to only position the
318. // popup once to squeeze a little extra performance, but
319. // that assumes that the textBox will never move once it's
320. // been added to its containing widget, which in an Ajax
321. // application is not always a safe bet. Besides, trying
322. // to optimize performance without empirical evidence that
323. // performance needs to be optimized is always questionable.
324. private void positionPopup() {
325.    popup.setPopupPosition(textBox.getAbsoluteLeft(),
326.        textBox.getAbsoluteTop()
327.            + textBox.getOffsetHeight());
328. }
329.
330. // SCRIPT.ACULO.US EFFECTS INTEGRATION
331.
332. // The JavaScript in this method sidesteps native extensions
333. // to account for some dubious behavior on Safari. See the
334. // Integrating JavaScript solution in the GWT Solutions book
```

continues

Listing 3.2   com.gwtsolutions.components.client.ui.AutoCompleteTextBox.java   *continued*

```
335.    // for more information about that dubious behavior.
336.    private native void applyEffect(String effect,
337.       Element element) /*-{
338.    var ne = $wnd._nativeExtensions;
339.    $wnd._nativeExtensions = false;
340.    $wnd.Effect[effect](element, {duration: 0.25});
341.    $wnd._nativeExtensions = ne;

342.    }-*/;
343.}
```

There's a lot to digest in the preceding listing, so let's discuss it in pieces. First, let's talk about composite widgets.

Composite Widgets and Pass-Through Methods

The first thing to note about the `AutoCompleteTextBox` class is that it extends the `Composite` class. The `Composite` class in turn extends `Widget`, so you can call any `Widget` methods or inherited `UIObject` methods, such as `setTitle()` or `setVisibleLength()`, on any composite. In fact, we call both of those methods on our autocomplete text box in Listing 3.1 on page 77 on lines 64 and 85, respectively.

Composites wrap a single widget, set by the `Composite.initWidget` method, which must be called in the composite's constructor before any `Widget` methods, such as `setTitle()`, are invoked on the composite. The `initWidget` method must also be called before you add the composite to a panel. In our widget, we invoke `initWidget` on line 76 in Listing 3.2 on page 81—it's the first thing we do in our constructor. The widget we wrap is the text box.

So what does it mean for a composite to wrap a widget? It means that when you add the composite to a panel, it's just like you added the wrapped widget to that panel, but *it does not mean that you can call class-specific methods on the wrapped widget*. For example, we wrap an instance of `TextBox` in our composite. The `TextBox` class extends `TextBoxBase`, which extends `FocusWidget`, which extends `Widget`. You cannot call any `TextBox`, `TextBoxBase`, or `FocusWidget` methods on the composite that wraps the text box. In effect, composites are opaque wrappers that can be manipulated as a *widget* but cannot be manipulated with methods further down the inheritance chain for the wrapped widget.

Having read all that, you may notice that we call `setVisibleLength()` on our composite on line 85 of Listing 3.1 on page 77. The `setVisibleLength` method originates in the `TextBox` class, so how is it possible that we can call that method on the text box's surrounding composite? We can call `setVisibleLength()` because we implemented a *pass-through method* in the `AutoCompleteTextBox` class that delegates to the enclosed text box. In fact, we pass through a number of methods to the composite's enclosed text box beginning on line 163 of Listing 3.2 on page 83:

- `void setFocus(boolean)`

- `void addKeyboardListener(KeyboardListener)`

- `void removeKeyboardListener(KeyboardListener)`

- `void setVisibleLength(int)`

- `int getVisibleLength()`

- `void setText(String)`

- `String getText()`

- `void setName(String)`

- `String getName()`

> ℹ️ **So What Exactly Is a Composite Widget?**
>
> Composites are opaque wrappers around a single widget, but you can selectively make the wrapped widget's methods available through the composite with pass-through methods.
>
> Composites give you fine-grained control over how users of your composite can manipulate the underlying widget.

Event Handlers

The second noteworthy thing about the autocomplete widget is its event handlers, which constitute the bulk of the widget's implementation. There are three event handlers: two keyboard listeners, one attached to the widget's text box, and the other to the widget's list box; and a click listener attached to the list box. Let's look at each event handler in turn.

The Text Box's Keyboard Listener

The text box's keyboard listener, starting on line 91, reacts to key down events in the text box. If the list box is not visible when a user types a key in the text box—or the list box is visible, but the key is not a down arrow—we populate completion items that match the text in the text box.

If the list box is visible and the user typed a down arrow in the text box, we give the list box focus, set its selected index to zero, and copy that corresponding item from the list box to the text box.

The List Box's Keyboard Listener

The list box's keyboard listener, starting on line 113, looks for up and down arrow keys. The listener reacts to those keys by copying the text of the list box's selected item to the text box. As a result of that copying, as the user traverses the list box's items with the up or down arrow keys, we keep the text box's text in sync with the selected item in the list box.

If the key pressed by the user was not an up or down arrow, we end the completion by invoking the `complete` method, which is listed starting on line 201. That method hides the popup and list box, gives focus back to the text box, and fires a change event to all change listeners registered with the autocomplete widget.

The List Box's Click Listener

The list box's click listener, starting on line 128, reacts to mouse clicks in the list box. When a user clicks the mouse in the list box, the listener ends the completion.

Firing Change Events

In our form completion application shown in Figure 3.1 on page 72, we created a change listener that listens to the autocomplete widget. When the autocomplete widget's text changes, that listener updates the city and state fields to match the selected zip code.

The autocomplete widget implements the `SourcesChangeEvents` interface, as do all GWT widgets that fire change events. The `SourcesChangeEvents` interface defines two methods: `addChangeListener()` and `removeChangeListener()`. See "Constructing Event Listeners and Firing Events with GWT" (page 259) for more information on sourcing and firing events in general.

Starting on line 142, we add support for change listeners. The `addChangeListener` method adds a change listener to an instance of `ChangeListenerCollection`. The `removeChangeListener` method, starting on line 154, removes a listener from that collection.

The `complete` method, starting on line 201, fires a change event to all registered change listeners by invoking `listeners.fireChange(this)`, where `listeners` is an instance of `ChangeListenerCollection`. We pass the widget that initiated the event—the autocomplete widget itself—to listeners so that they can extract information from the autocomplete widget, such as which completion item the user selected.

Implementing the HasText and HasName Interfaces

Besides `SourcesChangeEvents`, the autocomplete widget also implements GWT's `HasText` and `HasName` interfaces.

The `HasText` interface is implemented by widgets that have text, such as labels and buttons. Starting on line 183, the autocomplete widget implements the two methods defined by that interface—void `setText(String)` and `String getText()`—by delegating to the autocomplete widget's enclosed text box. So, when you call `getText()`, you get the text in the text box.

The `HasName` interface is more interesting than `HasText`. The `HasName` interface is implemented by widgets that can be submitted from inside a GWT form panel, such as text boxes, text areas, and file uploads. GWT's form panel, represented by the `FormPanel` class, has a bona fide HTML form for its DOM element, and you can submit that underlying form to the server. Widgets that reside in a form panel and that have a value to submit to the server must also have a name, because HTML fields are transmitted to the server in name/value pairs. So, because the autocomplete widget implements `HasName`, you can use autocomplete widgets in GWT form panels. Starting on line 191, we implement the two methods defined by `HasName`—String `getName()` and void `setName()`—by delegating to the enclosed text box. That works because the `TextBox` class also implements the `HasName` interface.

Incorporating the Script.aculo.us Blind Down Effect

When we show the pop-up containing the completion items, we apply a Script.aculo.us blind down effect, as shown in Figure 3.2 on page 73.

We've already covered integrating JavaScript in Solution 2, so we won't revisit that topic here, other than to note that this time, instead of integrating JavaScript directly in an application, we've embedded it in a custom widget. Because the effect is encapsulated in a widget that resides in our `Components` module, we import the requisite JavaScript in our module's configuration file instead of in the application's HTML file. That way, you can use autocomplete widgets, replete with Script.aculo.us effects, simply by using our module—you don't have to import the JavaScript that we need for our effect because that importation is encapsulated in our module. Listing 3.3 lists our module's configuration file.

Listing 3.3   Components.gwt.xml

```
1.<module>
2.
3.   <!— Inherit the core Web Toolkit stuff.               —>
4.   <inherits name='com.google.gwt.user.User'/>
5.   <inherits name='com.google.gwt.xml.XML' />
6.   <inherits name='com.google.gwt.i18n.I18N' />
7.   <inherits name='com.google.gwt.http.HTTP' />
8.   <inherits name='com.google.gwt.json.JSON' />
9.
10.  <!— Specify the app entry point class.               —>
```

continues

Listing 3.3   Components.gwt.xml   *continued*

```
11.  <entry-point class='com.gwtsolutions.components.client.Components'/>
12.
13.  <script src="javascript/prototype.js">
14.     if ($wnd.$) {
15.        return true;
16.     }
17.     else {
18.        return false;
19.     }
20.  </script>
21.
22.  <script src="javascript/effects.js">
23.     if ($wnd.Effect) {
24.        return true;
25.     }
26.     else {
27.        return false;
28.     }
29.  </script>
30.
31.</module>
32.
```

That's all for our autocomplete widget. Next, we look at a low-level custom widget.

com.google.gwt.user.client.ui.UIObject

- `int getAbsoluteLeft()`

  Returns a widget's absolute left position, meaning the offset from the top-left corner of the browser's client area.

- `int getAbsoluteTop()`

  Returns a widget's absolute top position, meaning the offset from the top-left corner of the browser's client area.

- `int getOffsetHeight()`

  Returns the height of a widget, including the widget's decorations, such as padding and border, but not including the widget's margin.

com.google.gwt.user.client.ui.Composite

- void initWidget(Widget w)

Sets the widget that a composite wraps.

This method is subject to three important restrictions: 1) You can only call it once; 2) you must call it before you invoke any Widget methods on the composite itself; 3) you must call it before you add the composite to a panel.

com.google.gwt.user.client.ui.SimplePanel

- void add(Widget w)

Adds a widget to a panel. The SimplePanel class, which is the superclass of PopupPanel, can have only one widget, and the one you pass to this method is that one widget.

com.google.gwt.user.client.ui.PopupPanel

- void show()

Shows the pop-up at the position previously specified by PopupPanel.setPopupPosition(int left, int top). You must add a child widget to a pop-up panel before invoking show() with the add method from the SimplePanel class.

- void hide()

Hides a pop-up panel. This method has no effect if you call it for a pop-up panel that is currently not showing.

com.google.gwt.user.client.ui.ListBox

- int getSelectedIndex()

Returns the index of the currently selected item. If a list box has multiple items selected, this method always returns the index of the first selected item (you can get indices of multiple selections by querying with isItemSelected(int index). This method returns -1 if no items are currently selected.

- void setSelectedIndex(int index)

Sets the selected index.

- `String getItemText(int index)`

Returns the text of the item at the specified index.

You can use this method in conjunction with the selected index to get the text of the currently (or first) selected item, like this: `String item = listBox.getItemText(listBox.getSelectedIndex());`

com.google.gwt.user.client.ui.TextBox

- `int getVisibleLength()`

Returns the visible length of the text box.

com.google.gwt.user.client.ui.SourcesChangeEvents

- `void addChangeListener(ChangeListener listener)`

Adds a change listener to the widget's list of change listeners.

Change listeners are notified of changes to the widget with which they are registered as a listener. The concept of "change" is defined by the widget class that sources change events.

- `void removeChangeListener(ChangeListener listener)`

Removes a change listener from the widget's list of change listeners.

com.google.gwt.user.client.ui.SourceKeyboardEvents

- `void addKeyboardListener(KeyboardListener listener)`

Adds a keyboard listener to a widget. Keyboard listeners are notified of keyboard events.

- `void removeKeyboardListener(KeyboardListener listener)`

Removes a keyboard listener from a widget.

> **com.google.gwt.user.client.ui.HasName**
>
> - setName(String name)
>
>   Sets a widget's name. The HasName interface is supported by GWT widgets, such as text boxes, text areas, and file uploads, that may be submitted from inside a GWT form panel.
>
> - String getText()
>
>   Returns a widget's text.

A Low-Level Custom Widget

In Solution 2, we showed you how to incorporate a Script.aculo.us effect in the form of a pulsating error message in a login application. In this section, we encapsulate an effect-fueled error message in a low-level widget. With a configurable effect for our error message widget, we can apply any Script.aculo.us effect. Figure 3.6 shows our error message widget fitted with the Shake effect, which, unlike the figure, shakes back and forth a few times, but you should get the idea.

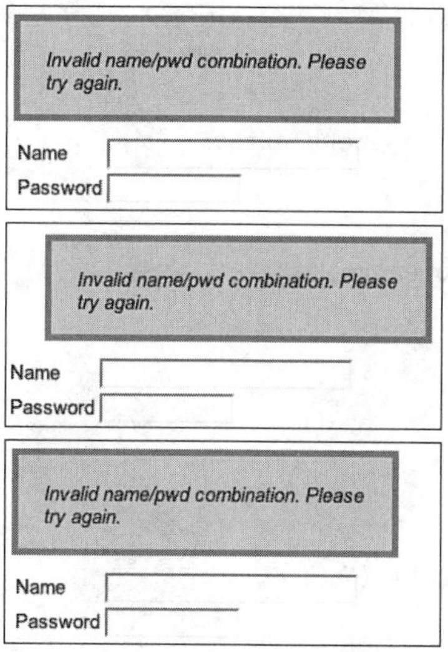

Figure 3.6   Shaking error message

Composites are handy for implementing custom widgets, as we saw in "Composite Custom Widgets" on page 72, but sometimes you want a low-level widget instead. The two main reasons to prefer a low-level widget to a composite are performance or a lack of existing widgets with which to compose a composite widget.

In the case of the error message, it seems like overkill to have a composite widget with an enclosed label, so we implement a low-level widget that uses the DOM class to create a DIV element. Then we bake in configurable Script.aculo.us effects for a whiz-bang error message component.

Listing 3.4 shows a login application, which is listed in its entirety in Listing 1.27 (page 47). In Listing 3.4, we highlight the use of the Message component.

Listing 3.4   com.gwtsolutions.client.Login.java

```
1.package com.gwtsolutions.client;
2.
3....
4.import com.gwtsolutions.components.client.ui.Message;
5.
6.public class Login implements EntryPoint, HistoryListener {
7.  ...
8.  private final Message message =
9.     new Message(constants.errorMsg(), Message.PULSATE, 0.75);
10. ...
11.  private void loadLoginView() {
12.    ...
13.    button.addClickListener(new ClickListener() {
14.      public void onClick(Widget sender) {
15.        ...
16.        ls.isValidLogin(nameTextbox.getText(), passwordTextbox
17.            .getText(), new AsyncCallback() {
18.          public void onSuccess(Object result) {
19.            if (true == ((Boolean) result).booleanValue()) {
20.              History.newItem(WELCOME_STATE);
21.            }
22.            else {
23.              message.setVisible(true);
24.            }
25.          }
26.          public void onFailure(Throwable caught) {
27.            Window.alert("rpc call failed: "
28.                + caught.getMessage());
29.          }
30.        });
31.      }
32.    });
33.    ...
34.    message.setVisible(false);
```

```
35.    ...
36.  }
37.  ...
38.}
```

The error message widget is instantiated on line 9 of the preceding listing. The ErrorMessage constructor that we call in the preceding application takes three arguments: the text of the error message, the Script.aculo.us effect to apply, and the duration of the effect.

On line 23 of the preceding listing, we set the visibility of the error message to true in response to a failed login attempt. We don't manually apply the Script.aculo.us effect because that's encapsulated in the component, which is listed in Listing 3.5.

Listing 3.5   com.gwtsolutions.components.client.ui.Message

```
1.package com.gwtsolutions.components.client.ui;
2.
3.import com.google.gwt.user.client.DOM;
4.import com.google.gwt.user.client.Element;
5.import com.google.gwt.user.client.ui.Widget;
6.
7.public class Message extends Widget {
8.    public static String GROW = "Grow";
9.    public static String SHAKE = "Shake";
10.    public static String PULSATE = "Pulsate";
11.
12.    private String[] effects = {
13.        GROW, PULSATE, SHAKE
14.    };
15.
16.    private String effect;
17.    private double duration = 0;
18.
19.    public Message() {
20.      setElement(DOM.createDiv());
21.      setStyleName("gwtsolutions-Message");
22.    }
23.    public Message(String text) {
24.      this();
25.      setText(text);
26.    }
27.    public Message(String text, String effect) {
```

continues

Listing 3.5 com.gwtsolutions.components.client.ui.ErrorMessage *continued*

```
28.    this(text);
29.    this.effect = effect;
30.  }
31.  public Message(String text, String effect, double duration) {
32.    this(text);
33.    this.effect = effect;
34.    this.duration = duration;
35.  }
36.  public void setText(String text) {
37.    DOM.setInnerText(getElement(), text);
38.  }
39.  public void setVisible(boolean visible) {
40.    super.setVisible(visible);
41.    if (visible && checkEffect()) {
42.      applyEffect(getElement(), effect, duration);
43.    }
44.  }
45.  public String getEffect() {
46.    return effect;
47.  }
48.  public void setEffect(String effect) {
49.    this.effect = effect;
50.  }
51.  public double getDuration() {
52.    return duration;
53.  }
54.  public void setDuration(double duration) {
55.    this.duration = duration;
56.  }
57.
58.  private boolean checkEffect() {
59.    for (int i = 0; i < effects.length; ++i) {
60.      if (effect == effects[i])
61.        return true;
62.    }
63.    return false;
64.  }
65.  private native void applyEffect(Element element,
66.      String effect, double duration) /*-{
67.    var ne = $wnd._nativeExtensions;
68.    $wnd._nativeExtensions = false;
```

```
69.    $wnd.Effect[effect](element, {duration: duration });
70.    $wnd._nativeExtensions = ne;
71.    }-*/;
72.}
```

Using the DOM Class in a Low-Level Custom Widget

Like all low-level widgets, our error message widget directly extends the Widget class. As we discussed in "GWT's Peers: DOM Elements" (page 32), all widgets are associated with a single DOM element. Our error message widget's DOM element is a DIV, which we create on line 20 with a call to DOM.createDiv(). The DOM class has numerous methods for creating all kinds of HTML elements. Subsequently, we call the widget's setElement method to set the widget's DOM element to the DIV.

Setting Default CSS Styles for a Custom Widget

On line 21, we set the style name for our widget to gwtSolutions-errorMessage. That means that developers can define a CSS style named gwtSolutions-errorMessage and GWT will automatically apply that style to all instances of our widget. Here's how the login application defines that style:

```
.gwtsolutions-ErrorMessage {
  padding: 20px;
  margin-bottom: 10px;
  font-style: italic;
  border: thick solid red;
  background: lightGray;
  width: 250px;
  height: 2em;
}
```

We don't force developers that use our widget to use a Script.aculo.us effect, so we provide constructors for creating an error message widget without one.

We also provide two public methods for you to use: setText(), starting on line 36, which sets the text of the error message; and setVisible(), starting on line 39, which lets you show and hide the error message.

Parameterizing Script.aculo.us Effects in a Custom Widget

As we did for the autocomplete custom widget, we have a native method for the message widget that implements a Script.aculo.us effect on our widget's DOM element. But for the message widget, we've added the ability to specify a duration for the effect, which adds a nice touch to the message widget.

The applyEffect method, starting on line 65, is passed a Java double representing the duration of the effect in seconds, and GWT turns that double into a JavaScript value in the body of the applyEffect method. We pass that duration to the Script.aculo.us effect as a JavaScript object with one property named duration whose value is the duration passed to the applyEffect method.

com.google.gwt.user.client.DOM

- Element createDIV()

  Creates an Element object that represents an underlying HTML DIV.

- void setStyleAttribute(Element element, String attribute, String value)

  Sets a CSS attribute for an HTML element.

- void setInnerText(Element element, String text)

  Sets the inner text for an HTML element. If you call this method on an element that has child elements, the child elements are replaced with the inner text.

com.google.gwt.user.client.ui.UIObject

- void setElement(Element element)

  Sets the underlying HTML element that every GWT widget represents. This method must be called before any other widget methods.

Stuff We Covered in This Solution

You can get by for a while with GWT's impressive set of out-of-the-box widgets, but chances are you're going to need a custom widget or two sooner or later. In this solution, we showed you how to implement both composite and low-level widgets.

Composite widgets are great for combining existing widgets, as we did for the auto-complete widget, which combines a text box, a pop-up panel, and a list box. Even though our autocomplete widget was fairly long-winded, composite widgets generally are pretty straightforward to implement, especially if you have a decent grasp of the underlying widgets you are combining.

Low-level widgets, on the other hand, are suitable when you don't have an appropriate set of existing widgets to combine or when you are concerned about performance. Low-level widgets extend the Widget class directly, create DOM elements and configure them by using the DOM class, and furnish a set of methods that developers can call to manipulate the widget.

For both of our widgets in this solution, we threw in some special effects, thanks to the Script.aculo.us JavaScript library. In the message widget, we took things a bit further by providing a way to customize the effect and its duration.

GWT provides a robust set of widgets out of the box, including trees, menu bars, and tab panels. Additionally, GWT gives you the infrastructure to implement custom widgets, either by composing existing widgets or by implementing low-level widgets where you create and manipulate DOM elements. With all of that support, you can effectively implement nearly anything you can think of that runs in the confines of the browser. In fact, in the next solution, we show you how to implement a custom widget that is impossible to implement with most existing Java-based web application frameworks such as Struts, Tapestry, or JavaServer Faces, without writing a great deal of JavaScript.

Solution 4
Viewports and Maps

When you start working with GWT, it doesn't take long before you realize that the possibilities are endless. Pretty much anything you can implement in a desktop application with frameworks like Swing or the SWT is also possible with GWT.

Swing provides a handy component known as a viewport, which serves as a port onto a larger view; thus the name. Viewports are handy for all sorts of things. For example, if you wanted to create a game with a scrolling background, you might use a viewport to show a portion of your background. As the game's characters approach the edges of the viewport, you could scroll the underlying background to let those characters explore other portions of your game's landscape.

Another use for viewports is an increasingly popular component of many websites: mapping. Google led the way with Google Maps, and nowadays many websites incorporate mapping; in fact, you can even create your own maps and share them with other web denizens at http://www.discovermachine.com.

Games and maps are only two examples of the usefulness of viewports. Unfortunately, GWT does not provide a viewport out of the box, but fortunately GWT provides all of the necessary ingredients so that you can easily write your own basic viewport class in a 100 or so lines of *pure Java* code. That's exactly what we're going to do in this solution.

But that's not all. Starting on page 117, we show you how to incorporate *user gestures* in a viewport to *animate* the underlying view, similar to the scrolling lists found in Apple's iPhone. Features such as that are typically reserved for desktop developer wizards (or cell phones from Apple), but when you're done with this solution, you'll see that anyone can do the same with just a little math and GWT.

Stuff You're Going to Learn

This solution explores the following aspects of GWT:

- Using the `AbsolutePanel` class to place widgets by pixel location (page 110)
- Dragging one widget inside another (page 110)
- Using an event preview to inhibit browser reactions to events (page 111)

- Capturing and releasing events for a specific widget (page 111)
- Changing cursors with CSS styles (page 112)
- Incorporating gestures in a viewport (page 129)
- Using GWT timers (page 120)

The final version of our Viewport class, listed in Listing 4.5 on page 120, weighs in at close to 350 lines of heavily commented code. In that class, we pack a lot of GWT stuff; in fact, everything listed above is contained in our Viewport class.

Viewports

Figure 4.1 illustrates a viewport. The top picture shows a viewport and a portion of the viewport's underlying view. The bottom picture demonstrates *viewport clipping*, whereby the underlying view is *clipped* to the confines of the viewport, meaning that only the portion of the view contained in the viewport is visible.

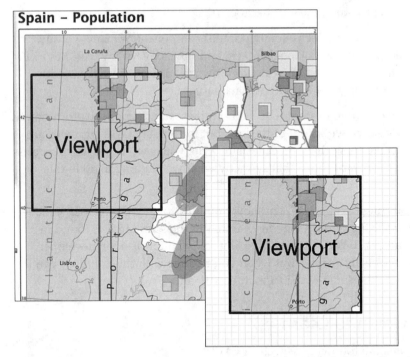

Figure 4.1   Viewports show a portion of a component that is larger than the viewport

Figure 4.2 shows our example application, which implements an actual viewport with a map image as the underlying view. Figure 4.2 also shows a user dragging the map toward the top-left corner inside the viewport.

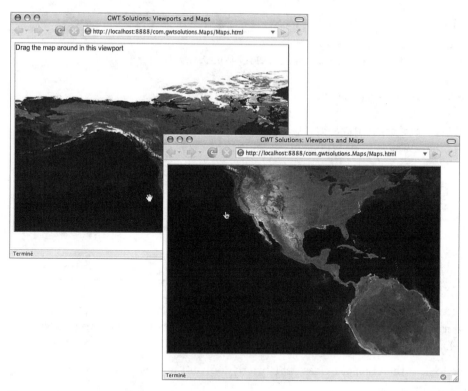

Figure 4.2   Dragging a map contained in a viewport

> **ℹ️ Mouse Cursors and Operating Systems**
>
> Different operating systems use different representations of the pointer and move cursors, so when you run the sample application, the cursors may look a little different than what you see in Figure 4.2.

Now that we've seen the example application for this solution, let's see how it's put together.

A General-Purpose Viewport Widget

The application shown in Figure 4.2, which is listed in Listing 4.1, is ridiculously simple because we've encapsulated all the complexity in our viewport widget.

Listing 4.1   com.gwtsolutions.client.Maps

```
1.package com.gwtsolutions.client;
2.
3.import com.google.gwt.core.client.EntryPoint;
```

continues

Listing 4.1   com.gwtsolutions.client.Maps   *continued*

```
4. import com.google.gwt.user.client.ui.*;
5. import com.gwtsolutions.components.client.ui.Viewport;
6.
7. public class Maps implements EntryPoint {
8.
9.   public void onModuleLoad() {
10.     final Viewport mapViewport = new Viewport();
11.
12.     mapViewport.setView(
13.         new Image("images/land_ocean_ice.jpg"));
14.
15.     RootPanel.get().add(mapViewport);
16.   }
17. }
```

In the preceding listing, we create a viewport and set the view to an image showing land, water, and ice on planet Earth. Then we add the viewport to the application's root panel, and we're done.

Before we look at the Viewport class, let's briefly look at the files and directories contained in our application.

The Map Application's Files and Directories

Our application's associated files and directories are shown in Figure 4.3.

Figure 4.3   The map application's files and directories

Notice that this application does not contain many files. We have the Maps class, which is our application, listed in Listing 4.1 on page 105, a CSS stylesheet, and the map image. The Viewport class is not shown in Figure 4.3, because it resides in our Components module, which contains the custom components we developed for this book.

The Viewport Implementation

Now that we've seen the implementation of the example application and its accompanying files, let's look at a first cut of the Viewport class, listed in Listing 4.2. Later on, in "A Viewport's View with Animated Gestures" on page 117, we discuss the final version of the Viewport class, which incorporates user gestures and view animation.

Listing 4.2   com.gwtsolutions.client.ui.Viewport

```
1. package com.gwtsolutions.client;
2.
3. import com.google.gwt.user.client.DOM;
4. import com.google.gwt.user.client.Event;
5. import com.google.gwt.user.client.EventPreview;
6. import com.google.gwt.user.client.ui.AbsolutePanel;
7. import com.google.gwt.user.client.ui.FocusPanel;
8. import com.google.gwt.user.client.ui.MouseListenerAdapter;
9. import com.google.gwt.user.client.ui.Widget;
10.
11.public class Viewport extends AbsolutePanel {
12.   private static final
13.     String DEFAULT_MOUSE_DOWN_CURSOR = "moveCursor";
14.   private static final
15.     String DEFAULT_MOUSE_DRAG_CURSOR = "pointerCursor";
16.
17.   private final FocusPanel focusPanel = new FocusPanel();
18.
19.   private String mouseDownCursor = DEFAULT_MOUSE_DOWN_CURSOR;
20.   private String mouseDragCursor = DEFAULT_MOUSE_DRAG_CURSOR;
21.
22.   private Widget view = null;
23.
24.   private boolean dragging = false;
25.   private int xoffset, yoffset;
26.
27.   private boolean eventPreviewAdded = false;
28.
29.   private static EventPreview preventDefaultMouseEvents =
```

continues

Listing 4.2   com.gwtsolutions.client.ui.Viewport   *continued*

```
30.     new EventPreview() {
31.       public boolean onEventPreview(Event event) {
32.         switch (DOM.eventGetType(event)) {
33.           case Event.ONMOUSEDOWN:
34.           case Event.ONMOUSEMOVE:
35.             DOM.eventPreventDefault(event);
36.         }
37.         return true;
38.       }
39.     };
40.
41.   public Viewport() {
42.     setStyleName("gwtsolutions-Viewport");
43.
44.     add(focusPanel);
45.
46.     focusPanel.addMouseListener(new MouseListenerAdapter() {
47.       public void onMouseEnter() {
48.         DOM.addEventPreview(preventDefaultMouseEvents);
49.       }
50.
51.       public void onMouseLeave() {
52.         DOM.removeEventPreview(preventDefaultMouseEvents);
53.       }
54.
55.       public void onMouseDown(Widget widget, int x, int y) {
56.         addStyleName(mouseDownCursor);
57.         dragging = true;
58.
59.         xoffset = x;
60.         yoffset = y;
61.         DOM.setCapture(focusPanel.getElement());
62.       }
63.
64.       public void onMouseMove(Widget widget, int x, int y) {
65.         if (dragging) {
66.           removeStyleName(mouseDownCursor);
67.           addStyleName(mouseDragCursor);
68.
69.           int newX = x + getWidgetLeft(focusPanel) - xoffset;
70.           int newY = y + getWidgetTop(focusPanel) - yoffset;
71.
```

```
72.              setWidgetPosition(focusPanel, newX, newY);
73.          }
74.      }
75.
76.      public void onMouseUp(Widget widget, int x, int y) {
77.          if (dragging) {
78.              dragging = false;
79.              removeStyleName(mouseDownCursor);
80.              removeStyleName(mouseDragCursor);
81.              DOM.releaseCapture(focusPanel.getElement());
82.          }
83.      }
84.  });
85.  }
86.
87.  public String getMouseDownCursor() {
88.      return mouseDownCursor;
89.  }
90.
91.  public void setMouseDownCursor(String mouseDownCursor) {
92.      this.mouseDownCursor = mouseDownCursor;
93.  }
94.
95.  public String getMouseDragCursor() {
96.      return mouseDragCursor;
97.  }
98.
99.  public void setMouseDragCursor(String mouseDragCursor) {
100.     this.mouseDragCursor = mouseDragCursor;
101.  }
102.
103.  public Widget getView() {
104.      return view;
105.  }
106.
107.  public void setView(Widget view) {
108.      this.view = view;
109.      focusPanel.setWidget(view);
110.  }
111.}
```

The preceding listing is just over 100 lines of code, but that code covers a number of GWT aspects:

- Using the `AbsolutePanel` GWT class

- Dragging the view inside the viewport

- Embedding a focus panel in an absolute panel to handle mouse events

- Using an event preview to inhibit the browser's reaction to mouse events

- Capturing events to funnel them to one particular widget

- Changing the mouse cursor with CSS styles

- Adding a default CSS style name for a custom widget

Let's take a look at each of those aspects.

Using an Instance of AbsolutePanel to Place Widgets at Pixel Locations

Our viewport lets users drag the underlying view, so we need to be able to place the view at specific pixel locations. In GWT, if you need to specify pixel locations for widgets, you put them in an instance of `AbsolutePanel`, which, as its name suggests, lets you place its widgets at absolute pixel locations.

Our `Viewport` class extends `AbsolutePanel`, as you can see on line 11 of Listing 4.2.

Dragging the View Inside the Viewport

You place widgets at specific pixel locations in an absolute panel with the `AbsolutePanel.setWidgetPosition` method. To drag a viewport's view inside the viewport, we use that method along with some simple math that constantly updates the view's position as the user drags the mouse. That method call and the corresponding math are listed on lines 69-72 in Listing 4.2.

Using a Focus Panel to React to Mouse Events

The `AbsolutePanel` class, however, has a drawback for our purposes: It does not support mouse listeners. In GWT-speak, `AbsolutePanel` does not source mouse events, and to drag the view within the viewport, we need to handle mouse events. So, to handle mouse events in the viewport, we place an instance of `FocusPanel`, which sources mouse events, inside the absolute panel at line 44 of the `Viewport` class. Subsequently, at line 109, we put the view widget in the focus panel. When the user drags the view, he is really dragging the focus panel, which contains the view widget.

By nesting a focus panel inside an absolute panel, we can place the view by pixel location and drag it inside the viewport.

Note, however, that using an instance of `FocusPanel` just to handle mouse events is a somewhat heavy-handed approach. In "The Viewport's Use of a Focus Panel: Revisted" on page 115, we discuss an alternative implementation.

Using an Event Preview to Inhibit the Browser's Default Reaction to Mouse Events

If you try to drag an image in an HTML page, your browser will oblige you by dragging an outline of the image. For our viewport, that browser feature is an unwanted intrusion that totally ruins our dragging effect.

In general, you will often want the browser to butt out of your event handling; for example, we see the same unwanted browser intrusion when we discuss drag-and-drop in Solution 6. How do you convince the browser to ignore events so that you can execute your code without interference?

The answer is an *event preview*. GWT lets you place an event preview on top of the event stack, meaning that your event preview gets first crack at every event. In addition, GWT's DOM class provides an `eventPreventDefault` method, that, as its name suggests, prevents the browser from exercising its default reaction to an event.

In the viewport's mouse listener's `onMouseEnter` method, on line 48, we place our event preview on the top of the event stack with a call to `DOM.addEventPreview()`.

In the mouse listener's `onMouseLeave` method, on line 52, we remove the event preview from the top of the stack, which returns event handling to its normal state.

Capturing Events

When the user drags the view inside our viewport, we want to funnel mouse events solely to our focus panel. If other DOM elements in the DOM tree are also handling those mouse events, even if they handle them as no-ops, we will surely pay a performance price for that event handling. So, to increase performance, we funnel events directly to our focus panel while the user drags it. We achieve that event funneling by invoking `DOM.setCapture()` on line 61 when the mouse is pressed.

We must, however, return event handling to normal once the user stops dragging the view. On line 81, when the user releases the mouse button, we invoke `DOM.releaseCapture()` so that events are no longer funneled strictly to the focus panel.

Clipping the Viewport's View

Because our view widget (the map) is much larger than its surrounding viewport, we must *clip* the view so that the only part of the view that's visible is what lies within the viewport.

Clipping graphics is not trivial. It takes some math and some underlying access to the internals of whatever you're clipping, such as an image. Luckily for us, however, GWT's `AbsolutePanel` class automatically clips anything outside of its bounds. So to clip the viewport's view, we have to do nothing other than extend `AbsolutePanel` in our `Viewport` class.

Changing the Mouse Cursor with CSS Styles

When the user clicks the mouse in our viewport's view, by default, we change the cursor to a pointer cursor. We accomplish that on line 56 of Listing 4.2, by adding the `pointerCursor` CSS style to the viewport.

When the user subsequently starts dragging the view, we set the cursor to a move cursor, by removing the `pointerCursor` CSS style and adding the `moveCursor` style, on lines 66 and 67, respectively.

Both the `pointerCursor` and `moveCursor` styles are defined in the stylesheet listed in Listing 4.3.

Changing mouse cursors is a fairly common occurrence in many applications. Fortunately, GWT makes it easy to accomplish.

Adding a Default CSS Style Name for a Custom Widget

In addition to adding and removing CSS styles to set the viewport's mouse cursor, in we also call `setStyleName()` on line 42 in Listing 4.2 on page 108 and specify a style named `gwtsolutions-Viewport`.

As we saw in the preceding section, you *add* CSS styles to a widget by invoking the widget's `addStyleName` method. All of the styles added by calling `addStyleName()` are applied to the widget. Conversely, you can selectively remove CSS styles by calling `removeStyleName()`.

You specify the *default* style name for a widget by invoking the widget's `setStyleName` method. GWT automatically applies default styles when they are defined. For example, even though we don't call `addStyleName("gwtsolutions-Viewport")` anywhere in our application, GWT still applies that style to our viewport if the style is defined, because the call to `setStyleName()` designates that style as the viewport's default style.

---

com.google.gwt.user.client.ui.MouseListener

- `void onMouseDown(Widget sender, int x, int y)`

  Is called by GWT when a mouse down event occurs in a widget to which you attach a mouse listener. The sender is the widget in which the mouse down event occurred, and the x and y coordinates are relative to that widget.

- `void onMouseUp(Widget sender, int x, int y)`

  Is called by GWT when a mouse up event occurs in a widget to which this listener is attached. Like `onMouseDown()`, the sender is the widget in which the event occurred, and the x and y coordinates are relative to that widget.

- void onMouseEnter(Widget sender)

Is called by GWT when the mouse enters a widget to which this listener is attached. The sender is the widget in which the event occurred.

- void onMouseLeave(Widget sender)

Is called by GWT when the mouse leaves a widget to which this listener is attached. The sender is the widget in which the event occurred.

- void onMouseMove(Widget sender, int x, int y)

Is called by GWT when a mouse move event occurs in a widget to which this listener is attached. Like the other MouseListener methods, the sender is the widget in which the event occurred, and like onMouseUp() and onMouseDown(), the x and y coordinates are relative to that widget.

com.google.gwt.user.client.ui.UIObject

- void addStyleName(String styleName)

Adds a CSS style to a widget. One of the methods of the UIObject class, which is the widget class's superclass and which inherits a number of methods that all widgets find useful.

- UIObject.setStyleName(String styleName)

Sets a widget's default style, which GWT automatically applies to the widget if the style is defined. You do not have to call addStyleName() to apply the style specified with setStyleName().

com.google.gwt.user.client.ui.AbsolutePanel

- void add(Widget w)

Adds a widget to the absolute panel. AbsolutePanel also has an add(Widget w, int x, int y) method that lets you add widgets by pixel location. This method, however, which takes no positional information, adds the specified widget as though the absolute panel were a vertical panel. If you just use add() to add widgets to an absolute panel, the absolute panel will lay out the widgets vertically.

- void setWidgetPosition(Widget w, int x, int y)

  Sets a widget's position by pixel location, relative to the containing absolute panel. The widget reference passed to the method must reside in the absolute panel on whose behalf the setWidgetPosition method is called.

- void getWidgetLeft(Widget w)

  Returns the x coordinate of a widget's left edge, relative to its enclosing absolute panel.

- void getWidgetTop(Widget w)

  Returns the y coordinate of a widget's top edge, relative to its enclosing absolute panel.

com.google.gwt.user.client.ui.FocusPanel

- void setWidget(Widget w)

  Sets the widget in an instance of FocusPanel. Instances of FocusPanel can contain only a single widget.

  Realize that although a focus panel can contain only a single widget, that widget can be a panel itself, which in turn may contain an unlimited number of widgets, so in practice you can add as many widgets as you want to a focus panel.

com.google.gwt.user.client.DOM

- static void addEventPreview(EventPreview ep)

  Adds an instance of EventPreview to the top of the event stack.

  Your event preview gets first crack at all events—even before the browser sees them—and you can use other DOM methods, such as DOM.eventPreventDefault() in your event preview to modify how events are handled.

- static void removeEventPreview(EventPreview ep)

  Removes an event preview from the event stack—you rarely want to leave an event preview on top of the event stack indefinitely.

- static void setCapture(Widget w)

  Funnels all events to the specified widget and only that widget has access to events. This method is handy for performance-intensive activities like dragging a widget so that other widgets don't waste time handling the event.

- `static void releaseCapture(Widget w)`

Releases event capture and returns event handling to normal.

Just as you will rarely want to leave an event preview on top of the event stack, you will rarely want to capture events for a particular widget indefinitely.

com.google.gwt.user.client.EventPreview

- `void EventPreview.onEventPreview(Event e)`

Is called by GWT for event previews that reside atop the event stack by virtue of a call to `DOM.addEventPreview()`.

The `onEventPreview` method is where you write code that typically circumvents, or modifies in some manner, normal event handling, as we did by preventing the browser from reacting to mouse dragging in Listing 4.2 on page 107.

The Viewport's Use of a Focus Panel: Revisited

In "Using a Focus Panel to React to Mouse Events" on page 110, we discussed how the `Viewport` class uses an instance of `FocusPanel` to handle mouse events. That implementation works, but it's a bit heavy-handed because focus panels provide additional infrastructure, such as support for dispatching focus events and keyboard navigation, which we don't need in our viewport.

Because of that extra infrastructure in the `FocusPanel` class, an option is to implement a more lightweight panel of our own that handles mouse events and then use an instance of that panel instead of a focus panel in our viewport. Listing 4.3 shows the implementation of that lightweight panel.

Listing 4.3   com.gwtsolutions.client.ui.MousePanel

```
1. package com.gwtsolutions.components.client.ui;
2.
3. import com.google.gwt.user.client.Event;
4. import com.google.gwt.user.client.ui.MouseListener;
5. import com.google.gwt.user.client.ui.MouseListenerCollection;
6. import com.google.gwt.user.client.ui.SimplePanel;
7. import com.google.gwt.user.client.ui.SourcesMouseEvents;
8.
```

continues

Listing 4.3   com.gwtsolutions.client.ui.MousePanel   *continued*

```
9.  // An extension of SimplePanel that sources mouse events
10. public class MousePanel extends SimplePanel
11.     implements SourcesMouseEvents {
12.   private MouseListenerCollection mouseListeners = null;
13.
14.   public MousePanel() {
15.     super();
16.
17.     // Sink mouse events, which means that GWT will
18.     // call our onBrowserEvent method whenever a mouse
19.     // event occurs in this panel
20.     sinkEvents(Event.MOUSEEVENTS);
21.   }
22.   public void onBrowserEvent(Event event) {
23.     // Fire the mouse event to listeners, if any listeners
24.     // are currently registered with this panel
25.     if (mouseListeners != null)
26.       mouseListeners.fireMouseEvent(this, event);
27.
28.     // Give the superclass the chance to handle the event
29.     super.onBrowserEvent(event);
30.   }
31.   public void addMouseListener(MouseListener listener) {
32.     // Lazily instantiate the mouse listener collection
33.     // when the first mouse listener is added to this
34.     // panel.
35.     if (mouseListeners == null)
36.       mouseListeners = new MouseListenerCollection();
37.
38.     mouseListeners.add(listener);
39.   }
40.   public void removeMouseListener(MouseListener listener) {
41.     // If there are no mouse listeners registered with this
42.     // panel, then this method is a no-op; otherwise, remove
43.     // the specified mouse listener from the panel
44.     if (mouseListeners != null)
45.       mouseListeners.remove(listener);
46.   }
47. }
```

The MousePanel class extends SimplePanel and maintains a collection of mouse listeners. It also implements the SourcesMouseEvents interface and implements the two methods defined by that interface: addMouseListener() and removeMouseListener().

The `MousePanel` class also *sinks mouse events* in its constructor. We discuss sinking events in general in more detail in "Sinking Events" (page 215), but here it suffices to understand that sinking mouse events causes GWT to invoke the `MousePanel`'s `onBrowserEvent()` whenever a mouse event occurs in an instance of `MousePanel`. In the `MousePanel`'s `onBrowserEvent` method, we fire the mouse event to all registered listeners, by invoking the `fireMouseEvent` method provided by the `MouseListenerCollection` class.

After the `MousePanel` class is implemented, it's a simple matter to modify the `Viewport` class to use an instance of `MousePanel` instead of a `FocusPanel`. On line 17 of Listing 4.2 on page 107, we replace the `FocusPanel` with an instance of `MousePanel`, and we're done with that change. In fact, Listing 4.5 on page 120 shows the final version of the `Viewport` class, which uses an instance of `MousePanel`.

A Viewport's View with Animated Gestures

Have you seen Apple's iPhone? That phone has a lot of cool features, but one of the coolest is its ability to animate scrolling of lists. Assuming you actually have more contacts than one screen can display, you can drag your finger up or down on the phone's display and the underlying list scrolls, without your intervention, until you stop scrolling by tapping your finger. Those finger drags and taps are known as user gestures.

Going back to our viewport, it's essential to be able to drag the view contained in our viewports. Without the ability to drag our map, for example, you'd only be able to see the portion of the map that was initially displayed in the viewport, rendering maps in a viewport virtually useless.

But if you want to see a place on the map that's a long way from the portion of the map that's initially visible, dragging can become a chore. You have to repeatedly move the mouse to one edge of the map, drag it to the desired edge, wheel back to the original edge, and then repeat until your desired location finally scrolls into view. Ugh.

So, to make it easy to quickly drag the map over great distances, we implemented animated scrolling, very similar to what Apple has done with its iPhone. Instead of finger dragging, mouse *quick*-dragging accomplishes our gestures.

The gesture that initiates animation of the viewport's underlying view is a mouse drag that lasts for less than a specified amount of time. By default, that time is a half-second, but we made that time limit configurable. So, by default, if the user drags the viewport's view for less than a half-second, we initiate the view's animation. On the other hand, if the drag lasts longer than a half-second, we don't initiate the animation. To stop the scrolling animation, the user makes another gesture, which is simply a mouse click somewhere within the confines of the scrolling map.

If the user accomplishes a drag in under the half-second time limit, we immediately start the scrolling animation shown in Figure 4.4. Notice that *the map scrolls in the same direction as the drag*. The user can set the map in motion simply by dragging quickly.

If the animation is not desired, most likely because the location of interest is already, or nearly, in view, then the user just needs to drag a the mouse for more than half a second.

Not only do we scroll in the same direction as the drag that constitutes the gesture, but we also *vary the speed of the scrolling animation depending on how fast the user dragged the mouse* while performing the gesture. If the drag lasted a quarter of a second and covered 100 pixels, we drag the mouse 10 times faster than a drag that also lasted for a quarter of a second but only covered 10 pixels. Of course, you can't see that in Figure 4.4; to check out that feature, you'll have to try it out for yourself.

Not only is animated scrolling a highly desirable feature and a really cool effect but it also illustrates a couple of things that you might need to implement in totally unrelated situations. For example, we use a GWT timer to perform and monitor the animation. Let's see how it works.

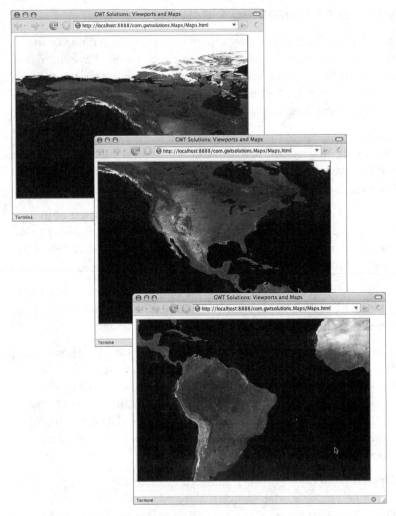

Figure 4.4   Animated scrolling

— From top to bottom, the map scrolls from lower-right to upper-left until the user clicks the mouse on the map.

Listing 4.4 shows our updated application, which configures the map's scrolling animation.

Listing 4.4   com.gwtsolutions.client.Maps

```
1.package com.gwtsolutions.client;
2.
3.import com.google.gwt.core.client.EntryPoint;
4.import com.google.gwt.user.client.ui.*;
5.import com.gwtsolutions.components.client.ui.Viewport;
6.
7.public class Maps implements EntryPoint {
8.
9.   public void onModuleLoad() {
10.     final Viewport mapViewport = new Viewport();
11.
12.     mapViewport.setGesturesEnabled(true);
13.     mapViewport.setGestureThreshold(1000);
14.     mapViewport.setView(
15.         new Image("images/land_ocean_ice.jpg"));
16.
17.     // Uncomment one of the following two lines of code
18.     // to restrict dragging in the horizontal or vertical
19.     // directions
20.
21.     //mapViewport.setRestrictDragHorizontal(true);
22.     //mapViewport.setRestrictDragVertical(true);
23.
24.     RootPanel.get().add(mapViewport);
25.   }
26.}
```

The final version of our `Viewport` class lets you restrict dragging either horizontally or vertically. If you uncomment out line 21 or 22, you can see that effect.

Additionally, our viewport lets you do two things with respect to animated scrolling. You can enable or disable animated scrolling, and you can also set the time threshold that distinguishes a simple drag from a gesture that initiates the scrolling animation.

On line 12, we call our viewport's `setGestureEnabled` method and specify `true` so that scrolling animations are enabled. That call is actually unnecessary because scrolling animations are enabled by default, but we added the call to the application so that you can easily experiment with turning animated scrolling on and off.

On line 15, we set the time threshold that distinguishes a simple drag from a gesture that initiates animated scrolling to one full second, for no other purpose than to illustrate how you can change that threshold.

Now that we've seen how to optionally configure the two configurable parameters we provide for animated scrolling, let's see how we actually implemented the gesture and the animation.

Animated Viewport Scrolling Really Showcases the Power of GWT

The fact that it's relatively easy to implement animated scrolling similar to Apple's iPhone's scrolling of contacts is a tribute to GWT.

By using mouse listeners, preventing the browser from reacting to mouse drags, and incorporating GWT timers, we are able to accomplish a feature that is unheard of in most Java-based web application frameworks and that rivals desktop applications built with frameworks such as the AWT or Swing.

The Final Version of the Viewport

Listing 4.5 lists the final version of our Viewport class.

Listing 4.5   The Final Version of com.gwtsolutions.client.Viewport

```
1. package com.gwtsolutions.components.client.ui;
2.
3. import com.google.gwt.user.client.DOM;
4. import com.google.gwt.user.client.Event;
5. import com.google.gwt.user.client.EventPreview;
6. import com.google.gwt.user.client.Timer;
7. import com.google.gwt.user.client.ui.AbsolutePanel;
8. import com.google.gwt.user.client.ui.MouseListenerAdapter;
9. import com.google.gwt.user.client.ui.Widget;
10.
11.public class Viewport extends AbsolutePanel {
12.   // Constants...
13.   private static final String DEFAULT_MOUSE_DOWN_CURSOR =
14.       "moveCursor";
15.   private static final String DEFAULT_MOUSE_DRAG_CURSOR =
16.       "pointerCursor";
17.
18.   // Defaults for time and space gesture thresholds
19.   private static final int DEFAULT_GESTURE_TIME_THRESHOLD =500;
20.   private static final int DEFAULT_GESTURE_PIXEL_THRESHOLD = 5;
21.
```

```
22.   // How often, in milliseconds, the animated scrolling
23.   // timer is called, and the speed factor multiplier
24.   private static final int TIMER_REPEAT_INTERVAL = 50;
25.   private static final int SPEED_FACTOR_MULTIPLIER = 20;
26.
27.   // Member variables...
28.
29.   // The mouse panel is the viewport's lone widget. When you
30.   // drag the mouse inside the viewport, the viewport drags
31.   // the mouse panel.
32.   // The view is the mouse panel's lone widget, which is
33.   // always at position (0,0) inside the mouse panel. As you
34.   // drag the mouse panel, the view goes with it.
35.   // Nesting the view inside the mouse panel makes sure we
36.   // can drag any widget inside a viewport.
37.   private final MousePanel mousePanel = new MousePanel();
38.   private Widget view = null;
39.
40.   // The mouse down and mouse drag cursors. You can set these
41.   // values with setter methods, but by default they are
42.   // the constants defined above.
43.   private String mouseDownCursor = DEFAULT_MOUSE_DOWN_CURSOR;
44.   private String mouseDragCursor = DEFAULT_MOUSE_DRAG_CURSOR;
45.
46.   // Keep track of whether the user is dragging the mouse
47.   // panel (and the view), or whether we are animating
48.   // scrolling in response to a user gesture.
49.   private boolean dragging = false;
50.   private boolean timerRunning = false;
51.
52.   // The offsets and starting values are set when the mouse
53.   // goes down. The offsets are used in onMouseMove() when
54.   // the user is dragging, and the starting values are used
55.   // in onMouseUp() to calculate how far, and in what
56.   // direction, the mouse moved while it was dragging.
57.   //
58.   // Time down is set in onMouseDown() and used in onMouseUp()
59.   // to calculate the elapsed time of a drag.
60.   //
61.   // Unit vector and speed factor are calculated in
62.   // onMouseUp(), and used by the timer that controls
63.   // animated scrolling.
64.   private int xoffset, yoffset;
```

continues

Solution 4: Viewports and Maps

```
65.   private int xstart, ystart;
66.   private long timeDown;
67.   private double unitVectorX, unitVectorY;
68.   private double speedFactor;
69.
70.   // Boolean values control whether gestures are enabled,
71.   // and whether dragging is restricted horizontally or
72.   // vertically
73.   private boolean gesturesEnabled = true;
74.   private boolean restrictDragHorizontal = false;
75.   private boolean restrictDragVertical = false;
76.
77.   // Thresholds for user gestures. Gestures initiate
78.   // animated scrolling if the user gesture falls within
79.   // both time and space thresholds.
80.   private int gestureTimeThreshold =
81.     DEFAULT_GESTURE_TIME_THRESHOLD;
82.   private int gesturePixelThreshold =
83.     DEFAULT_GESTURE_PIXEL_THRESHOLD;
84.
85.   // This is the timer that controls animated scrolling. It
86.   // is created in onMouseDown().
87.   private Timer timer = null;
88.
89.   // This event preview prevents the browser from reacting
90.   // to mouse drags while the user is dragging the mouse
91.   // panel (and its widget,the view)
92.   private EventPreview preventDefaultMouseEvents =
93.       new EventPreview() {
94.         public boolean onEventPreview(Event event) {
95.           switch (DOM.eventGetType(event)) {
96.             case Event.ONMOUSEDOWN:
97.             case Event.ONMOUSEMOVE:
98.               DOM.eventPreventDefault(event);
99.           }
100.          return true;
101.        }
102.      };
103.
104.  public Viewport() {
105.    // If you create a CSS class with this name, GWT
106.    // will automatically apply it to all viewports
```

```
107.    setStyleName("gwtsolutions-Viewport");
108.
109.    // Add the mouse panel to the viewport
110.    add(mousePanel);
111.
112.    mousePanel.addMouseListener(new MouseListenerAdapter() {
113.       public void onMouseEnter(Widget sender) {
114.          // Prevent the browser from reacting to mouse drags
115.          DOM.addEventPreview(preventDefaultMouseEvents);
116.       }
117.       public void onMouseLeave(Widget sender) {
118.          // Reset the browser's event handling to normal
119.          DOM.removeEventPreview(preventDefaultMouseEvents);
120.       }
121.       public void onMouseDown(Widget widget, int x, int y) {
122.          if (isGesturesEnabled() && timerRunning) {
123.             // On a mouse down, if the timer is running, stop it.
124.             timerRunning = false;
125.             timer.cancel();
126.          }
127.
128.          // Change the mouse cursor when the mouse goes down
129.          // and set the dragging flag to true.
130.          addStyleName(mouseDownCursor);
131.          dragging = true;
132.
133.          // Store the offsets of the mouse click inside the
134.          // view for later reference
135.          xoffset = x;
136.          yoffset = y;
137.
138.          // Capture mouse events for the view until the mouse
139.          // is released
140.          DOM.setCapture(mousePanel.getElement());
141.
142.          if (isGesturesEnabled()) {
143.             // If gestures are enabled, save the time when
144.             // the mouse went down, and the coordinates of
145.             // the mouse panel at the time for later reference
146.             timeDown = System.currentTimeMillis();
147.             xstart = getWidgetLeft(mousePanel);
148.             ystart = getWidgetTop(mousePanel);
149.
```

continues

Listing 4.5   The Final Version of com.gwtsolutions.client.Viewport   *continued*

```
150.            if (timer == null) {
151.               // If the timer hasn't been created, create it.
152.               timer = new Timer() {
153.                 public void run() {
154.                   // Calculate new X and Y locations for the
155.                   // mouse panel, and reposition it.
156.                   int newX =
157.                       getWidgetLeft(mousePanel)
158.                         - (int) (unitVectorX * speedFactor);
159.                   int newY =
160.                       getWidgetTop(mousePanel)
161.                         - (int) (unitVectorY * speedFactor);
162.
163.                   repositionView(newX, newY);
164.                 }
165.               };
166.            }
167.          }
168.       }
169.
170.       public void onMouseMove(Widget widget, int x, int y) {
171.          if (isGesturesEnabled() && timerRunning) {
172.             // If we're doing animated scrolling, ignore
173.             // mouse move events
174.             return;
175.          }
176.          if (dragging) {
177.             // If we're dragging, set the drag cursor, calculate
178.             // the new X and Y positions for the mouse panel,
179.             // and reposition it.
180.             removeStyleName(mouseDownCursor);
181.             addStyleName(mouseDragCursor);
182.
183.             int newX = x + getWidgetLeft(mousePanel) - xoffset;
184.             int newY = y + getWidgetTop(mousePanel) - yoffset;
185.
186.             repositionView(newX, newY);
187.          }
188.       }
189.
190.       public void onMouseUp(Widget widget, int x, int y) {
191.          if (dragging) {
```

```
192.            // If we were dragging, the mouse up stops the drag
193.            dragging = false;
194.
195.            // Get rid of the mouse drag and mouse down cursors
196.            removeStyleName(mouseDownCursor);
197.            removeStyleName(mouseDragCursor);
198.
199.            // Release event capture for the view. Event capture
200.            // was set when the mouse went down
201.            DOM.releaseCapture(mousePanel.getElement());
202.
203.            if (isGesturesEnabled()) {
204.              // If we're doing animated scrolling, get the time
205.              // when the mouse went up, calculate mouse movement
206.              // and elapsed time for the drag, and the unit
207.              // vector that represents the direction of the drag
208.              long timeUp = System.currentTimeMillis();
209.
210.              int xend = getWidgetLeft(mousePanel);
211.              int yend = getWidgetTop(mousePanel);
212.              double deltaX = Math.abs(xend - xstart);
213.              double deltaY = Math.abs(yend - ystart);
214.              long deltaTime = timeUp - timeDown;
215.
216.              if (deltaX > deltaY) {
217.                unitVectorX = xend < xstart ? 1 : -1;
218.                unitVectorY = (double) deltaY / (double) deltaX;
219.                unitVectorY =
220.                    yend < ystart ? unitVectorY : -unitVectorY;
221.              }
222.              else {
223.                unitVectorX = (double) deltaX / (double) deltaY;
224.                unitVectorX =
225.                    xend < xstart ? unitVectorX : -unitVectorX;
226.                unitVectorY = yend < ystart ? 1 : -1;
227.              }
228.
229.              // If the drag was within time and space
230.              // thresholds, set the speed factor, and start
231.              // the timer that controls animated scrolling
232.              if (deltaTime < gestureTimeThreshold
233.                  && (deltaX > gesturePixelThreshold
234.                      || deltaY > gesturePixelThreshold)) {
```

continues

Listing 4.5   The Final Version of com.gwtsolutions.client.Viewport *continued*

```
235.              speedFactor =
236.                 ((deltaX + deltaY) / (timeUp - timeDown))
237.                    * SPEED_FACTOR_MULTIPLIER;
238.              timerRunning = true;
239.              timer.scheduleRepeating(TIMER_REPEAT_INTERVAL);
240.            }
241.          }
242.        }
243.      }
244.    private void repositionView(int newX, int newY) {
245.       // Check to see if the view scrolled out of sight;
246.       // if so, bring it back in view
247.       if (newX > getOffsetWidth())
248.         newX = 0;
249.       else if (newX < 0-view.getOffsetWidth())
250.         newX = getOffsetWidth();
251.
252.       if (newY > getOffsetHeight())
253.         newY = 0;
254.       else if (newY < 0-view.getOffsetHeight())
255.         newY = getOffsetHeight();
256.
257.       // Reposition the mouse panel, taking dragging
258.       // restrictions into account
259.       if (isRestrictDragVertical())
260.         setWidgetPosition(mousePanel, xstart, newY);
261.       else if (isRestrictDragHorizontal())
262.         setWidgetPosition(mousePanel, newX, ystart);
263.       else
264.         setWidgetPosition(mousePanel, newX, newY);
265.     }
266.   });
267. }
268.
269. // Property setters and getters follow...
270.
271. public String getMouseDownCursor() {
272.   return mouseDownCursor;
273. }
274.
275. public void setMouseDownCursor(String mouseDownCursor) {
276.   this.mouseDownCursor = mouseDownCursor;
```

```
277.    }
278.
279.    public String getMouseDragCursor() {
280.        return mouseDragCursor;
281.    }
282.
283.    public void setMouseDragCursor(String mouseDragCursor) {
284.        this.mouseDragCursor = mouseDragCursor;
285.    }
286.
287.    public Widget getView() {
288.        return view;
289.    }
290.
291.    public void setView(Widget view) {
292.        this.view = view;
293.        mousePanel.setWidget(view);
294.    }
295.
296.    public void setViewPosition(int x, int y) {
297.        setWidgetPosition(mousePanel, x, y);
298.    }
299.
300.    public int getViewLeft() {
301.        return getWidgetLeft(mousePanel);
302.    }
303.    public int getViewTop() {
304.        return getWidgetTop(mousePanel);
305.    }
306.
307.    public boolean isRestrictDragHorizontal() {
308.        return restrictDragHorizontal;
309.    }
310.    public void setRestrictDragHorizontal(
311.        boolean restrictDragHorizontal) {
312.        this.restrictDragHorizontal = restrictDragHorizontal;
313.    }
314.
315.    public boolean isRestrictDragVertical() {
316.        return restrictDragVertical;
317.    }
318.
319.    public void setRestrictDragVertical(
```

continues

Listing 4.5   The Final Version of com.gwtsolutions.client.Viewport   *continued*

```
320.         boolean restrictDragVertical) {
321.       this.restrictDragVertical = restrictDragVertical;
322.     }
323.
324.     public boolean isGesturesEnabled() {
325.       return gesturesEnabled;
326.     }
327.
328.     public void setGesturesEnabled(boolean gesturesEnabled) {
329.       this.gesturesEnabled = gesturesEnabled;
330.     }
331.
332.     public int getGestureTimeThreshold() {
333.       return gestureTimeThreshold;
334.     }
335.
336.     public void setGestureThreshold(int gestureTimeThreshold) {
337.       this.gestureTimeThreshold = gestureTimeThreshold;
338.     }
339.
340.     public int getGesturePixelThreshold() {
341.       return gesturePixelThreshold;
342.     }
343.
344.     public void setGesturePixelThreshold(int gesturePixelThreshold) {
345.       this.gesturePixelThreshold = gesturePixelThreshold;
346.     }
347. }
```

The preceding listing incorporates four features that were not present in the original version of the class listed in Listing 4.2 on page 107:

- Incorporating the drag gesture

- Animating scrolling in response to the drag gesture

- Animating scrolling in the same direction as the drag gesture

- Varying the speed of the scrolling animation according to how fast the user performed the gesture

Let's discuss how we implemented each of those features.

Incorporating the Drag Gesture

To distinguish between a simple drag and a gesture that initiates animated scrolling, we use Java's `System.currentTimeMillis()` to measure the time that elapses during a mouse drag. If gestures are enabled, we call that method the first time on line 146 in reaction to a mouse down event. Subsequently, we call `System.currentTimeMillis()` again on line 208 in reaction to a mouse up event. If the elapsed time is less than the gesture threshold (which remember is configurable), we initiate the animation. Pretty simple.

Animating Scrolling in Response to the Drag Gesture

We implement animated scrolling with a GWT timer. On line 152, we instantiate a `Timer` instance and implement its `run` method to perform the scrolling. When we detect the user gesture, we start the timer on line 239 by invoking `Timer.scheduleRepeating()`, which causes GWT to repeatedly call the timer's `run` method at the interval we specify. That interval is 50 milliseconds, which is stored in a constant declared on line 24. Also pretty simple.

Animating Scrolling in the Same Direction as the Drag Gesture

To scroll in the same direction as the user gesture, we take a page from a mechanical engineer's playbook.

Mechanical engineers spend a fair amount of time figuring out how things move. One of the tricks they use to establish direction is to calculate a *unit vector*. A unit vector is a vector, composed of directions along both the x and y axis, that is one unit in length. Figure 4.5 illustrates a unit vector.[1]

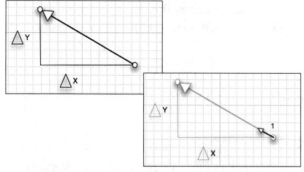

Figure 4.5   Unit vector

— *Unit vectors establish direction.*

---

[1] If your background is mechanical engineering, you may notice that our unit vector is not a true unit vector, but it's close enough that the concept applies.

The top figure illustrates some arbitrary mouse drag, which covers ground in both the x and y directions. Those distances are referred to as delta X and delta Y, respectively.

The corresponding unit vector doesn't care about the *magnitude* of the delta X and delta Y that constitute the mouse drag; instead, it's only concerned with the *direction* of the drag. For our viewport, we calculate a unit vector from the corresponding drag gesture on lines 216 to 227. Essentially, we divide both the delta X and delta Y values by the larger of either delta X or delta Y. For example, if delta X is 50 pixels and delta Y is 10 pixels, we wind up with a unit vector whose delta X is 1 pixel and a delta Y that's 10/50, or 0.20. We use that tuple (1, 0.20) as multiplying factors on lines 157 and 160 to move the map in the right direction.

Varying the Speed of the Scrolling Animation

If the user drags the mouse for less than the gesture threshold, which by default is 1/2 second but which is configured to 1 second in our application, we initiate animated scrolling. If the user dragged the mouse fast during that period of time, meaning the mouse cursor covered a lot of ground, then we scroll fast. If the user dragged the mouse slowly, then we scroll slowly.

We calculate the speed of the scrolling animation on line 236 by adding the delta X and delta Y that the drag covered divided by the elapsed time of the drag. Since that will often be a small number, we multiply it by a constant, SPEED_FACTOR-MULTIPLIER, which we set to 20 on line 25. In practice, we found that constant to provide excellent results.

com.google.gwt.user.client.Timer

- Timer.run()

  Is called by GWT, either once or repeatedly, depending on whether the timer was activated with Timer.schedule() or Timer.scheduleRepeating(), respectively.

- Timer.schedule(int delayMillis)

  Schedules a timer's run method to be called by GWT once, after the delay, in milliseconds, has elapsed.

- Timer.scheduleRepeating(int periodMillis)

  Schedules a timer's run method to be called by GWT repeatedly, at intervals specified by the period, in milliseconds.

Stuff We Covered in This Solution

Viewports are handy widgets that afford a view onto a portion of another widget that's larger than the viewport itself. Viewports find respectable employment in applications as far-ranging as games and mapping-related software.

It's a tribute to GWT that we were able to create a viewport, complete with user gestures and animated scrolling, in a couple of thoroughly enjoyable evenings. Not only is it difficult to do the same in other Java-based web application frameworks, but with most frameworks, it is *impossible* without resorting to JavaScript and integrating that JavaScript with your application. Try creating a viewport by using Struts, for example.

Apart from the viewport widget that we developed in this solution, we've also explored some interesting corners of GWT, such as: changing a widget's cursor; capturing and releasing events for a specific widget; using event previews to inhibit the browser's reactions to events; and using GWT timers. That knowledge will come in handy as you construct your own components, whether or not you use them in the context of a viewport widget.

In the next solution, we use our viewports to display maps that we download from Yahoo!s Maps web service, so you can see how to incorporate online web services in your GWT applications. Then, in Solution 6, we take dragging a bit further and create a nascent drag-and-drop framework. In Solution 7, we will employ many of the techniques we discussed in this solution and a few more for good measure. As always, our goal is to expose the raw power of GWT through cool and useful widgets and let you use those techniques in your own applications. Let's continue our quest.

Access to Online Web Services

At the end of the last century, software development underwent a profound paradigm shift. Instead of primarily developing applications for specific operating systems, as had been the norm since the dawn of computer science, people began writing web applications that ran in a browser—any browser, for the most part—without regard to the operating system in which that browser ran.

Today, we are undergoing another paradigm shift. Instead of writing monolithic applications, people are beginning to stitch together applications from *web services*. Web services provide information over the Web, information that you can incorporate into your applications or websites. Like many things in computer science, web services arrived on the scene before their time, and it's taken awhile for them to take hold, but their time has finally arrived. Not only are people using web services, but recently folks began integrating information from multiple web services to form seamless, coherent applications. Those applications are known as *mashups*.

In this solution, we show you how to integrate web services in your GWT applications. We use GWT's remote procedure call (RPC) mechanism to access a web service, and we use some of the custom widgets that we've discussed in previous solutions to put together a pretty cool application that displays maps, obtained from Yahoo!'s Maps web service, in multiple windows.

Stuff You're Going to Learn

This solution explores the following aspects of GWT:

- Using deferred commands (page 141)
- Loading images from URLs on the Web (page 143)
- Monitoring image loading (page 143)
- Temporarily changing a widget's cursor to a wait cursor (page 136)
- Temporarily adding a widget to a panel (page 143)
- Using Apache Jakarta's HttpClient to access online web services (page 146)
- Returning an object from a remote procedure call (page 142)

- Returning an array of objects from a remote procedure call (page 155)

- Making a widget hover above another widget (page 162)

Besides looking at integrating web services into GWT applications, which is the main thrust of this solution, we also look at GWT images, deferred commands, hovering widgets, removal of widgets from a panel, and temporary changes to a widget's cursor.

Yahoo! Maps Web Service

Yahoo! provides a Maps web service that returns a map image, given either an address or latitude and longitude. Figure 5.1 shows the homepage for the Yahoo! Maps web service.

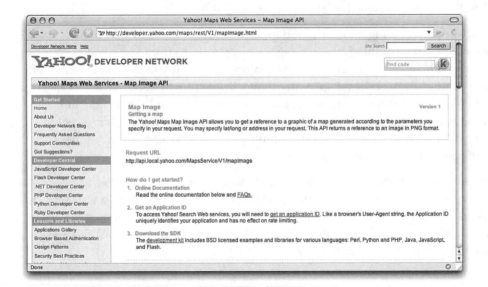

Figure 5.1   The Yahoo! Maps web services homepage

The premise behind Yahoo! Maps is simple. You access a Yahoo! URL with parameters that specify a location, and Yahoo! returns a reference to a map image from their server. Once you have that image reference, you can download the corresponding image over the Web and display it in your application. Let's see how it works.

Exploring the Example Application

Figure 5.2 shows the Yahoo! Maps example application. You type in an address, and when you click the Get Map button, the application opens a window and populates it with the map returned by the Yahoo! web service. The window is an instance of the `SimpleWindow` class, which is not a GWT class; rather, it is a custom widget that extends GWT's `PopupPanel` class that we discuss in Solution 7.

Also, the map that's returned from the Yahoo! Maps web service does not fit in its enclosing window. Because of that size mismatch, we put the map image inside a viewport. That viewport lets you drag the map so that you can see the portion of the map in which you're interested. Like the `SimpleWindow` class, the `Viewport` class is also a custom widget, as discussed in Solution 4.

Finally, notice the innocent-looking `State` text box. That widget is not simply a GWT text box, but it is an instance of our custom `AutoComplete` widget, which we introduced in Solution 2.

All in all, the application shown in Figure 5.2 sports three custom widgets: viewports, simple windows, and an autocomplete text box.

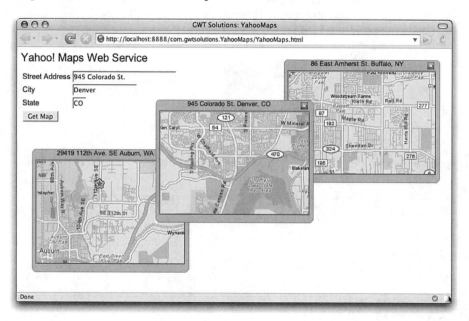

Figure 5.2   The example application

Three maps are shown in Figure 5.2 because we entered three addresses and clicked the Get Map button for each address. Every time we click the Get Map button, the application opens another simple window and populates the enclosed viewport with a map image returned from Yahoo!'s web service. You can view as many maps as you like as long as you keep supplying addresses and subsequently clicking the Get Map button.

What Figure 5.2 doesn't show is what happens immediately after you click the Get Map button. For that information, take a look at Figure 5.3.

After you supply an address and click the Get Map button, the application opens a window, but you must wait for a certain period of time—which varies depending on the speed of your internet connection—while the application downloads the corresponding map image from the Yahoo! server. Because of that delay, the application shows a message (Loading image, please wait) in the window's viewport that will ultimately display the map. Additionally, the application changes the mouse cursor for the window to a *wait* cursor while the map loads. That cursor's look depends on your operating system. You can probably tell from the wait cursor in Figure 5.3 that we took the screenshots on a Macintosh.

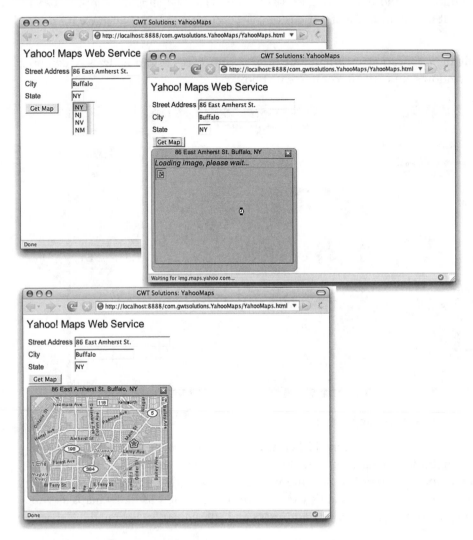

Figure 5.3   Loading a map from Yahoo!'s web service

When the map image is downloaded, the application removes the message from the window, adds the map to the viewport, and returns the cursor to its normal representation.

Remember that the viewport is the custom widget that we discussed in Solution 4. That widget has a neat feature, similar to Apple's iPhone, that recognizes a user gesture—in this case, that gesture is a quick (less than a half-second) drag—that initiates animated scrolling so you that don't have to incrementally drag the map over and over to get to the portion of the map that interests you. That feature is depicted in Figure 5.4, where the map is scrolling from bottom-right to top-left.

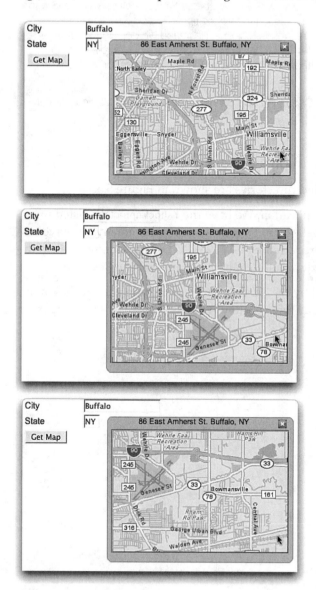

Figure 5.4   Animated scrolling in a simple window's viewport

For more information about user gestures, animated scrolling, and our implementation of those features, see Solution 7.

Now that we've seen the example application for this solution, let's look at its files and directories.

> **i** **Two Example Applications**
>
> In this section, we've referred to the example application for this solution, but this solution actually has two example applications.
>
> Starting at "Zoom!" on page 151, we show you how to use Yahoo!'s Maps web service to add zooming to the first example application in this solution. We add a list box that lets you select a zoom level, which corresponds to a specific image we downloaded from Yahoo!'s Maps web service. That list box *hovers* over the map. As you scroll the map underneath the hovering list box, the list box remains stationary, waiting for you to select your next zoom level.
>
> If you're curious about the second example application for this solution that incorporates zooming, see Figure 5.8 on page 153.

Summarizing the Map Application's Files and Directories

Our application's associated files and directories are shown in Figure 5.5.

We don't have many files in this application. We have the YahooMaps class, listed in Listing 5.1 on page 139, a CSS stylesheet, and some images. Additionally, we have two interfaces and one servlet class, as required by GWT's RPC mechanism, which together combine to form a remote procedure call to Yahoo!'s Maps web service.

Realize that other Java classes used by the Yahoo! Maps application are not shown in Figure 5.5, namely, the classes for our three custom widgets. Those classes reside in our Components module.

Figure 5.5   The Yahoo! Maps application's files and directories

Now that we've seen the files and directories for this solution, let's see how it's implemented.

Implementing the YahooMaps Application

Listing 5.1 shows the Yahoo! maps application.

Listing 5.1   com.gwtsolutions.client.YahooMaps

```
1. package com.gwtsolutions.client;
2.
3. import com.google.gwt.core.client.EntryPoint;
4. import com.google.gwt.core.client.GWT;
5. import com.google.gwt.user.client.Command;
6. import com.google.gwt.user.client.DeferredCommand;
7. import com.google.gwt.user.client.Window;
8. import com.google.gwt.user.client.rpc.AsyncCallback;
9. import com.google.gwt.user.client.rpc.ServiceDefTarget;
10.import com.google.gwt.user.client.ui.Button;
11.import com.google.gwt.user.client.ui.ClickListener;
12.import com.google.gwt.user.client.ui.Grid;
13.import com.google.gwt.user.client.ui.Image;
14.import com.google.gwt.user.client.ui.Label;
15.import com.google.gwt.user.client.ui.LoadListener;
16.import com.google.gwt.user.client.ui.RootPanel;
17.import com.google.gwt.user.client.ui.SimplePanel;
18.import com.google.gwt.user.client.ui.TextBox;
19.import com.google.gwt.user.client.ui.VerticalPanel;
20.import com.google.gwt.user.client.ui.Widget;
21.import com.gwtsolutions.components.client.ui.AutoCompleteTextBox;
22.import com.gwtsolutions.components.client.ui.Viewport;
23.import com.gwtsolutions.components.client.ui.sw.SimpleWindow;
24.
25.public class YahooMaps implements EntryPoint {
26.  private static final String[] states =
27.     {
28.          "CO", "NY", "NJ", "CA", "VT", "SC", "FL", "Al",
29.          "LA", "OR", "WA", "NV", "NM", "TX"
30.     };
31.
32.  public void onModuleLoad() {
33.    final Label heading = new Label("Yahoo! Maps Web Service");
34.    heading.addStyleName("heading");
```

continues

Listing 5.1   com.gwtsolutions.client.YahooMaps   *continued*

```
35.
36.    final Label streetAddressLabel =
37.        new Label("Street Address");
38.    final TextBox streetAddressTextBox = new TextBox();
39.    streetAddressTextBox.setVisibleLength(25);
40.
41.    final Label cityLabel = new Label("City");
42.    final TextBox cityTextBox = new TextBox();
43.    cityTextBox.setVisibleLength(15);
44.
45.    final Label stateLabel = new Label("State");
46.    final AutoCompleteTextBox stateTextBox =
47.        new AutoCompleteTextBox() {
48.          public String[] getCompletionCandidates() {
49.            return states;
50.          }
51.        };
52.
53.    stateTextBox.setVisibleLength(2);
54.
55.    final Button button = new Button("Get Map");
56.
57.    Grid grid = new Grid(4, 2);
58.    grid.setWidget(0, 0, streetAddressLabel);
59.    grid.setWidget(0, 1, streetAddressTextBox);
60.    grid.setWidget(1, 0, cityLabel);
61.    grid.setWidget(1, 1, cityTextBox);
62.    grid.setWidget(2, 0, stateLabel);
63.    grid.setWidget(2, 1, stateTextBox);
64.    grid.setWidget(3, 0, button);
65.
66.    DeferredCommand.addCommand(new Command() {
67.      public void execute() {
68.        streetAddressTextBox.setFocus(true);
69.      }
70.    });
71.
72.    button.addClickListener(new ClickListener() {
73.      public void onClick(Widget sender) {
74.        // Get the service from the GWT
75.        MapServiceAsync ws =
```

```
76.                    (MapServiceAsync) GWT.create(MapService.class);
77.
78.             ServiceDefTarget target = (ServiceDefTarget) ws;
79.             target.setServiceEntryPoint(GWT.getModuleBaseURL()
80.                 + "/mapService");
81.
82.             ws.getMap(streetAddressTextBox.getText(), cityTextBox
83.                 .getText(), stateTextBox.getText(),
84.                 new AsyncCallback() {
85.                   public void onSuccess(Object result) {
86.                     String title =
87.                         streetAddressTextBox.getText() + " "
88.                             + cityTextBox.getText() + ", "
89.                             + stateTextBox.getText();
90.
91.                     final MapWindow mw =
92.                         new MapWindow(title, result.toString(),
93.                             150, 150, 300, 200);
94.                   }
95.                   public void onFailure(Throwable throwable) {
96.                     Window.alert(throwable.getMessage());
97.                   }
98.                 });
99.         }
100.     });
101.     RootPanel.get().add(heading);
102.     RootPanel.get().add(grid);
103.   }
104.}
```

The preceding listing creates widgets, puts them in a grid panel, and makes a remote procedure call (RPC).

One interesting aspect of the preceding listing is on line 66, which defines a *deferred command* that gives focus to the street address text box. GWT executes that deferred command after the street address text box has been displayed. If you remove the deferred command and just call the text box's setFocus method directly, that method call will not stick—because the widget's DOM element hasn't yet been attached to the DOM tree—and the text box will not have focus when the application starts. Placing that method call in a deferred command causes GWT to execute the command, and therefore setFocus(), after the current event stack has been processed. At that point, GWT has displayed the text box, and the setFocus method works as expected.

A click listener for the Get Map button invokes the RPC. If that call is successful, the application creates a *map window* on line 91, passing the map window's constructor the window title and the map image returned from the RPC.

The MapWindow class is listed in Listing 5.2.

Listing 5.2   com.gwtsolutions.client.MapWindow

```
1. package com.gwtsolutions.client;
2.
3. import com.google.gwt.user.client.Window;
4. import com.google.gwt.user.client.ui.AbsolutePanel;
5. import com.google.gwt.user.client.ui.Image;
6. import com.google.gwt.user.client.ui.Label;
7. import com.google.gwt.user.client.ui.LoadListener;
8. import com.google.gwt.user.client.ui.VerticalPanel;
9. import com.google.gwt.user.client.ui.Widget;
10.import com.gwtsolutions.components.client.ui.Viewport;
11.import com.gwtsolutions.components.client.ui.sw.SimpleWindow;
12.
13.public class MapWindow extends SimpleWindow {
14.    private AbsolutePanel ap = new AbsolutePanel();
15.
16.    public MapWindow(String title, String imageURL,
17.        int left, int top, int width, int height) {
18.        final Viewport viewport = new Viewport();
19.        final VerticalPanel vp = new VerticalPanel();
20.        final Label loadingLabel =
21.            new Label("Loading image, please wait...");
22.        Image im = new Image(imageURL);
23.
24.        viewport.setView(im);
25.        vp.add(loadingLabel);
26.        vp.add(viewport);
27.        ap.add(vp);
28.
29.        addStyleName("busyCursor");
30.
31.        im.addLoadListener(new LoadListener() {
32.            public void onError(Widget sender) {
33.                Window.alert("Couldn't load map");
34.            }
35.
36.            public void onLoad(Widget sender) {
```

```
37.              vp.remove(loadingLabel);
38.              removeStyleName("busyCursor");
39.          }
40.      });
41.
42.      im.setUrl(imageURL);
43.
44.      setContent(ap);
45.      setTitle(title);
46.      setWidth("300px");
47.      setHeight("200px");
48.      setWindowPosition(left, top);
49.
50.      show();
51.  }
52.}
53.
```

The MapWindow class extends SimpleWindow, which is a custom widget class that we discuss in Solution 7. The MapWindow constructor creates a vertical panel that contains a label (Loading image, please wait...) at the top and a viewport underneath the label. The map window displays the label only while the map image is loading. When the label is loaded, the map window removes the label from the vertical panel (line 37), leaving the viewport as the sole occupant of the vertical panel.

The map window does something else while the map image loads: It changes its cursor to a busy cursor (line 29). When the image is loaded, in addition to removing the label from the vertical panel, the map window returns the cursor to its initial state (line 38).

The MapWindow constructor sets the window's content, title, width, height, and position, and then calls SimpleWindow.show() to display the window.

Because images take time to load, especially when the images are downloaded over the Internet, it is often necessary to monitor image loading, as is the case for the MapWindow class. When you set an image's URL with Image.setUrl(), as we did on line 42 of the preceding listing, GWT starts loading the image. If you've attached a load listener to your image, GWT calls the listener's onLoad method when the image is loaded, or onFailure() if the image fails to load. In the meantime, it's often a good idea to give the user some visual cue that indicates an image is being loaded. The map window gives the user two indicators by changing the cursor and temporarily displaying a message.

GWT's DOM Elements Are Reminiscent of the AWT's Peers

The Abstract Window Toolkit (AWT) is a peer-based framework, meaning that its widgets are thin veneers on top of operating-system-specific controls. Because of that design, some method calls for AWT widgets won't work until the widget's peer has been displayed onscreen.

GWT also uses a peer-based approach, but GWT's peers are DOM elements instead of operating system-specific widgets. When you create a GWT widget, what ultimately is shown in the browser is a DOM element that you can effectively manipulate through its associated widget.

Like AWT widgets, some method calls on GWT widgets, such as `setFocus()`, do not work until the underlying peer has been attached to the DOM tree. To make those method calls work, you can wrap them in a deferred command, as we did to give the street address text box focus when the application is first displayed.

 com.google.gwt.user.client.ui.Grid

- `setWidget(int row, int column, Widget w)`

Specifies a particular row and column for a widget that you add to a grid. The method is useful because `Grid` class is a panel that arranges its widgets in rows and columns.

 com.google.gwt.user.client.ui.TextBox

- `setVisibleLength(int length)`

Sets the number of characters that are visible in a text box. You can set the maximum number of characters that can be typed into a text box with `setMaxLength()`.

 com.google.gwt.user.client.GWT

- `create(Class class)`

Given a class of a particular type of object, returns a corresponding object that implements that class's interface. Use this method for obtaining references to remote services and also for GWT internationalization.

com.google.gwt.user.client.rpc.ServiceDefTarget

- setServiceEntryPoint(String entryPoint)

Sets an entry point for mapping to a servlet used for remote procedure calls. You should always prepend the module base, obtained with GWT.getModuleBaseURL(), to the entry point to make sure that GWT will find the RPC servlet when your application runs in an external server.

See Solution 11 for more information on running your application in an external server.

com.google.gwt.user.client.rpc.AsyncCallback

- onSuccess(Object result)

Is called by GWT after a successful RPC. The result object is the result of the RPC. That object can be a number of different types, including user-defined types that adhere to GWT's serialization.

See GWT's online documentation for more information about the data types that you can return from an RPC.

- onFailure(Throwable exception)

Is called by GWT when an RPC fails; the method passes the corresponding exception.

RPC calls can fail for numerous reasons, including network problems.

com.google.gwt.user.client.ui.LoadListener

- onLoad(Widget sender)

Is called by GWT when an image, to which you attached a load listener, successfully loads; GWT passes to the method the image widget on whose behalf the image was loaded.

- onError(Widget sender)

Is called by GWT when an image, to which you attached a load listener, fails to load; GWT passes to the method the image on whose behalf the image failed to load.

com.google.gwt.user.client.ui.Image

- setUrl(String url)

    Begins the loading process for an image at the specified URL. If you have attached a load listener to an image, that listener will be invoked when the image is loaded, or when the image fails to load. The URL that you pass to setUrl() must not violate the *same origin policy* enforced by web browser. If the URL references an image packaged as a part of a reusable component, the URL string must be constructed using GWT.getModuleBaseURL() so that the image can be loaded from the reusable module's public path. If the URL string is not prepended with the module base, the URL is interpreted relative to the location of the page which references it.

Access to Yahoo!'s Web Service

Now that we've seen the requisite code on the client, let's turn our attention to the server, where our remote procedure call is implemented.

To access the Yahoo! Maps web service, we need to invoke an HTTP GET method on an appropriate URL on the Yahoo! server, passing attributes that represent the desired street address, city, and state. How do you invoke an HTTP GET method on an arbitrary URL on the Internet?

Fortunately, you don't need to know how to programmatically invoke an HTTP GET, because you can use Apache Jakarta's HttpClient. All we have to do is use their API and let HttpClient do all the heavy lifting for us. The HttpClient homepage is shown in Figure 5.6.

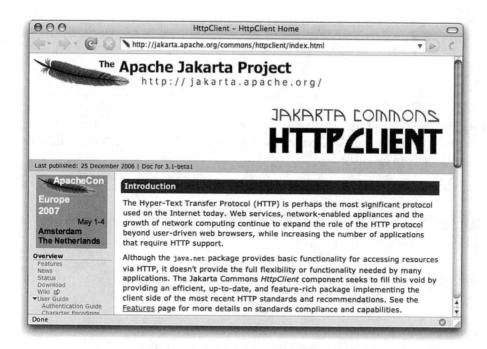

Figure 5.6   Apache's Jakarta Commons HttpClient homepage

Before we discuss the details of using HttpClient, let's look at Listing 5.3 and Listing 5.4, which list the interfaces we need for our RPC.

Listing 5.3   com.gwtsolutions.client.MapService

```
1.package com.gwtsolutions.client;
2.
3.import com.google.gwt.user.client.rpc.RemoteService;
4.
5.public interface MapService extends RemoteService {
6.   String getMap(String streetAddress, String city,
7.       String state);
8.}
9.
```

Listing 5.4   com.gwtsolutions.client.MapServiceAsync

```
1.package com.gwtsolutions.client;
2.
3.import com.google.gwt.user.client.rpc.AsyncCallback;
4.
5.public interface MapServiceAsync {
6.   void getMap(String streetAddress, String city, String state,
```

continues

Listing 5.4   com.gwtsolutions.client.MapServiceAsync   continued

```
7.        AsyncCallback callback);
8.}
9.
```

GWT uses the MapService interface to invoke our remote service on the server. The MapServiceAsync interface is what we used in Listing 5.1 on page 139 to asynchronously call the remote service.

Listing 5.5 shows the implementation of the MapService interface.

Listing 5.5   com.gwtsolutions.server.MapServiceImpl

```
1. package com.gwtsolutions.server;
2.
3. import java.io.InputStream;
4. import javax.xml.parsers.DocumentBuilderFactory;
5.
6. import org.apache.commons.httpclient.HttpClient;
7. import org.apache.commons.httpclient.methods.GetMethod;
8. import org.w3c.dom.Document;
9. import org.w3c.dom.Element;
10.import org.w3c.dom.NodeList;
11.
12.import com.google.gwt.user.server.rpc.RemoteServiceServlet;
13.import com.gwtsolutions.client.MapService;
14.
15.public class MapServiceImpl extends RemoteServiceServlet
16.    implements MapService {
17.    private static final String APPID = "PUT_YOUR_ID_HERE";
18.    private static final long serialVersionUID = 1L;
19.
20.    public String getMap(String streetAddress, String city,
21.        String state) {
22.        return getMapUrlFromDocument(
23.            getMapDocumentFromWebService(
24.                streetAddress, city, state, APPID));
25.    }
26.    private String getMapUrlFromDocument(Document document) {
27.        NodeList result =
28.            (NodeList) document.getElementsByTagName("Result");
29.
30.        Element mapUrl = (Element) result.item(0);
```

```
31.        return mapUrl.getFirstChild().getNodeValue();
32.    }
33.    private Document getMapDocumentFromWebService(
34.        String streetAddress, String city, String state,
35.        String appid) {
36.      String url =
37.          "http://api.local.yahoo.com/MapsService/V1"
38.              + "/mapImage?appid=" + appid + "&street="
39.              + encode(streetAddress) + "&city=" + city
40.              + "&state=" + state + "&image_width=2000"
41.              + "&image_height=2000";
42.      return getDocumentFromUrl(url);
43.    }
44.    private Document getDocumentFromUrl(String url) {
45.      HttpClient client = new HttpClient();
46.      GetMethod get = new GetMethod(url);
47.      Document document = null;
48.
49.      try {
50.        int result = client.executeMethod(get);
51.        if (result == 200) {
52.          InputStream in = get.getResponseBodyAsStream();
53.          document =
54.              DocumentBuilderFactory.newInstance()
55.                  .newDocumentBuilder().parse(in);
56.        }
57.      }
58.      catch (Exception e) {
59.        try {
60.          document =
61.              DocumentBuilderFactory.newInstance()
62.                  .newDocumentBuilder().parse("map.xml");
63.        }
64.        catch (Exception e1) {
65.          e1.printStackTrace();
66.        }
67.      }
68.      return document;
69.    }
70.    private String encode(String streetAddress) {
71.      StringBuffer buffer = new StringBuffer();
72.      for (int i = 0; i < streetAddress.length(); ++i) {
73.        if (streetAddress.charAt(i) == ' ')
```

continues

Listing 5.5   com.gwtsolutions.server.MapServiceImpl   *continued*

```
74.        buffer.append('+');
75.     else
76.        buffer.append(streetAddress.charAt(i));
77.     }
78.   return buffer.toString();
79.  }
80.}
```

GWT passes the `getMap` method—which is defined by the `MapService` interface and whose implementation starts on line 20 of the preceding listing—the street address, city, and state that the user entered into our user interface on the client.

The `getMap` method gets the XML document from the Yahoo! web service with the `getMapDocumentFromWebService` method (line 33). With the XML document in hand, the `getMap` method then extracts the map URL from the document with the `getMapUrlFromDocument` method (line 26).

The XML document returned from the Yahoo! Maps web service is simple; here's a sample document:

```
<?xml version="1.0" encoding="UTF-8"?>

<Result xmlns:xsi="http://www.w3.org/2001/XMLSchema-instance">
http://img.maps.yahoo.com/mapimage?MAP
DATA=eJz6K.d6wXVM6myr2yRPfx6.kl.uMGgD3Tu4JtDQzr_33pFEsTTSaosZ90CtsiDrsLv9t65fzjz
0CJm6JO2v_ZIHLflY9gto.xWMK9ovlRJVmrBLO4FoSsh3Ipsr
</Result>
```

The XML document returned from Yahoo!'s Maps web service contains only a single element—`Result`—that contains a map URL. XML documents returned from online web services are typically more complex because they often return more than one piece of information.

To get the XML document from the Yahoo! web service, we construct a URL on line 36, complete with parameters for street address, city, and state, and then we use an `HttpClient GetMethod` instance to make an HTTP GET request to that URL on line. We make that GET request by invoking `HttpClient.executeMethod()` on line 50, which returns an HTTP status code. If that status is 200, we know the call succeeded, so we get the response stream and turn it into a corresponding XML document with the aid of Java's `DocumentBuilderFactory` class from the `java.xml.parsers` package on line 53. Once we have the XML document, we return the enclosed map URL to the client. Recall from Listing 5.1 on page 139 that we pass that URL to GWT's `Image.setUrl` method to load the corresponding image over the Internet. Then we're done.

There's one more piece to the RPC puzzle, and that's the servlet mapping, contained in our application's module configuration file, which is listed in Listing 5.6.

Listing 5.6   YahooMaps.gwt.xml

```
1.<module>
2.
3.<!— Inherit the core Web Toolkit stuff.              —>
4.   <inherits name='com.google.gwt.user.User'/>
5.   <inherits name='com.gwtsolutions.components.Components'/>
6.
7.   <servlet path="/mapService"
8.            class="com.gwtsolutions.server.MapServiceImpl"/>
9.
10.   <stylesheet src="css/styles.css"/>
11.
12.<!— Specify the app entry point class.              —>
13.<entry-point class='com.gwtsolutions.client.YahooMaps'/>
14.
15.</module>
```

Recall that we invoked GWT.create() to create our remote service in Listing 5.1 on page 139 and subsequently set the service's entry point like this:

```
MapServiceAsync ws = (MapServiceAsync) GWT.create(MapService.class);
ServiceDefTarget target = (ServiceDefTarget) ws;
target.setServiceEntryPoint(GWT.getModuleBaseURL() + "/mapService");
```

Notice that the URL passed to ServiceDefTarget.setServiceEntryPoint ends in /mapService, which corresponds to the mapping on line 7 of Listing 5.6.

Zoom!

Now that we've seen how to implement an RPC call that obtains information from an online web service, let's see how we can extend the example shown in Figure 5.1 on page 134 by implementing zoom levels.

Figure 5.7 shows the parameters that you can send to Yahoo!'s Maps web service. We are concerned with the zoom parameter, which specifies the zoom level for a map. That value is an integer from 1, which signifies street level, to 12, which signifies country level.

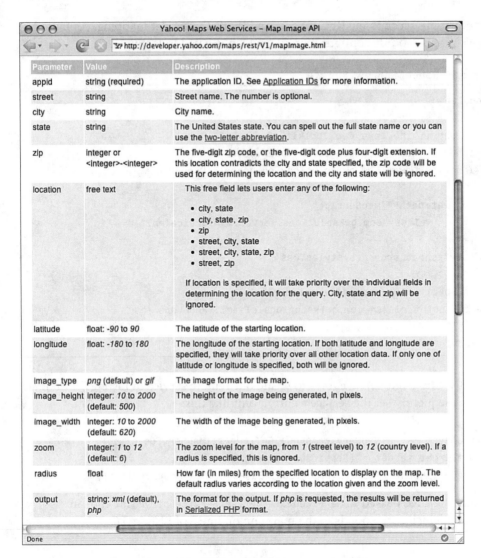

Parameter	Value	Description
appid	string (required)	The application ID. See Application IDs for more information.
street	string	Street name. The number is optional.
city	string	City name.
state	string	The United States state. You can spell out the full state name or you can use the two-letter abbreviation.
zip	integer or <integer>-<integer>	The five-digit zip code, or the five-digit code plus four-digit extension. If this location contradicts the city and state specified, the zip code will be used for determining the location and the city and state will be ignored.
location	free text	This free field lets users enter any of the following: • city, state • city, state, zip • zip • street, city, state • street, city, state, zip • street, zip If location is specified, it will take priority over the individual fields in determining the location for the query. City, state and zip will be ignored.
latitude	float: -90 to 90	The latitude of the starting location.
longitude	float: -180 to 180	The longitude of the starting location. If both latitude and longitude are specified, they will take priority over all other location data. If only one of latitude or longitude is specified, both will be ignored.
image_type	png (default) or gif	The image format for the map.
image_height	integer: 10 to 2000 (default: 500)	The height of the image being generated, in pixels.
image_width	integer: 10 to 2000 (default: 620)	The width of the image being generated, in pixels.
zoom	integer: 1 to 12 (default: 6)	The zoom level for the map, from 1 (street level) to 12 (country level). If a radius is specified, this is ignored.
radius	float	How far (in miles) from the specified location to display on the map. The default radius varies according to the location given and the zoom level.
output	string: xml (default), php	The format for the output. If php is requested, the results will be returned in Serialized PHP format.

Figure 5.7   Parameters for URLs sent to Yahoo! Maps web service

As shown in Figure 5.8, we give our application a zoom-level list box that hovers over the map. When users change the zoom level, we load the corresponding map in the window.

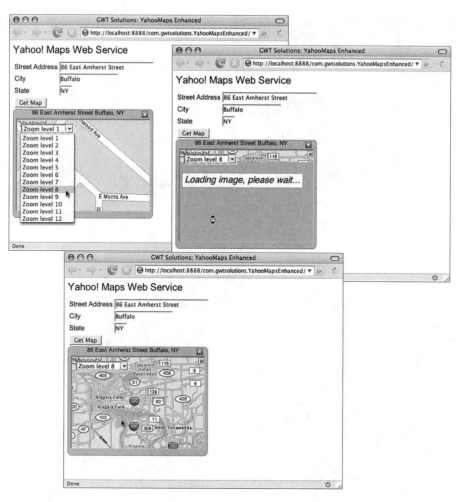

Figure 5.8   Changing a map Image's zoom level

When a user drags the map in the viewport, the map moves underneath the hovering zoom-level list box, as illustrated in Figure 5.9.

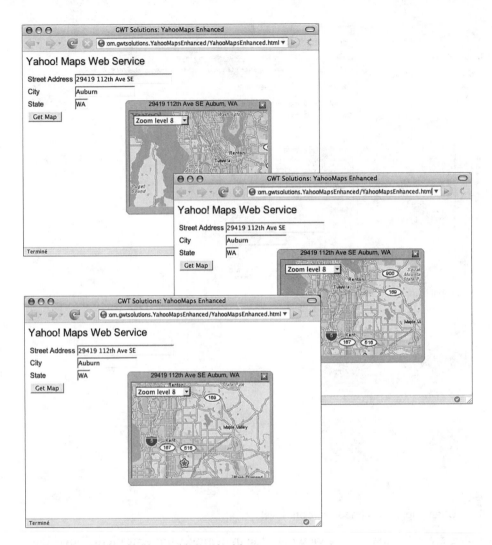

Figure 5.9   The hovering zoom level widget

Instead of making one call to Yahoo!'s web service for a particular address, as we did in the first example application in this solution, we now make *twelve* calls, one for each zoom level. With every call, we add a zoom parameter to the URL; when the RPC is finished, we have twelve map URLs, one for each zoom level.

The first order of business is to change the remote service interface that we originally listed in Listing 5.3 on page 147. The updated version of that interface is listed in Listing 5.7.

Listing 5.7   com.gwtsolutions.MapService

```
1.package com.gwtsolutions.client;
2.
3.import com.google.gwt.user.client.rpc.RemoteService;
4.
5.public interface MapService extends RemoteService {
6.  String[] getMap(String streetAddress, String city,
7.      String state);
8.}
```

The only change we made to the interface is on line 6, where we specify that the RPC returns an array of map URLs instead of a single URL.

Interestingly enough, the corresponding asynchronous interface, originally listed in Listing 5.4 on page 147, remains unchanged because all asynchronous methods for an RPC return void. Because the arguments to the asynchronous call are unchanged, we need not make any changes to the asynchronous interface.

A severely truncated listing of the updated implementation of the remote service is listed in Listing 5.8.

Listing 5.8   com.gwtsolutions.server.MapServiceImpl (truncated)

```
1.package com.gwtsolutions.server;
2....
3.import com.google.gwt.user.server.rpc.RemoteServiceServlet;
4.import com.gwtsolutions.client.MapService;
5.
6.public class MapServiceImpl extends RemoteServiceServlet
7.    implements MapService {
8.  ...
9.  public String[] getMap(String streetAddress, String city,
10.      String state) {
11.    String[] urls = new String[12];
12.
13.    for (int i=1; i <= urls.length; ++i) {
14.      urls[i-1] = getMapUrlFromDocument(
15.          getMapDocumentFromWebService(
16.              streetAddress, city, state, APPID, i));
17.    }
18.    return urls;
19.  }
20.  ...
21.}
```

Most of the code for the remote service interface is unchanged, except for the `getMap` method itself, which we modified to fetch twelve map URLs instead of one.

The modified application on the client is listed in Listing 5.9.

Listing 5.9   com.gwtsolutions.client.YahooMapsEnhanced

```
1. package com.gwtsolutions.client;
2.
3. import com.google.gwt.core.client.EntryPoint;
4. import com.google.gwt.core.client.GWT;
5. import com.google.gwt.user.client.Command;
6. import com.google.gwt.user.client.DeferredCommand;
7. import com.google.gwt.user.client.Window;
8. import com.google.gwt.user.client.rpc.AsyncCallback;
9. import com.google.gwt.user.client.rpc.ServiceDefTarget;
10.import com.google.gwt.user.client.ui.Button;
11.import com.google.gwt.user.client.ui.ClickListener;
12.import com.google.gwt.user.client.ui.Grid;
13.import com.google.gwt.user.client.ui.Label;
14.import com.google.gwt.user.client.ui.RootPanel;
15.import com.google.gwt.user.client.ui.TextBox;
16.import com.google.gwt.user.client.ui.Widget;
17.import com.gwtsolutions.components.client.ui.AutoCompleteTextBox;
18.
19.public class YahooMapsEnhanced implements EntryPoint {
20.   private static final int FIRST_MAP_WINDOW_TOP = 150;
21.   private static final int FIRST_MAP_WINDOW_LEFT = 150;
22.
23.   private static final int TOP_OFFSET = 20;
24.   private static final int LEFT_OFFSET = 20;
25.
26.   private static final int MAP_WINDOW_WIDTH = 500;
27.   private static final int MAP_WINDOW_HEIGHT = 300;
28.
29.   private int lastWindowLeft = FIRST_MAP_WINDOW_LEFT;
30.   private int lastWindowTop = FIRST_MAP_WINDOW_TOP;
31.
32.   private MapServiceAsync ws =
33.       (MapServiceAsync) GWT.create(MapService.class);
34.   private ServiceDefTarget target = (ServiceDefTarget) ws;
35.
36.   private static final String[] states =
37.       {
38.           "CO", "NY", "NJ", "CA", "VT", "SC", "FL", "Al",
```

```
39.              "LA", "OR", "WA", "NV", "NM", "TX"
40.        };
41.
42.    public void onModuleLoad() {
43.      final Label heading = new Label("Yahoo! Maps Web Service");
44.      heading.addStyleName("heading");
45.
46.      final Label streetAddressLabel =
47.          new Label("Street Address");
48.      final TextBox streetAddressTextBox = new TextBox();
49.      streetAddressTextBox.setVisibleLength(25);
50.
51.      final Label cityLabel = new Label("City");
52.      final TextBox cityTextBox = new TextBox();
53.      cityTextBox.setVisibleLength(15);
54.
55.      final Label stateLabel = new Label("State");
56.      final AutoCompleteTextBox stateTextBox =
57.          new AutoCompleteTextBox() {
58.            public String[] getCompletionCandidates() {
59.              return states;
60.            }
61.          };
62.
63.      streetAddressTextBox.setTabIndex(1);
64.      cityTextBox.setTabIndex(2);
65.      stateTextBox.setTabIndex(3);
66.
67.      stateTextBox.setVisibleLength(2);
68.
69.      final Button button = new Button("Get Map");
70.
71.      Grid grid = new Grid(4, 2);
72.      grid.setWidget(0, 0, streetAddressLabel);
73.      grid.setWidget(0, 1, streetAddressTextBox);
74.      grid.setWidget(1, 0, cityLabel);
75.      grid.setWidget(1, 1, cityTextBox);
76.      grid.setWidget(2, 0, stateLabel);
77.      grid.setWidget(2, 1, stateTextBox);
78.      grid.setWidget(3, 0, button);
79.
80.      DeferredCommand.addCommand(new Command() {
```

continues

Listing 5.9   com.gwtsolutions.client.YahooMapsEnhanced   *continued*

```
81.       public void execute() {
82.          streetAddressTextBox.setFocus(true);
83.       }
84.    });
85.
86.    target.setServiceEntryPoint(GWT.getModuleBaseURL()
87.       + "/mapService");
88.
89.    button.addClickListener(new ClickListener() {
90.       public void onClick(Widget sender) {
91.          ws.getMap(streetAddressTextBox.getText(), cityTextBox
92.             .getText(), stateTextBox.getText(),
93.             new AsyncCallback() {
94.                public void onSuccess(Object result) {
95.                   String title =
96.                      streetAddressTextBox.getText() + " "
97.                         + cityTextBox.getText() + ", "
98.                         + stateTextBox.getText();
99.
100.                   new MapWindow(title, (String[])result,
101.                      lastWindowLeft + LEFT_OFFSET,
102.                      lastWindowTop + TOP_OFFSET,
103.                      MAP_WINDOW_WIDTH, MAP_WINDOW_HEIGHT);
104.
105.                   lastWindowLeft += LEFT_OFFSET;
106.                   lastWindowTop  += TOP_OFFSET;
107.                }
108.                public void onFailure(Throwable throwable) {
109.                   Window.alert(throwable.getMessage());
110.                }
111.             });
112.       }
113.    });
114.    RootPanel.get().add(heading);
115.    RootPanel.get().add(grid);
116. }
117.}
```

On line 100 of the preceding listing, we cast the result of the RPC as an array of strings instead of a single string. Most of the other changes for the second example application are encapsulated in the MapWindow class, which is listed in Listing 5.10.

Listing 5.10   com.gwtsolutions.client.MapWindow

```
1. package com.gwtsolutions.client;
2.
3. import com.google.gwt.user.client.Window;
4. import com.google.gwt.user.client.ui.AbsolutePanel;
5. import com.google.gwt.user.client.ui.ChangeListener;
6. import com.google.gwt.user.client.ui.Image;
7. import com.google.gwt.user.client.ui.Label;
8. import com.google.gwt.user.client.ui.ListBox;
9. import com.google.gwt.user.client.ui.LoadListener;
10.import com.google.gwt.user.client.ui.Widget;
11.import com.gwtsolutions.components.client.ui.Viewport;
12.import com.gwtsolutions.components.client.ui.sw.SimpleWindow;
13.
14.public class MapWindow extends SimpleWindow {
15.    private final AbsolutePanel ap = new AbsolutePanel();
16.    private final Viewport viewport = new Viewport();
17.    private final ListBox zoomLevels = new ListBox();
18.    private final Image[] images;
19.    private final String[] imageUrls;
20.    private final Label loadingLabel =
21.        new Label("Loading image, please wait...");
22.
23.    public MapWindow(String title, String[] imageUrls,
24.        int left, int top, int width, int height) {
25.       images = new Image[imageUrls.length];
26.       this.imageUrls = imageUrls;
27.       int cnt = 0;
28.
29.       showLoadingIndicators();
30.
31.       // Iterate over image URLs, create a new image for each
32.       // URL and set the image's URL. Also add a load listener
33.       // to every image
34.       while (cnt < images.length) {
35.          images[cnt] = new Image();
36.
37.          if (cnt == 0) // initially, only load the first image
38.              images[cnt].setUrl(imageUrls[cnt]);
39.
40.          images[cnt++].addLoadListener(new MapLoadListener());
41.          zoomLevels.addItem("Zoom level " + cnt);
```

continues

Listing 5.10   com.gwtsolutions.client.MapWindow   *continued*

```
42.    }
43.
44.    loadingLabel.addStyleName("loadingLabel");
45.    zoomLevels.addStyleName("zoomListBox");
46.    viewport.setView(images[0]);
47.
48.    ap.add(viewport);
49.    setContent(ap);
50.    setTitle(title);
51.
52.    zoomLevels.addChangeListener(new ZoomChangeListener());
53.
54.    setPixelSize(width, height);
55.    viewport.setPixelSize(width, height);
56.    setWindowPosition(left, top);
57.    show(true);
58.    }
59.
60.    // This method keeps the viewport's size in sync with
61.    // the window when the window is resized.
62.    public void windowResized(int width, int height) {
63.      // viewport can be null if setPixelSize() is called
64.      // in the superclass's constructor
65.      if (viewport != null) {
66.        viewport.setPixelSize(width - 2*SIDE_FRAME_WIDTH,
67.            height - TOP_FRAME_HEIGHT + BOTTOM_FRAME_HEIGHT);
68.      }
69.    }
70.
71.    private void showLoadingIndicators() {
72.      ap.add(loadingLabel, 5, 50);
73.      addStyleName("busyCursor");
74.    }
75.
76.    private class ZoomChangeListener implements ChangeListener {
77.      public void onChange(Widget sender) {
78.        int selectedIndex =
79.            ((ListBox) sender).getSelectedIndex();
80.        Image image = images[selectedIndex];
81.        String u = image.getUrl();
82.        if (image.getUrl().equals("")) {
83.          String url = imageUrls[selectedIndex];
```

```
84.          showLoadingIndicators();
85.          image.setUrl(url);
86.       }
87.       viewport.setView(image);
88.    }
89.  }
90.
91.  private class MapLoadListener implements LoadListener {
92.    public void onError(Widget sender) {
93.      Window.alert("Couldn't load map");
94.    }
95.
96.    public void onLoad(Widget sender) {
97.      ap.remove(loadingLabel);
98.      removeStyleName("busyCursor");
99.      if (!zoomLevels.isAttached()) {
100.       ap.add(zoomLevels, 10, 10);
101.     }
102.   }
103. }
104.}
```

The preceding version of `MapWindow` differs from the original listed in Listing 5.2 on page 142 in three respects:

- It maintains an array of map images instead of a single image.

- It causes the `Loading image, please wait...` label to hover over the viewport, instead of above it.

- It adds a zoom-level list box that also hovers over the viewport.

Instead of maintaining a single map image, as was the case for our first implementation of `MapWindow`, in the preceding listing, we maintain an array of images. On line 25, we create an array of images, and on line 34, we iterate over the array of image URLs that we passed to the `MapWindow` constructor on line 100 of Listing 5.9 on page 156.

On line 38 of the preceding listing, we set the URL for the *first* map image. That call to `Image.setUrl()` causes GWT to load the first image in our array of images (the one at zoom level 1).

We load only the first image because it's very likely that few, if any, users will access all twelve zoom levels. From then on, we *lazily* load map images when the user accesses a particular zoom level. By implementing lazy loading, we only load images associated with a particular zoom level when the user first accesses that zoom level.

To implement a hovering loading message and a hovering zoom-level list box, we changed the contents of our map window. In the original version of MapWindow class, we had a vertical panel with a label in the top and a viewport in the bottom. To achieve hovering widgets, we replaced the vertical panel with an instance of AbsolutePanel. Absolute panels let you place widgets at pixel locations and, more importantly, allow widgets to overlap one another.

So, instead of a vertical panel, our map window now contains an absolute panel, which we create on line 15 of the preceding listing. We add the viewport to the absolute panel on line 48. On line 29, we invoke showLoadingIndicators(). That method, starting on line 71, adds the Loading image, please wait... label to the absolute panel at a pixel location of 5 pixels from the left edge of the panel and 50 pixels from the top. Notice that when we add the viewport to the absolute panel, we don't specify a pixel location. In the absence of a specific pixel location, the absolute panel adds the viewport at (0,0).

To display map images at appropriate zoom levels and to add and remove hovering widgets, we create two event listeners: a load listener and a change listener.

On line 40, we attach a load listener to each image maintained by the map window. That load listener, starting on line 91, reacts to the loading of an image by removing the hovering Loading image, please wait... label from the absolute panel and restoring the cursor to its original representation, on lines 97 and 98, respectively. That load listener also adds the zoom-level list box to the map window's absolute panel at a pixel location of (10, 10) *immediately after the first image loads*.

We don't want to add the zoom-level list box to the absolute panel every time an image is loaded, so we add it only if the list box is not already attached to the absolute panel. We check for the presence of the zoom-level list box by invoking the list box's isAttached method, which returns true if the list box is attached to a parent widget.

When the user selects a zoom level from the zoom-level list box, we check to see if the associated image has an empty string for its URL (line 82); if so, we call the image's setUrl method on line 85 to begin the image-loading process. On line 84, we once again invoke showLoadingIndicators() to show the hovering Loading image, please wait... label and to change the cursor to a busy cursor. Then, on line 87, we set the viewport's view to the image associated with the zoom level selected from the list box.

com.google.gwt.user.client.ui.AbsolutePanel

- add(Widget w)

Adds a widget to an absolute panel.

This method does not specify a pixel location for the widget that's added to the panel. In response to the absence of a pixel location, absolute panels add widgets as though the absolute panel were a vertical panel. If the first widget added to an absolute panel is added with this method, it is placed at (0,0) within the panel. If the second widget is also added with this method, it is placed at (0, bottom of first widget), and so on.

- add(Widget w, int x, int y)

Adds a widget to an absolute panel at a specific pixel location.

Absolute panels support overlapping widgets, so you can add one widget on top of another. The first overlapping widget added to an absolute panel is shown underneath the second overlapping widget added to the panel.

com.google.gwt.user.client.ui.Widget

- isAttached()

Returns true if a widget is attached to a parent widget, as long as the parent widget and its ancestors are also attached to a parent widget; an exception is the root panel, which has no parent. If a widget is not attached to a panel, this method returns false.

com.google.gwt.user.client.ui.ChangeListener

- onChange(Widget sender)

Is called when a widget has been changed by a user; the method is passed the widget that was changed. An example is a user changing the currently selected item in a list box.

GWT May Invoke Load Listeners Immediately After You Set an Image's URL

You may notice that on lines 29 and 84 of the previous listing, we showed loading indicators—meaning we added a status message and changed the cursor—*before* we set image URLs. In the image load listener, we remove those indicators.

We set the loading indicators before setting image URLs—not the other way around—because on some browsers, load listeners can be called as soon as the call to load the images URL (setURL()) returns. Therefore, if we set loading indicators after calling the image's setURL(), the load listener will already have been called, and our loading indicators will not be removed by the load listener.

The moral of the story: Load listeners may be called immediately after you call setURL() on an image, so do any setup that's undone by load listeners prior to calling setURL().

Stuff We Covered in This Solution

It took awhile for web services to catch on, but nowadays most popular sites such as Flickr and YouTube (see Figure 5.10) provide web services so that you can access their data. Web services enable all kinds of interesting applications, including mashups that combine information from multiple web services.

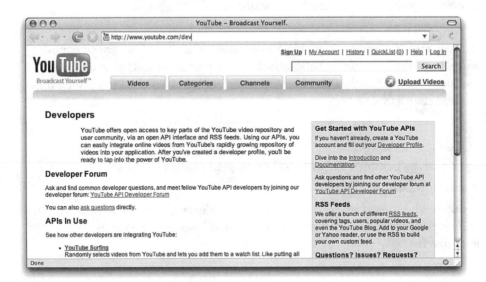

Figure 5.10   YouTube's web services

GWT lets you easily make RPCs to the server, where you can access online web services, but GWT doesn't directly support access to online web services. Fortunately, the Java landscape is rich enough that you can easily find a solid, open-source API to make GET requests over the Web. In this solution, we used Apache Jakarta's

HttpClient to do our heavy lifting on the server. In just a few lines of code, we obtained an XML document from the Yahoo! Maps web service that provided a URL to a map image associated with an address.

The application discussed in this solution really shows the potential of GWT. Not only did we access maps from a web service, but our application displays multiple maps in windows that reside within the confines of the browser. Not only that, the windows contain viewports that implement animated scrolling similar to Apple's iPhone to make it easy to get around on maps. While we were at it, we showed you some techniques that you will undoubtedly find useful in unrelated applications, such as monitoring image loading, implementing RPCs, using deferred commands, making widgets hover, and creating images from URLs on the Internet.

Including the implementation of the three custom widgets used in this solution and the two example applications, we probably spent two man-weeks' worth of time putting the whole thing together. Not bad for a couple of guys who also had a lot of writing to do. Imagine what you could do with more time and a few more developers.

Drag and Drop

The ultimate in user interactivity, drag and drop is taken for granted in desktop applications but is a litmus test of sorts for web applications: If you can easily implement drag and drop with your web application framework, then you know you've got something special.

Until now, drag and drop for web applications has, for the most part, been limited to specialized JavaScript frameworks such as Script.aculo.us and Rico.[1] No more. With the advent of GWT, we have drag-and-drop capabilities in a Java-based web application framework. Although GWT does not explicitly support drag and drop (drag and drop is an anticipated feature in the future), it provides us with all the necessary ingredients to make our own drag-and-drop module.

In this solution, we explore drag-and-drop implementation with GWT. We implement drag and drop in a module of its own so that you can easily incorporate drag and drop into your applications.

Stuff You're Going to Learn

This solution explores the following aspects of GWT:

- Implementing composite widgets with the `Composite` class (page 174)
- Removing widgets from panels (page 169)
- Changing cursors for widgets with CSS styles (page 200)
- Implementing a GWT module (page 182)
- Adding multiple listeners to a widget (page 186)
- Using the `AbsolutePanel` class to place widgets by pixel location (page 211)
- Capturing and releasing events for a specific widget (page 191)
- Using an event preview to inhibit browser reactions to events (page 196)

---

[1] See http://www.script.aculo.us and http://openrico.org for more information about Script.aculo.us and Rico, respectively.

See Solution 1 and Solution 2 for more in-depth discussions of implementing GWT modules and implementing composite widgets, respectively.

The Drag-and-Drop Example Application

Our discussion of drag and drop (dnd) starts with a sample application that uses our drag-and-drop module. Then we peel back the layers of the drag-and-drop onion to reveal the underlying implementation.

Figure 6.1 shows the drag-and-drop example application in action. The application contains iPods and Zunes that can be dragged into their respective shopping carts. When you start dragging a music player, the cursor changes to the *pointer* cursor to indicate that a drag is underway, just in case the actual movement of the music player is not enough evidence of that fact.

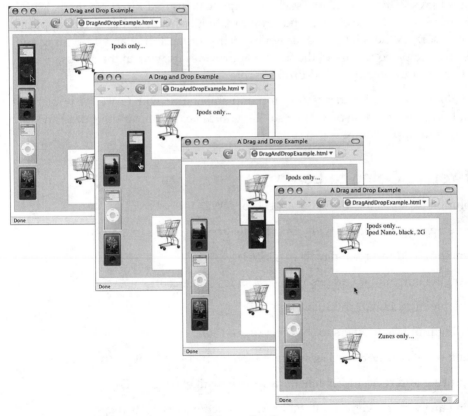

Figure 6.1   The drag-and-drop example application

If a user drags a music player, which in dnd parlance is known as a drag source, over its shopping cart (referred to as a drop target), two things happen: We once again change the cursor, this time to a *move* cursor, to indicate that a drop is acceptable for this drop target (known as a drag-over effect), and we change the border of the drop target (known as a drag-under effect). If the user subsequently releases the mouse while the drag source is over the drop target, we remove the drag source from the page and update the drop target to reflect the fact that it now contains the music player that was dropped.

If the user starts dragging a music player and then decides against dropping it on its shopping cart panel, we scoot the music player back to its original position, as illustrated in Figure 6.2. This is standard drag-and-drop behavior.

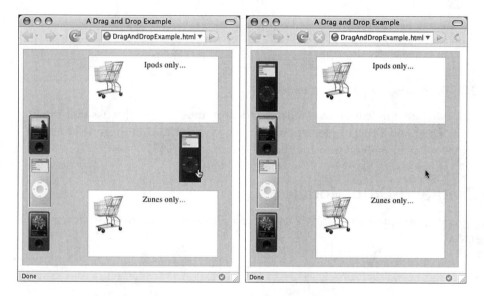

Figure 6.2   Drag sources snap back when dropped outside a drop target

Finally, notice that we have two drop targets: one for iPods and another for Zunes. Users cannot drag an iPod into the Zune shopping cart, or vice versa. If they try to do so, the cursor changes to the no-drop cursor when the music player enters the forbidden shopping cart, as shown in Figure 6.3. When a user drops a music player over a forbidden shopping cart, the music player moves back to its original position, just as it does when dropped outside any drop target.

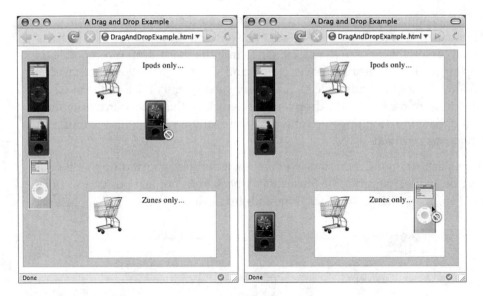

Figure 6.3   Disallowing drops in drop targets

Our drag-and-drop application uses a drag-and-drop module. We discuss that module in detail in "Drag and Drop Implementation in a GWT Module" on page 182, but for now let's see what's involved in using that module.

The Drag-and-Drop Module

The drag-and-drop application and its associated files and directories are shown in Figure 6.4.

Figure 6.4   The drag-and-drop application's files and directories

The application is made up primarily of five things: Java source files; images; a CSS file; a configuration file; and an HTML page. In Solution 1, we showed you how to use custom widgets that were packaged in a module. For the drag-and-drop application, we employ the same technique—a two-step process—to use the drag-and-drop module:

- Inherit the module with an `inherits` element in the configuration file.

- Include the module's JAR file in our application's classpath.

We showed you how to include GWT Solutions `Components` module in your application's classpath in "Custom Widget Use" (page 40), so we don't cover that ground again, but we do show you how we inherit the drag-and-drop module in the application's configuration file.

Inheriting the Drag-and-Drop Module in an Application's Configuration File

The XML configuration file for our application is shown in Listing 6.1.

Listing 6.1   com/gwtsolutions/DragAndDrop.gwt.xml

```
1.<module>
2.
3.    <!— Inherit the core Web Toolkit stuff. —>
4.    <inherits name='com.google.gwt.user.User'/>
5.
6.    <!— Inherit the I18N stuff. —>
7.    <inherits name="com.google.gwt.i18n.I18N"/>
8.
9.    <!— Inherit the drag and drop stuff. —>
10.    <inherits name='com.gwtsolutions.components.Components'/>
11.    <inherits name='com.gwtsolutions.components.client.ui.Dnd'/>
12.
13.    <!— Include CSS stylesheet. —>
14.    <stylesheet src="styles.css"/>
15.
16.    <!— Specify the app entry point class. —>
17.    <entry-point class='com.gwtsolutions.client.DragAndDrop'/>
18.
19.</module>
```

The drag-and-drop application uses GWT internationalization, so we inherit GWT's I18N module in addition to the User module.

The drag-and-drop module resides in the GWT Solutions Components module, so we inherit both of those modules in our application's configuration file.

The configuration file also includes its CSS stylesheet in the configuration file. We could have included the stylesheet with a standard link element in the application's HTML page, but including stylesheets in GWT configuration files is a more reusable solution because users can reuse your stylesheet along with your module. No one's ever going to reuse our application's module, but just the same, we prefer including stylesheets in configuration files to HTML pages in general.

Finally, we specify the entry point class for our application, com.gwtsolutions.client. DragAndDrop.

Now that we've seen how the drag-and-drop application uses the drag-and-drop module, let's look at the code for the application. We revisit the drag-and-drop module in "Drag and Drop Implementation in a GWT Module" on page 182, where we look at the module's implementation.

Implementation of the Drag-and-Drop Application

Listing 6.2 shows the drag-and-drop application's class.

Listing 6.2   com.gwtsolutions.client.DragAndDrop

```
20. package com.gwtsolutions.client;
21.
22. import com.google.gwt.core.client.EntryPoint;
23. import com.google.gwt.core.client.GWT;
24. import com.google.gwt.user.client.ui.AbsolutePanel;
25. import com.google.gwt.user.client.ui.RootPanel;
26.
27. public class DragAndDrop implements EntryPoint {
28.   public void onModuleLoad() {
29.     DragAndDropConstants constants =
30.         (DragAndDropConstants) GWT
31.             .create(DragAndDropConstants.class);
32.
33.     final AbsolutePanel ap = new AbsolutePanel();
34.
35.     ap.add(new IpodDropTarget(new ShoppingCartPanel(constants
36.         .iPodsOnly())), 125, 10);
37.
38.     ap.add(new ZuneDropTarget(new ShoppingCartPanel(constants
39.         .zunesOnly())), 125, 260);
40.
41.     final MusicPlayer blackIpod =
42.         new MusicPlayer("images/ipod-nano-black.jpg",
43.             constants.blackIPodInfo());
44.
45.     final MusicPlayer blackZune =
46.         new MusicPlayer("images/zune-black.jpg", constants
47.             .blackZuneInfo());
48.
49.     final MusicPlayer silverIpod =
50.         new MusicPlayer("images/ipod-nano-silver.jpg",
51.             constants.silverIPodInfo());
52.
53.     final MusicPlayer brownZune =
54.         new MusicPlayer("images/zune-brown.jpg", constants
55.             .brownZuneInfo());
56.
57.     ap.add(new MusicPlayerDragSource(blackIpod), 10, 20);
```

continues

Listing 6.2   com.gwtsolutions.client.DragAndDrop   *continued*

```
58.    ap.add(new MusicPlayerDragSource(brownZune), 10, 120);
59.    ap.add(new MusicPlayerDragSource(silverIpod), 10, 200);
60.    ap.add(new MusicPlayerDragSource(blackZune), 10, 300);
61.
62.    ap.addStyleName("dragPanel");
63.    RootPanel.get().add(ap);
64.  }
65.}
```

The preceding code is straightforward. We create an absolute panel, to which we add two shopping cart panels, each wrapped in a drop target. Then we create four music players and add each of them, wrapped in music player drag sources, to the absolute panel. After that flurry of activity, we have an absolute panel with four drag sources and two drop targets. Finally, we attach a CSS style to the absolute panel and add it to the root panel of the page.

The MusicPlayer and ShoppingCartPanel classes are GWT composite widgets. Let's look at their implementations before we dive into the dnd module.

Using the Music Player and Shopping Cart Panel Components

The MusicPlayer class is listed in Listing 6.3.

Listing 6.3   com.gwtsolutions.client.MusicPlayer

```
1.package com.gwtsolutions.client;
2.
3.import com.google.gwt.user.client.ui.Composite;
4.import com.google.gwt.user.client.ui.Image;
5.
6.public class MusicPlayer extends Composite {
7.   private Image image;
8.   private String info;
9.
10.   public MusicPlayer(String imageUrl, String info) {
11.      image = new Image(imageUrl);
12.      this.info = info;
13.      initWidget(image);
14.   }
15.
16.   public String getInfo() {
```

```
17.    return info;
18.  }
19.}
```

This is about as simple as a composite widget gets. The music player composite contains an image and some information about the player. Notice the call to the Composite class's initWidget method. As with all composite widgets that extend Composite, you must call that method in the constructor.

The shopping cart panel composite is listed in Listing 6.4.

Listing 6.4   com.gwtsolutions.client.ShoppingCartPanel

```
1.package com.gwtsolutions.client;
2.
3.import com.google.gwt.user.client.ui.Composite;
4.import com.google.gwt.user.client.ui.HorizontalPanel;
5.import com.google.gwt.user.client.ui.Image;
6.import com.google.gwt.user.client.ui.Label;
7.import com.google.gwt.user.client.ui.VerticalPanel;
8.
9.public class ShoppingCartPanel extends Composite {
10.   private final HorizontalPanel hp = new HorizontalPanel();
11.   private final VerticalPanel vp = new VerticalPanel();
12.
13.   public ShoppingCartPanel(String title) {
14.      initWidget(hp);
15.      hp.add(new Image("images/shopping_cart.gif"));
16.      hp.addStyleName("cartPanel");
17.      vp.add(new Label(title));
18.      hp.add(vp);
19.   }
20.
21.   public void add(MusicPlayer ipod) {
22.      vp.add(new Label(ipod.getInfo()));
23.   }
24.}
```

This composite contains a horizontal panel that in turn contains the shopping cart image and a vertical panel. The vertical panel initially contains only a title. When a music player is dropped on a drop target, the drop target invokes ShoppingCartPanel. add() to add the music player to the cart. That add method simply adds the music player's information, in the form of a GWT label, to the vertical panel.

com.google.gwt.user.client.ui.HorizontalPanel

- void add(Widget w)

  Adds a widget to a horizontal panel. This method creates a table data (<td>) element, places the widget's DOM element in the table data, and adds the table data to the lone table row created by the horizontal panel. That table row resides in a table that's created by the vertical panel's subclass, CellPanel. The method then sets the horizontal and vertical alignments for the widget to left and top, respectively.

com.google.gwt.user.client.ui.VerticalPanel

- void add(Widget w)

  Adds a widget to a vertical panel. This method creates a table row (<tr>) and a table data (<td>) element, adds the widget's DOM element to the table data, and adds the table row to the table that's created by the vertical panel's subclass, CellPanel. The method then sets the horizontal and vertical alignments for the widget to left and top, respectively.

Using Drag Sources and Drop Targets

We've seen the application and its two composite widgets. Now things start to get interesting because next we look at how you implement your own drag sources and drop targets by using the drag-and-drop module.

Our sample application implements a single drag source—the MusicPlayerDragSource class—and two drop targets: IpodDropTarget and ZuneDropTarget. Let's start with the drag source, which is listed in Listing 6.5.

Listing 6.5   com.gwtsolutions.client.MusicPlayerDragSource

```
1.package com.gwtsolutions.client;
2.
3.import com.gwtsolutions.components.client.ui.dnd.DragSource;
4.import com.gwtsolutions.components.client.ui.dnd.DropTarget;
5.
6.public class MusicPlayerDragSource extends DragSource {
7.  public MusicPlayerDragSource(MusicPlayer musicPlayer) {
8.    super(musicPlayer);
9.  }
10.
```

```
11.   public void dragStarted() {
12.      addStyleName("pointerCursor");
13.   }
14.
15.   public void droppedOutsideDropTarget() {
16.      super.droppedOutsideDropTarget();
17.      removeStyleName("pointerCursor");
18.   }
19.
20.   public void acceptedByDropTarget(DropTarget dt) {
21.      removeStyleName("pointerCursor");
22.   }
23.
24.   public void rejectedByDropTarget(DropTarget dt) {
25.      super.rejectedByDropTarget(dt);
26.      removeStyleName("pointerCursor");
27.   }
28.}
```

This class extends the DragSource class, which is part of our dnd module. That DragSource class implements four methods that subclasses are likely to override:

- void dragStarted()

- void droppedOutsideDropTarget()

- void acceptedByDropTarget(DropTarget dt)

- void rejectedByDropTarget(DropTarget dt)

The preceding methods are called by the dnd module when one of the following occurs: The drag starts; the drag source is dropped outside a drop target; or the drop is accepted or rejected by a drop target.

When the drag starts, the music player drag source adds to itself the CSS style named pointerCursor. That style defines a single property, the cursor property, with the value pointer. Setting that style effectively changes the cursor when it's over our drag source. See Listing 6.9 on page 181 for the definition of that CSS style.

When a music player drag source is dropped outside any drop target, we invoke super.droppedOutsideDropTarget(), which returns the drag source to its original position, and we reset the cursor by removing the pointerCursor style from the drag source widget.

When a music player drag source is dropped on a drop target that rejects the drop, we invoke super.droppedOutsideDropTarget(), which returns the drag source to its original position and resets the cursor. Notice that in this case, dropping a music player outside a drop target has the same effect, from the point of view of the drag source, as being rejected by a drop target.

When a music player drag source is dropped on a drop target that accepts the drop, we simply reset the cursor. It's up to the drop target to add the music player to the drop target's enclosed panel.

We only have one drag source class, because iPods and Zunes react identically when they are dragged and dropped; however, we need two drop targets because the iPod drop target only accepts iPods and the Zune drop target only accepts Zunes. That said, however, the two kinds of drop targets are much more similar than they are different, so we have a base class that encapsulates those similarities. That drop target base class is listed in Listing 6.6.

Listing 6.6   com.gwtsolutions.client.MusicPlayerDropTarget

```
1.package com.gwtsolutions.client;
2.
3.import com.google.gwt.user.client.ui.AbsolutePanel;
4.import com.google.gwt.user.client.ui.Widget;
5.import com.gwtsolutions.components.client.ui.dnd.DragSource;
6.import com.gwtsolutions.components.client.ui.dnd.DropTarget;
7.
8.public abstract class MusicPlayerDropTarget extends DropTarget {
9.   public MusicPlayerDropTarget(Widget w) {
10.      super(w);
11.   }
12.
13.   public void dragSourceEntered(DragSource ds) {
14.      if (acceptsDragSource(ds)) {
15.         ds.addStyleName("moveCursor");
16.         addStyleName("moveCursor");
17.         addStyleName("blueBorder");
18.      }
19.      else {
20.         ds.addStyleName("noDropCursor");
21.         addStyleName("noDropCursor");
22.      }
23.   }
24.
25.   public void dragSourceExited(DragSource ds) {
26.      if (acceptsDragSource(ds)) {
27.         ds.removeStyleName("moveCursor");
```

```
28.         removeStyleName("moveCursor");
29.         removeStyleName("blueBorder");
30.      }
31.      else {
32.         ds.removeStyleName("noDropCursor");
33.         removeStyleName("noDropCursor");
34.      }
35.   }
36.
37.   public void dragSourceDropped(DragSource ds) {
38.      super.dragSourceDropped(ds);
39.
40.      if (acceptsDragSource(ds)) {
41.         ((ShoppingCartPanel) getWidget()).add((MusicPlayer) ds
42.            .getWidget());
43.
44.         ((AbsolutePanel) ds.getParent()).remove(ds);
45.
46.         removeStyleName("moveCursor");
47.         removeStyleName("blueBorder");
48.      }
49.      else {
50.         ds.removeStyleName("noDropCursor");
51.         removeStyleName("noDropCursor");
52.      }
53.   }
54.}
```

This class extends the `DropTarget` class, which is also part of our dnd module. That class implements three methods that subclasses typically override:

- `void dragSourceEntered(DragSource ds)`
- `void dragSourceDropped(DragSource ds)`
- `void dragSourceExited(DragSource ds)`

The preceding methods are called by the dnd module when a drag source enters, exits, or is dropped on a drop target. The drop target superclass also defines one abstract method that subclasses must implement: `boolean acceptsDragSource(DragSource ds)`, which determines whether a drop target will accept a given drag source.

When a music player drag source enters or exits a drop target, we manipulate styles depending on whether the drag source is acceptable to the drop target to achieve drag-over and drag-under effects.

When a music player drag source is dropped on the drop target, we call `super.dragSourceDropped()`, which notifies the drag source of the drop by calling the drag source's `acceptedByDropTarget` method or `rejectedByDropTarget` method, depending on whether or not the drop target accepts the drop.

Now that we've encapsulated common drop target behavior in a base class, let's look at the subclasses specific to iPods and Zunes, listed in Listing 6.7 and Listing 6.8.

Listing 6.7   com.gwtsolutions.public.IpodDropTarget

```
1.package com.gwtsolutions.client;
2.
3.import com.google.gwt.user.client.ui.Widget;
4.import com.gwtsolutions.components.client.ui.dnd.DragSource;
5.
6.public class IpodDropTarget extends MusicPlayerDropTarget {
7.   public IpodDropTarget(Widget w) {
8.     super(w);
9.   }
10.
11.   public boolean acceptsDragSource(DragSource ds) {
12.     MusicPlayer mp =
13.        (MusicPlayer) ((MusicPlayerDragSource) ds).getWidget();
14.
15.     return mp.getInfo().startsWith("iPod");
16.   }
17.}
```

Listing 6.8   com.gwtsolutions.public.ZuneDropTarget

```
1.package com.gwtsolutions.client;
2.
3.import com.google.gwt.user.client.ui.Widget;
4.import com.gwtsolutions.components.client.ui.dnd.DragSource;
5.
6.public class ZuneDropTarget extends MusicPlayerDropTarget {
7.   public ZuneDropTarget(Widget w) {
8.     super(w);
9.   }
10.
11.   public boolean acceptsDragSource(DragSource ds) {
12.     MusicPlayer mp =
13.        (MusicPlayer) ((MusicPlayerDragSource) ds).getWidget();
```

```
14.
15.    return mp.getInfo().startsWith("Zune");
16.  }
17.}
```

The only thing that the drop targets specific to the music player do is define what kind of music player they will accept, by checking whether the component wrapped in the drag source is an iPod or a Zune.

com.google.gwt.user.client.ui.UIObject

- removeStyleName(String style)

  Removes a CSS style from the set of styles applied to a single GWT widget.

  Because you can selectively add and remove styles to a widget, you can change the way the widget looks under certain conditions, such as changing a drop target's border to indicate that a hovering draggable is acceptable (or not) for dropping on the drop target.

com.google.gwt.user.client.ui.AbsolutePanel

- remove(Widget w)

  Removes the specified widget from the absolute panel. AbsolutePanel inherits this method from its superclass, ComplexPanel. If the widget is not a child of the panel, the method does nothing; otherwise, it removes the widget's DOM element from the panel's DOM element.

Defining the CSS Classes

Listing 6.9 shows the CSS styles used by the application's drag source and drop targets.

Listing 6.9   com/gwtsolutions/public/css/styles.css

```
1. <style>
2.     body,td,a,div,.p{font-family:arial,sans-serif}
3.     div,td{color:#000000}
4.     a:link,.w,.w a:link{color:#0000cc}
5.     a:visited{color:#551a8b}
6.     a:active{color:#ff0000}
7.
8.     .dragPanel {
9.       border: thin solid darkGray;
```

continues

Listing 6.9   com/gwtsolutions/public/css/styles.css   *continued*

```
10.        width: 400px;
11.        height: 400px;
12.        background: lightGray;
13.    }
14.
15.    .cartPanel {
16.        padding: 10px;
17.        border: thin solid darkGray;
18.        background: white;
19.        width: 250px;
20.        height: 125px;
21.    }
22.
23.    .pointerCursor {
24.        cursor: pointer;
25.    }
26.    .moveCursor {
27.        cursor: move;
28.    }
29.    .blueBorder {
30.        border: thin solid blue;
31.    }
32.    .noDropCursor {
33.        cursor: no-drop;
34.    }
35. </style>
```

Take note of the cursor styles—pointerCursor, moveCursor, noDropCursor—and the blueBorder style. Each of those styles has only one attribute, and the styles are added and removed from widgets. With GWT, it is not uncommon to define CSS styles with one attribute that are *mixed in* with other CSS styles for a single widget.

Drag and Drop Implementation in a GWT Module

Now that we have a good grasp of how to use the dnd module, let's look at how it's implemented.

The drag-and-drop module is implemented inside, our Components module. Figure 6.5 shows the drag and drop's pertinent files and directories.

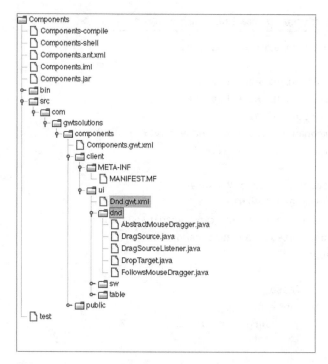

Figure 6.5   Drag-and-drop module's files and directories

Like all GWT modules, our drag-and-drop module has an XML configuration file. Like most modules, our drag-and-drop module also has some Java classes and interfaces.

The Module Configuration File

Every GWT module must provide a configuration file. The dnd module's configuration file is listed in Listing 6.10.

Listing 6.10   com/gwtsolutions/dnd/Dnd.gwt.xml

```
1.<module>
2.    <inherits name='com.google.gwt.core.Core'/>
3.</module>
```

It doesn't get any simpler than that. All we need for our dnd module is the core GWT classes, so that's what we inherit.

Now let's look at the Java classes in the dnd module.

The Abstract Drag Source and Drop Target Classes

The DragSource class is listed in Listing 6.11.

Listing 6.11   com.gwtsolutions.components.client.ui.dnd.DragSource

```
1.package com.gwtsolutions.components.client.ui.dnd;
2.
3.import com.google.gwt.user.client.ui.AbsolutePanel;
4.import com.google.gwt.user.client.ui.MouseListener;
5.import com.google.gwt.user.client.ui.Widget;
6.import com.gwtsolutions.components.client.ui.MousePanel;
7.import com.gwtsolutions.components.client.ui.Point;
8.
9.public abstract class DragSource extends MousePanel {
10.    private static final String BAD_PARENT =
11.        "Drag sources must have a parent of type AbsolutePanel";
12.    private static final MouseListener defaultDragger =
13.        new FollowsMouseDragger();
14.
15.    private boolean dragging = false;
16.    private Point originalLocation = null;
17.    private DropTarget enclosingDropTarget = null;
18.
19.    public DragSource(Widget w) {
20.        // Drag sources contain only one widget, which is
21.        // the widget passed to this constructor
22.        add(w);
23.
24.        // Listener order is significant. See the text
25.        // of GWT Solutions for more information
26.        addMouseListener(new DragSourceListener());
27.        addMouseListener(getMouseListener());
28.    }
29.
30.    public void onLoad() {
31.        // GWT calls this method when the drag source's
32.        // DOM element is added to the browser's DOM tree.
33.        if ( ! (getParent() instanceof AbsolutePanel))
34.          throw new IllegalStateException(BAD_PARENT);
35.    }
36.
37.    public void dragStarted() {
38.        // subclasses can override this no-op method
39.        // as needed
40.    }
41.
42.    public void droppedOutsideDropTarget() {
```

```
43.      // By default, when a drag source is dropped outside
44.      // of any drop target, it is returned to its original
45.      // position. Subclasses can override this method to
46.      // change or augment that behavior
47.      returnToOriginalPosition();
48.  }
49.
50.  public void acceptedByDropTarget(DropTarget dt) {
51.      // subclasses can override this no-op method
52.      // as needed
53.  }
54.
55.  public void rejectedByDropTarget(DropTarget dt) {
56.      // By default, when a drag source is rejected by
57.      // a drop target, it is returned to its original
58.      // position. Subclasses can override this method to
59.      // change or augment that behavior
60.      returnToOriginalPosition();
61.  }
62.
63.  public boolean isDragging() {
64.    return dragging;
65.  }
66.
67.  public void setDragging(boolean dragging) {
68.    this.dragging = dragging;
69.  }
70.
71.  public void setOriginalLocation(Point originalLocation) {
72.    this.originalLocation = originalLocation;
73.  }
74.
75.  public DropTarget getEnclosingDropTarget() {
76.    return enclosingDropTarget;
77.  }
78.
79.  public void setEnclosingDropTarget(
80.      DropTarget enclosingDropTarget) {
81.    this.enclosingDropTarget = enclosingDropTarget;
82.  }
83.
84.  protected void returnToOriginalPosition() {
85.    AbsolutePanel ap = (AbsolutePanel) getParent();
```

continues

Listing 6.11   com.gwtsolutions.components.client.ui.dnd.DragSource   *continued*

```
86.    ap.setWidgetPosition(this, originalLocation.x,
87.        originalLocation.y);
88.  }
89.
90.  protected MouseListener getMouseListener() {
91.    return defaultDragger;
92.  }
93.}
```

This simple extension of the `MousePanel` we discussed in "The Viewport's Use of a Focus Panel: Revisited" (page 115) defines three properties and implements four methods that subclasses are likely to use: `dragStarted()`, `droppedOutsideDropTarget()`, `acceptedByDropTarget()`, and `rejectedByDropTarget()`.

The properties keep track of whether the mouse panel is currently being dragged, its position before the drag began, and the enclosing drop target, if any. The methods are typically overridden by subclasses, as is the case for the `MusicPlayerPanelDropTarget`, listed in Listing 6.6 on page 178.

You may wonder why `DragSource` extends `MousePanel`. Here's why: Not all GWT widgets support mouse listeners; in fact, most do not, and we want to be able to drag any GWT component. So we wrap widgets in a mouse panel, which does support mouse listeners. Unbeknownst to users of the dnd module, they are really dragging mouse panels, which contain a single widget. We used this same technique in The Viewport's Use of a Focus Panel: Revisited" (page 115). See that section for more information about mouse panels and mouse listeners.

The `DragSource` class adds two mouse listeners to the widget that it wraps. The first listener, an instance of `DragSourceListener`, which is listed in Listing 6.15 on page 192, monitors the drag and invokes the abstract methods defined by the `DragSource` and `DropTarget` classes at the appropriate times.

The second listener, by default, is an instance of `FollowsMouseDragger`, which is listed in Listing 6.14 on page 191. That implementation of the `MouseListener` interface drags the drag source wherever the mouse goes. Notice that the mouse listener—an instance of `FollowsMouseListener`—is pluggable; `DragSource` subclasses can override `getMouseListener()` to provide a different dragger.

Oh, one more thing: The order in which we add listeners is significant because that is the order in which GWT will invoke them.[2] For the drag-and-drop module to function properly, the drag source listener must be added first because the `DragSourceListener`'s `onMouseUp` method turns into a no-op if the drag source is not being dragged (we don't want the drag source listener to react to mouse up events if the drag source is not

---

[2.] That's a big improvement over the Abstract Window Toolkit (AWT), which does not guarantee the order in which listeners are invoked.

being dragged). Because `AbstractMouseDragger.onMouseUp()` sets the drag source's dragged property to `false`, that method must be called *after* the `DragSourceListener.onMouseUp()`. If you reverse the order of the addition of the mouse listeners, you will see that the drag-and-drop module never reacts to mouse up events.

The `DropTarget` class is listed in Listing 6.12.

---

com.google.gwt.user.client.ui.Widget

- void onLoad()

    The GWT calls this method when a widget's DOM element is attached to the browser's DOM tree. The onLoad method is a protected method in the `Widget` class, so it is available for overriding by subclasses, but you cannot call it directly outside a widget subclass. The onLoad method is overridden in the drag-and-drop module discussed in this section by the `DragSource` class to make sure that the drag source's parent widget is an instance of `AbsolutePanel`.

Listing 6.12   com.gwtsolutions.components.client.ui.dnd.DropTarget

```
1.package com.gwtsolutions.components.client.ui.dnd;
2.
3.import com.google.gwt.user.client.ui.Widget;
4.import com.gwtsolutions.components.client.ui.MousePanel;
5.
6.public abstract class DropTarget extends MousePanel {
7.    public abstract boolean acceptsDragSource(DragSource ds);
8.
9.    public DropTarget(Widget w) {
10.       // This panel conatians only one widget, which is the
11.       // widget passed to this constructor
12.       add(w);
13.   }
14.
15.    public void dragSourceEntered(DragSource ds) {
16.       // subclasses can override this no-op method
17.       // as needed
18.   }
19.
20.    public void dragSourceExited(DragSource ds) {
21.       // subclasses can override this no-op method
22.       // as needed
23.   }
24.
```

continues

Listing 6.12   com.gwtsolutions.components.client.ui.dnd.DropTarget *continued*

```
25.  public void dragSourceDropped(DragSource ds) {
26.    // If the drag source dropped on this drop target
27.    // is acceptable, notify the drag source that it's been
28.    // dropped on this drop target; otherwise, notify the
29.    // drag source that it was rejected by this drop target
30.    if (acceptsDragSource(ds))
31.      ds.acceptedByDropTarget(this);
32.    else
33.      ds.rejectedByDropTarget(this);
34.  }
35.}
```

This is another extension of `MousePanel` because we want any GWT widget to be able to function as a drop target. This class provides no-op defaults for two of the three methods that subclasses are likely to override: `dragSourceEntered()` and `dragSourceExited()`.

For `dragSourceDropped()`, if the drag source is acceptable to the drop target—indicated by the return value of `acceptsDragSource()`, which is an abstract method subclasses must implement—we tell the drag source that it was accepted by the drop target; otherwise, we notify the drag source that, sadly enough, it was rejected by the drop target.

Mouse Listeners

The final pieces of the dnd puzzle are the mouse listeners, where most of the complexity lies. Listing 6.13 lists the `AbstractMouseDragger` class, which blithely drags widgets around on an absolute panel.

Listing 6.13   com.gwtsolutions.components.client.ui.dnd.AbstractMouseDragger

```
1.package com.gwtsolutions.components.client.ui.dnd;
2.
3.import com.google.gwt.user.client.DOM;
4.import com.google.gwt.user.client.ui.AbsolutePanel;
5.import com.google.gwt.user.client.ui.MouseListenerAdapter;
6.
7.public abstract class AbstractMouseDragger extends
8.    MouseListenerAdapter {
9.  private int xoffset, yoffset;
10.
11.  // Subclasses implement this method to override the
12.  // proposed left edge of the dragSource after a drag
13.  protected abstract int getNextLeft(int proposedLeft,
```

```
14.        DragSource ds);
15.
16.    // Subclasses implement this method to override the
17.    // proposed top edge of the dragSource after a drag
18.    protected abstract int getNextTop(int proposedTop,
19.        DragSource ds);
20.
21.    public void onMouseDown(DragSource ds, int x, int y) {
22.        xoffset = x;
23.        yoffset = y;
24.
25.        // Enable event capturing, so that subsequent mouse
26.        // events are all sent directly to the ds's
27.        // DOM element
28.        DOM.setCapture(ds.getElement());
29.
30.        // Tell the drag source that dragging has begun
31.        ds.setDragging(true);
32.    }
33.
34.    public void onMouseMove(DragSource ds, int x, int y) {
35.        if (ds.isDragging()) {
36.            // If the drag source is being dragged, calculate
37.            // the proposed left and top, and give subclasses
38.            // a chance to adjust those values
39.            AbsolutePanel ap = (AbsolutePanel) ds.getParent();
40.            int proposedLeft = x + ap.getWidgetLeft(ds) - xoffset;
41.            int proposedRight = y + ap.getWidgetTop(ds) - yoffset;
42.
43.            int nextLeft = getNextLeft(proposedLeft, ds);
44.            int nextRight = getNextTop(proposedRight, ds);
45.
46.            // Set the drag source's position to the next
47.            // left and next right
48.            ap.setWidgetPosition(ds, nextLeft, nextRight);
49.        }
50.    }
51.
52.    public void onMouseUp(DragSource ds, int x, int y) {
53.        // Tell the drag source that dragging is done and
54.        // release the capture of mouse events that was set
55.        // in onMouseDown()
56.        ds.setDragging(false);
```

```
57.      DOM.releaseCapture(ds.getElement());
58.    }
59.
60.    protected int checkLeftBounds(int proposedLeft,
61.        DragSource dragSource) {
62.      // Adjust the left edge of the dragSource if it's outside
63.      // the bounds of it's parent panel
64.      AbsolutePanel panel =
65.          (AbsolutePanel) dragSource.getParent();
66.      int dragSourceWidth = dragSource.getOffsetWidth();
67.      int panelWidth = panel.getOffsetWidth();
68.      int nextLeft = proposedLeft;
69.
70.      if (proposedLeft + dragSourceWidth > panelWidth)
71.        nextLeft = panelWidth - dragSourceWidth;
72.
73.      nextLeft = nextLeft < 0 ? 0 : nextLeft;
74.      return nextLeft;
75.    }
76.
77.    protected int checkTopBounds(
78.      // Adjust the top edge of the dragSource if it's outside
79.      // the bounds of it's parent panel
80.      int proposedTop, DragSource dragSource) {
81.      AbsolutePanel panel =
82.          (AbsolutePanel) dragSource.getParent();
83.      int dragSourceHeight = dragSource.getOffsetHeight();
84.      int panelHeight = panel.getOffsetHeight();
85.      int nextRight = proposedTop;
86.
87.      if (proposedTop + dragSourceHeight > panelHeight)
88.        nextRight = panelHeight - dragSourceHeight;
89.
90.      nextRight = nextRight < 0 ? 0 : nextRight;
91.      return nextRight;
92.    }
93.}
```

This class knows nothing about drag sources or drop targets; all it does is drag widgets. Most of the logic consists of basic math that calculates the next position of a widget and checks boundaries to make sure the widget does not escape its enclosing absolute panel.

The interesting parts of the class are the calls to DOM.setCapture() and
DOM.releaseCapture(), in onMouseDown() and onMouseUp(), respectively.
DOM.setCapture() captures all mouse events and makes them available only to the
widget that it is passed until DOM.releaseCapture() is invoked, returning event handling to normal. That provides a significant boost to performance while a widget is
being dragged, which gives us time to make sophisticated calculations, like those in
the DragSourceListener class, listed in Listing 6.15.

One other interesting thing about the AbstractMouseDragger class: It's abstract because
it defines two abstract methods that can be implemented by subclasses to plug in a different dragging algorithm. Those methods—getNextLeft() and getNextTop()—are
passed proposed locations that follow the mouse and return final locations for the current mouse movement. Those methods can be implemented by subclasses for specialized dragging, such as dragging widgets only in the horizontal or vertical directions.
One of those subclasses is the FollowsMouseDragger class, listed in Listing 6.14, which
follows the mouse but restricts the widget being dragged to the bounds of its enclosing absolute panel by invoking the inherited methods checkLeftBounds() and
checkTopBounds().

Listing 6.14   com.gwtsolutions.components.client.ui.dnd.FollowsMouseDragger

```
1.package com.gwtsolutions.components.client.ui.dnd;
2.
3.// This extension of AbstractMouseDragger drags a drag source
4.// so that it follows the mouse.
5.public class FollowsMouseDragger extends AbstractMouseDragger {
6.   protected int getNextLeft(int proposedLeft,
7.       DragSource dragSource) {
8.     // Adjust left edge if the left edge is outside the
9.     // bounds of the drag source's parent panel
10.    return checkLeftBounds(proposedLeft, dragSource);
11.  }
12.
13.   protected int getNextTop(int proposedTop,
14.       DragSource dragSource) {
15.     // Adjust left edge if the top edge is outside the
16.     // bounds of the drag source's parent panel
17.    return checkTopBounds(proposedTop, dragSource);
18.  }
19.}
```

The DragSourceListener class, which makes callbacks to drag sources and drop targets
as a widget is dragged, is listed in Listing 6.15.

Listing 6.15   com.gwtsolutions.components.client.ui.dnd.DragSourceListener

```
1. package com.gwtsolutions.components.client.ui.dnd;
2.
3. import com.google.gwt.user.client.DOM;
4. import com.google.gwt.user.client.Event;
5. import com.google.gwt.user.client.EventPreview;
6. import com.google.gwt.user.client.ui.AbsolutePanel;
7. import com.google.gwt.user.client.ui.MouseListenerAdapter;
8. import com.google.gwt.user.client.ui.Widget;
9. import com.google.gwt.user.client.ui.WidgetCollection;
10.import com.gwtsolutions.components.client.ui.Point;
11.
12.import java.util.Iterator;
13.
14.public class DragSourceListener extends MouseListenerAdapter {
15.   private final Point[] dsCorners = new Point[4];
16.   private final WidgetCollection dropTargets =
17.       new WidgetCollection(null);
18.
19.   // The following event preview prevents the browser
20.   // from reacting to mouse drags as the user drags
21.   // drag sources
22.   private static EventPreview preventDefaultMouseEvents =
23.     new EventPreview() {
24.       public boolean onEventPreview(Event event) {
25.         switch (DOM.eventGetType(event)) {
26.           case Event.ONMOUSEDOWN:
27.           case Event.ONMOUSEMOVE:
28.             DOM.eventPreventDefault(event);
29.         }
30.         return true;
31.       }
32.     };
33.
34.   public void onMouseEnter(Widget sender) {
35.     // Prevent the browser from reacting to mouse
36.     // events once the cursor enters the drag source
37.     DOM.addEventPreview(preventDefaultMouseEvents);
38.   }
39.   public void onMouseLeave(Widget sender) {
40.     // Restore browser event handling when the cursor
41.     // leaves the drag source
```

```
42.      DOM.removeEventPreview(preventDefaultMouseEvents);
43.    }
44.    public void onMouseDown(Widget sender, int x, int y) {
45.      // All drag sources must have an AbsolutePanel for a
46.      // parent. This restriction is enforced in the
47.      // drag source's onLoad method
48.      AbsolutePanel parent = (AbsolutePanel)sender.getParent();
49.      Iterator widgetIterator = parent.iterator();
50.
51.      // Iterate over the parent's widgets and put all
52.      // drop targets in the dropTargets widget collection
53.      // for future reference (see intersectsDropTarget(),
54.      // implemented below)
55.      while (widgetIterator.hasNext()) {
56.        Widget w = (Widget) widgetIterator.next();
57.        if (w instanceof DropTarget) {
58.          dropTargets.add(w);
59.        }
60.      }
61.
62.      // Set the original location of the drag source in
63.      // case the drag source is dropped outside any drop
64.      // targets or is dropped on a drop target that rejects
65.      // the drag source
66.      DragSource ds = (DragSource) sender;
67.      ds.setOriginalLocation(new Point(parent.getWidgetLeft(ds),
68.          parent.getWidgetTop(ds)));
69.
70.      // Notify the drag source that a drag has been
71.      // initiated
72.      ds.dragStarted();
73.    }
74.
75.    public void onMouseMove(Widget sender, int x, int y) {
76.      DragSource ds = (DragSource) sender;
77.      if (!ds.isDragging()) {
78.        // Don't do anything if the drag source is
79.        // not being dragged
80.        return;
81.      }
82.
83.      Widget dsWidget = ds.getWidget();
84.      DropTarget dt = intersectsDropTarget(dsWidget);
```

continues

Listing 6.15   **com.gwtsolutions.components.client.ui.dnd.DragSourceListener**   *continued*

```
85.
86.    // If the drag source intersects a drop target...
87.    if (dt != null) {
88.      // ...and if the drag source just entered
89.      // the drop target...
90.      if (ds.getEnclosingDropTarget() == null) {
91.        // ...set the enclosing drop target and
92.        // notify the drop target that the drag source
93.        // has entered
94.        ds.setEnclosingDropTarget(dt);
95.        dt.dragSourceEntered(ds);
96.      }
97.    }
98.    // If the drag source is not intersecting a drop
99.    // target...
100.    else {
101.      DropTarget enclosingDropTarget =
102.          ds.getEnclosingDropTarget();
103.
104.      // ...and the drag source was inside a drop target
105.      // previously...
106.      if (enclosingDropTarget != null) {
107.        // ...set the enclosing drop target to null
108.        // and notify the drop target that the drag
109.        // source has exited
110.        ds.setEnclosingDropTarget(null);
111.        enclosingDropTarget.dragSourceExited(ds);
112.      }
113.    }
114.  }
115.
116.  public void onMouseUp(Widget sender, int x, int y) {
117.    DragSource ds = (DragSource) sender;
118.    Widget dsWidget = ds.getWidget();
119.
120.    if (!ds.isDragging()) {
121.      // If the drag source is not being dragged,
122.      // do nothing
123.      return;
124.    }
125.
126.    DropTarget dt = intersectsDropTarget(dsWidget);
```

```
127.     if (dt != null) {
128.       // If the drag source intersects a drop target,
129.       // notify the drop target that the drag source
130.       // was dropped
131.       dt.dragSourceDropped(ds);
132.     }
133.     else {
134.       // If the drag source doesn't intersect a drop
135.       // target, notify the drag source that it was
136.       // dropped outside of any drop target
137.       ds.droppedOutsideDropTarget();
138.     }
139.   }
140.
141.   private DropTarget intersectsDropTarget(Widget dsWidget) {
142.     // Iterate over the collection of drop targets in the
143.     // drag source's enclosing panel and see if the drag
144.     // source intersects any of those drop targets; if so,
145.     // return that drop target
146.     Iterator it = dropTargets.iterator();
147.     while (it.hasNext()) {
148.       DropTarget dt = (DropTarget) it.next();
149.       int dtLeft = dt.getAbsoluteLeft();
150.       int dtTop = dt.getAbsoluteTop();
151.       int dtWidth = dt.getOffsetWidth();
152.       int dtHeight = dt.getOffsetHeight();
153.       int dsLeft = dsWidget.getAbsoluteLeft();
154.       int dsTop = dsWidget.getAbsoluteTop();
155.       int dsWidth = dsWidget.getOffsetWidth();
156.       int dsHeight = dsWidget.getOffsetHeight();
157.       dsCorners[0] = new Point(dsLeft, dsTop);
158.       dsCorners[1] = new Point(dsLeft + dsWidth, dsTop);
159.       dsCorners[2] =
160.           new Point(dsLeft + dsWidth, dsTop + dsHeight);
161.       dsCorners[3] = new Point(dsLeft, dsTop + dsHeight);
162.
163.       for (int i = 0; i < dsCorners.length; ++i) {
164.         int x = dsCorners[i].x;
165.         int y = dsCorners[i].y;
166.         if (x > dtLeft && x < dtLeft + dtWidth && y > dtTop
167.             && y < dtTop + dtHeight) {
168.           return dt;
169.         }
```

continues

Listing 6.15   com.gwtsolutions.components.client.ui.dnd.DragSourceListener   *continued*

```
170.        }
171.    }
172.    return null;
173.  }
174.}
```

This is where most of the heavy lifting in the dnd module occurs. On a mouse down event, `onMouseDown()` finds all the drop targets in the drag source's enclosing absolute panel and stores them in an instance of `WidgetCollection` for further reference. That method also stores the drag source's location and invokes its `startDragging` method.

When the drag source is dragged, `onMouseMove()` checks to see if the drag source intersects one of the drop targets discovered in `onMouseDown()`; if so, it sets the drag source's `enclosingDropTarget` property and informs the drop target that a drag source has entered. If the drag source does not intersect a drop target but currently has an enclosing drop target, the listener informs the drop target that the drag source has exited and sets the drag source's `enclosingDropTarget` property to `null`.

When a drag source is dropped, either inside or outside a drop target, `onMouseUp()` informs both the drag source and drop target of the event.

Finally, notice that in `onMouseEnter()`, we call GWT's `DOM.addEventPreview` method to add an event preview to the top of the JavaScript event stack to prevent the browser from reacting to mouse drags. If we don't do that, then when a user drags an image, *the browser will drag around an outline of the image as the user drags the mouse*. It will not drag the image itself. Without that event preview, our drag and drop turns into mush (you might want to try removing the event preview and see the results for yourself). Subsequently, `onMouseLeave()` removes the event preview so that event handling returns to normal. See "Overriding a Pop-Up Panel's Default Event Handling Behavior" (page 211) for a more in-depth discussion of `DOM.addEventPreview()` and `DOM.eventPreventDefault()`.

com.google.gwt.user.client.ui.Widget

- `getParent()`

  Returns the widget's parent widget. This method returns `null` for the root panel and for widgets whose DOM elements have not yet been added to the DOM tree.

One final detail of our drag-and-drop module: The `DragSourceListener` class uses instances of the `Component` module's `Point` class, which is listed in Listing 6.16.

Listing 6.16   com.gwtsolutions.components.client.ui.Point

```
1.package com.gwtsolutions.components.client.ui;
2.
3.public class Point { // immutable
4.   final public int x;
5.   final public int y;
6.
7.   public Point(int x, int y) {
8.     this.x = x;
9.     this.y = y;
10.  }
11.}
```

Stuff We Covered in This Solution

GWT gives us all the tools we need to achieve drag and drop, and now that you have the code discussed in this solution, you don't have to do it yourself. With that code in hand, it's easy to use drag and drop in your own applications by developing the appropriate drag sources and drop targets, which can enclose any GWT widget, and then adding them to an absolute panel.

Apart from drag and drop itself, we've also explored some interesting corners of GWT, such as creating a GWT module to encapsulate reusable code, changing a widget's cursor, capturing and releasing events for a specific widget, and using event previews to inhibit the browser's reactions to events. That knowledge will come in handy as you create your own components, whether or not they are related to drag and drop.

Simple Windows

Out of the box, GWT provides a very useful widget that's almost unheard of in other Java-based web application frameworks: a pop-up panel.

Pop-up panels, or pop-ups for short, afford a more interactive experience than your typical, run-of-the-mill web application. For example, in Solution 10, you can see how to use a pop-up in a Rolodex application to change contact information without loading a new screen to edit that information; instead, we let users edit contact information in a pop-up.

But GWT's pop-up panel is very basic. Pop-ups have no border, and their background color, by default, is the same color as the browser, so unadorned pop-ups are rather bland. Figure 7.1 shows a pop-up from our Rolodex application that underscores the simplicity of GWT's pop-up. Using CSS, we applied a border to that pop-up, because by default, GWT pop-ups have no border.

Figure 7.1   Simple pop-up panel

Although pop-ups are useful, they're lacking in a number of areas besides their looks. Pop-ups do not have any accoutrements such as a window bar or Close button, and users cannot resize pop-ups or drag them around.

While we were writing the code for this book, we longed for a more robust pop-up that could serve as a simple window, so we implemented a SimpleWindow class, along with a small supporting cast of other classes, that we discuss in this solution. Our simple windows have a nice-looking border and a window bar with a Close button, and users can resize and drag them.

When we developed our simple windows, by necessity we implemented a number of useful techniques that we are certain you will find useful outside the realm of simple windows themselves. Let's take a broad look at those techniques before we discuss them in detail.

> **ⓘ By Default, GWT Pop-Up Panels Are Modal**
>
> By default, when you show a GWT pop-up, that pop-up consumes all mouse events outside the pop-up itself. So in effect, pop-ups are modal, meaning that you cannot manipulate any GWT widgets outside the pop-up itself while the pop-up is showing.
>
> Pop-ups also have an autohide feature that hides the pop-up when you click outside the pop-up. If that feature is turned on for a particular pop-up and you click outside the pop-up while it is showing, the pop-up hides itself and lets the mouse click go through to other widgets. In effect then, activating autohide makes a pop-up nonmodal. By default, autohide is not activated for pop-ups.
>
> Neither feature—modality or autohide—is appropriate for the simple windows we implement in this solution, because we want our windows to remain showing and to allow manipulation of widgets outside the window. In "Overriding a Pop-Up Panel's Default Event Handling Behavior" on page 211, we show you how to work around modality and autohide.

Stuff You're Going to Learn

This solution explores the following aspects of GWT:

- Using GWT's `FlexTable` (page 201)
- Using GWT's pop-up panels (page 210)
- Overriding a pop-up's default event handling (page 210)
- Previewing events (page 211)
- Handling browser events (page 211)
- Loading an image with a URL (page 214)
- Formatting table elements with table formatters (page 214)
- Sinking events (page 215)
- Accessing a widget's DOM element (page 217)
- Controlling a widget's Z index (page 217)
- Resizing pop-ups (page 219)
- Using a *sender* widget sent to a mouse listener method (page 221)
- Capturing events (page 221)
- Preventing unwanted browser effects (page 222)
- Extending GWT's `HorizontalPanel` (page 228)

- Aligning widgets within cells in a horizontal panel (page 228)
- Using GWT's event adapter classes (page 256)
- Simulating 3-D buttons with mouse listeners and images (page 229)

Simple windows, shown in Figure 7.2, are implemented as an extension of the PopupPanel class. Pop-up panels contain a single widget, which often is a panel that contains other widgets. Our simple window class, however, does not contain a panel; instead, we chose to use an instance of FlexTable because we could place the pieces of our simple windows in table cells, as shown in Figure 7.3 on page 203, which let us use conveniences such as table cell formatters. As a result of that choice, in this solution, we introduce GWT tables. In Solution 8, we take a closer look at tables when we implement dynamic column resizing and paging.

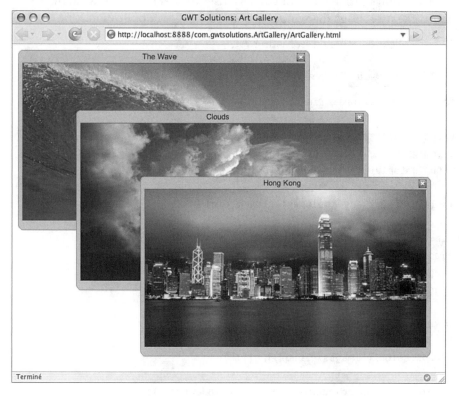

Figure 7.2   The art gallery

Dragging and resizing simple windows proved to be somewhat challenging. We had to deal with nefarious browser effects whenever we dragged the mouse, as you can see from Figure 7.6 on page 222 and Figure 7.10 on page 234. To deal with those effects we had to prevent the browser from reacting to mouse events whenever users were dragging or resizing a window.

When a user clicks in a simple window outside the Close button or inside the pop-up's content, we bring the window to the front of all the other windows currently displayed in the browser. To implement that feature, we had to set the Z index for our window's DOM element.

Finally, we ran across a number of other interesting techniques, such as simulating a 3-D button with a mouse listener and some images, implementing rounded corners for our windows, and capturing and sinking events.

We've already used our simple windows in an earlier example in this book in the Solution 5 solution, in which we displayed maps from the Yahoo! Maps web service in simple windows. For this solution, we implemented the application shown in Figure 7.2.

Our application contains three simple windows, each of which shows a picture. By default, simple windows resize their content as a user resizes the window, so the images resize as the user drags the windows in the art gallery application.

The art gallery application is listed in Listing 7.1.

Listing 7.1   com.gwtsolutions.client.ArtGallery

```
1.package com.gwtsolutions.client;
2.
3.import com.google.gwt.core.client.EntryPoint;
4.import com.google.gwt.user.client.ui.*;
5.import com.gwtsolutions.components.client.ui.sw.SimpleWindow;
6.
7.public class ArtGallery implements EntryPoint {
8.
9.   public void onModuleLoad() {
10.      Image wave = new Image();
11.      Image hongkong = new Image();
12.      Image clouds = new Image();
13.
14.      wave.setUrl("images/wave.jpg");
15.      hongkong.setUrl("images/hongkong.jpg");
16.      clouds.setUrl("images/clouds.jpg");
17.
18.      SimpleWindow waveWindow = new SimpleWindow(wave);
19.      SimpleWindow cloudsWindow = new SimpleWindow(clouds);
20.      SimpleWindow hongkongWindow = new SimpleWindow(hongkong);
21.
22.      waveWindow.setTitle("The Wave");
23.      waveWindow.setWindowPosition(10, 10);
24.
25.      cloudsWindow.setTitle("Clouds");
```

```
26.        cloudsWindow.setWindowPosition(110, 110);
27.
28.        hongkongWindow.setTitle("Hong Kong");
29.        hongkongWindow.setWindowPosition(220, 220);
30.
31.        waveWindow.show();
32.        cloudsWindow.show();
33.        hongkongWindow.show();
34.    }
35. }
```

The preceding application is straightforward. We created three images and set their URLs to JPG files. Then we created three simple windows, passing an image to the SimpleWindow constructor. Finally, we set each window's title and position and showed the windows.

> ### Some Performance Considerations
>
> Our art gallery application performs admirably in most browsers, but if windows are resized quickly enough on Firefox, that browser has some difficulty keeping up with the constant resizing, and subsequent scaling, of images.
>
> By dynamically scaling and resizing images, we are pushing the performance envelope here, so it's not surprising to see some browsers struggling to keep up with rapid resizing. Our Yahoo! Maps web services application in Solution 5, which also uses simple windows, performed admirably on all browsers because we do not resize the map images contained in the simple windows.

A Window Built from a Flex Table

Simple windows directly contain a single widget—an instance of FlexTable—that contains all the constituents of a simple window, as shown in Figure 7.3.

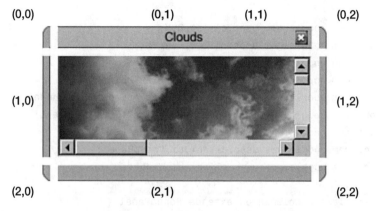

Figure 7.3   A Simple window contains a flex table with nine table cells

The simple window's flex table contains nine table cells, which are populated as outlined in Table 7. 1.

Table 7. 1   Constituents of a Simple Window

(Row,Column)	Component	Description
(0,0)	Image	Top-left corner
(0,1)	WindowBar	Title bar, including the Close button
(0,2)	Image	Top-right corner
(1,0)	Image	Left side
(1,1)	Any widget	Window contents, which can be any widget. When a user resizes the window, the window resizes the content.
(1,2)	Image	Right side
(2,0)	Image	Lower-left corner
(2,1)	Image	Bottom
(2,2)	Image	Lower-right corner

Our discussion of simple windows is split into two parts. In the first part, we look at the `SimpleWindow` class, and on page 219, resizing windows with the `SimpleWindowResizer` class. In the second part, we look at the implementation of the `WindowBar` class on page 219 and moving windows with the `SimpleWindowMover` class on page 219.

The Simple Window

The `SimpleWindow` class is listed in Listing 7.2.

Listing 7.2   com.gwtsolutions.components.client.ui.sw.SimpleWindow

```
1. package com.gwtsolutions.components.client.ui.sw;
2.
3. import com.google.gwt.user.client.DOM;
4. import com.google.gwt.user.client.Element;
5. import com.google.gwt.user.client.Event;
6. import com.google.gwt.user.client.ui.FlexTable;
7. import com.google.gwt.user.client.ui.HasHorizontalAlignment;
8. import com.google.gwt.user.client.ui.HasVerticalAlignment;
9. import com.google.gwt.user.client.ui.Image;
10.import com.google.gwt.user.client.ui.PopupPanel;
11.import com.google.gwt.user.client.ui.Widget;
12.
13.public class SimpleWindow extends PopupPanel {
14.   private static final int DEFAULT_WIDTH = 500;
```

```
15.   private static final int DEFAULT_HEIGHT = 300;
16.
17.   protected static final int SIDE_FRAME_WIDTH = 8;
18.   protected static final int TOP_FRAME_HEIGHT = 22;
19.   protected static final int BOTTOM_FRAME_HEIGHT = 16;
20.
21.   // Z index of top-most window. This value is incremented
22.   // relentlessly in incrementZIndex().
23.   private static int topZIndex = 0;
24.
25.   private WindowBar windowBar; // The window bar
26.   private Widget contentWidget; // Widget displayed in window
27.   private FlexTable table; // The popup panel's widget
28.
29.   // The following mouse listener adapter prevents the
30.   // browser from reacting to drag events. All pieces of
31.   // the window use this listener, except for the window's
32.   // content.
33.   private PreventDefaultDuringDragging
34.     preventDefaultDuringDragging =
35.       new PreventDefaultDuringDragging();
36.
37.   // This constructor is for subclasses that need to
38.   // instantiate a window without content. To set content
39.   // later, call setContent(Widget)
40.   public SimpleWindow() {
41.     this(null);
42.   }
43.   public SimpleWindow(Widget widget) {
44.     this(widget, DEFAULT_WIDTH, DEFAULT_HEIGHT);
45.   }
46.   public SimpleWindow(Widget widget, int width, int height) {
47.     setPixelSize(width, height);
48.
49.     if (widget != null) // If no widget is supplied here,
50.       setContent(widget); // you must call setContent() later
51.   }
52.
53.   public void show() {
54.     show(true); // By default, move windows to front when shown
55.   }
56.
57.   public void show(boolean moveToFront) {
```

continues

```
58.    super.show();
59.
60.    if (moveToFront) {
61.       moveToFront();
62.    }
63. }
64.
65. public void setContent(Widget widget) {
66.    contentWidget = widget;
67.    contentWidget
68.       .addStyleName("gwtsolutions-SimpleWindow-content");
69.
70.    createAndPopulateTable();
71. }
72.
73. // This method is overridden by subclasses that are
74. // interested in reacting to window resizing
75. protected void windowResized(int width, int height) {
76. }
77.
78. private void createAndPopulateTable() {
79.    table = new FlexTable();
80.    table.setWidth("100%");  // Make sure the table fills
81.    table.setHeight("100%"); // the popup window
82.
83.    table.setBorderWidth(0); // Make all cells in the table
84.    table.setCellPadding(0); // fit together, with no gaps
85.    table.setCellSpacing(0);
86.
87.    // Create the pieces of the table
88.    createTopLeft();
89.    createTop();
90.    createTopRight();
91.    createLeftEdge();
92.
93.    createContent();
94.
95.    createRightEdge();
96.    createBottomLeft();
97.    createBottom();
98.    createBottomRight();
99.
```

```
100.     // The popup panel's lone widget is the flex table
101.     setWidget(table);
102.
103.     // Sink onClick events so that GWT will call
104.     // onBrowserEvent() for mouse clicks
105.     sinkEvents(Event.ONCLICK);
106. }
107.
108. public void onBrowserEvent(Event event) {
109.     moveToFront();
110. }
111.
112. public void moveToFront() { // Move this window to the front
113.     incrementZIndex(getElement());
114. }
115.
116. // By default, PopupPanel eats mouse events outside of the
117. // popup (unless it's a mouse click and autohide
118. // enabled) by returning false from onEventPreview.
119. // That's fine for a popup, but for our window,
120. // we don't want to disallow mouse events outside of the
121. // window, so we override onEventPreview to return true.
122. public boolean onEventPreview(Event event) {
123.     return true;
124. }
125.
126. // Convenience method: even though we extend popup, this
127. // this class conceptually represents windows
128. public void setWindowPosition(int left, int top) {
129.     setPopupPosition(left, top);
130. }
131.
132. // Delegate setting of the title to the window bar
133. public void setTitle(String title) {
134.     windowBar.setTitle(title);
135. }
136.
137. // PRIVATE HELPER METHODS FOR CONSTRUCTING THE INDIVIDUAL
138. // PIECES OF THE POPUP'S FLEX TABLE FOLLOW
139. private void createTopLeft() {
140.     Image topLeft = new Image();
141.     topLeft.setUrl("images/topleft.png");
142.     table.setWidget(0, 0, topLeft);
```

continues

```
143.      topLeft.addMouseListener(preventDefaultDuringDragging);
144.   }
145.
146.   private void createTop() {
147.      windowBar = new WindowBar(this, "images/top.png");
148.      windowBar.setWidth("100%");
149.      windowBar.setHeight(TOP_FRAME_HEIGHT + "px");
150.      table.setWidget(0, 1, windowBar);
151.   }
152.
153.   private void createTopRight() {
154.      Image topRight = new Image();
155.      topRight.setUrl("images/topright.png");
156.      table.setWidget(0, 2, topRight);
157.      topRight.addMouseListener(preventDefaultDuringDragging);
158.   }
159.
160.   private void createLeftEdge() {
161.      Image leftEdge = new Image();
162.      leftEdge.setUrl("images/leftedge.png");
163.      leftEdge.setHeight("100%");
164.      leftEdge.setWidth(SIDE_FRAME_WIDTH + "px");
165.      table.setWidget(1, 0, leftEdge);
166.      leftEdge.addMouseListener(preventDefaultDuringDragging);
167.   }
168.
169.   private void createRightEdge() {
170.      Image rightEdge = new Image();
171.      rightEdge.setUrl("images/rightedge.png");
172.      rightEdge.setHeight("100%");
173.      rightEdge.setWidth(SIDE_FRAME_WIDTH + "px");
174.      table.setWidget(1, 2, rightEdge);
175.      rightEdge.addMouseListener(preventDefaultDuringDragging);
176.   }
177.
178.   private void createBottomLeft() {
179.      Image bottomLeft = new Image();
180.      bottomLeft.setUrl("images/bottomleft.png");
181.      table.setWidget(2, 0, bottomLeft);
182.      bottomLeft.addMouseListener(preventDefaultDuringDragging);
183.   }
184.
```

```
185.  private void createBottom() {
186.    Image bottom = new Image();
187.    bottom.setUrl("images/bottom.png");
188.    bottom.setWidth("100%");
189.    bottom.setHeight(BOTTOM_FRAME_HEIGHT + "px");
190.    table.setWidget(2, 1, bottom);
191.    bottom.addMouseListener(preventDefaultDuringDragging);
192.  }
193.
194.  private void createBottomRight() {
195.    final Image bottomRight = new Image();
196.    bottomRight.setUrl("images/bottomright.png");
197.
198.    table.setWidget(2, 2, bottomRight);
199.
200.    bottomRight.addMouseListener(preventDefaultDuringDragging);
201.    bottomRight.addMouseListener(
202.        new SimpleWindowResizer(this));
203.  }
204.  private void createContent() {
205.    table.setWidget(1, 1, contentWidget);
206.    table.getCellFormatter().setWidth(1, 1, "100%");
207.    table.getCellFormatter().setHeight(1, 1, "100%");
208.  }
209.
210.  // Relentlessly increment the Z index. Called by
211.  // moveToFront() only
212.  private void incrementZIndex(Element element) {
213.    DOM.setIntStyleAttribute(element, "zIndex", ++topZIndex);
214.  }
215.}
```

The SimpleWindow class encompasses a number of general GWT techniques:

- Using pop-up panels
- Overriding a pop-up panel's default event handling behavior
- Using a GWT flex table and formatting its cells
- Sinking events
- Manipulating the Z index for a widget's DOM element
- Resizing pop-up panels
- Preventing unwanted browser effects

Although the `SimpleWindow` class is more than 200 lines of code, much of that code is concerned with creating the individual widgets shown in Figure 7.3 and adding them to the window's flex table. To help you understand the techniques employed by `SimpleWindow`, we look at each of the techniques listed previously.

Using Pop-Up Panels

Simple windows are pop-up panels by virtue of the fact that `SimpleWindow` extends `PopupPanel`. Simple windows use three methods that they inherit from `PopupPanel`: `setWidget()`, `show()`, and `setPopupPosition()`.

When you set a simple window's content, either by passing the content widget to a `SimpleWindow` constructor or by calling the `setContent` method, the `SimpleWindow` class calls a private `createAndPopuplateTable` method.

After creating the flex table and the widgets it contains, `createAndPopuplateTable()` calls the `setWidget` method inherited from `PopupPanel`'s superclass, `SimplePanel`. Simple panels, such as pop-ups, can have only one direct child widget, and for simple windows, that widget is a flex table.

On line 53 of the preceding listing, we override the `show` method to move the window to the front when it is shown, which is the default behavior for simple windows. You can also call the `show` method that takes a `boolean`, which starts on line 57, to show a simple window without bringing it to the front of all the other windows.

Finally, we wrap the `setPopupPosition` method in a method named `setWindowPosition` on line 129. We could have let simple window users call `setPopupPosition()` directly, but we wanted to provide a method that was consistently named for the window abstraction.

`com.google.gwt.user.client.ui.PopupPanel`

- `void show()`

  Attaches a pop-up panel if one is not currently attached to the browser's DOM, and subsequently shows the pop-up, but only if the pop-up's visibility is `true`.

  Pop-up panels, like all widgets, are visible by default; we just want to emphasize that `show()` does not make a pop-up visible if the pop-up's visibility is `false`. The `show()` method shows the pop-up at the coordinates specified by `PopupPanel.setPopupPosition()`. **Note:** You must call `SimplePanel.setWidget (Widget)` or `SimplePanel.add(Widget)` before calling `show()`; otherwise, GWT does not show your pop-up.

- void setPopupPosition(int left, int top)

   Sets a pop-up panel's position relative to the browser's client area (the browser's client area is the inside the browser window, not including address bars, toolbars, or status panels). That position is where the show method shows the pop-up panel. If you do not call setPopupPosition() before you call show(), the show method adds the pop-up panel to the root panel according to the root panel's layout algorithm.

com.google.gwt.user.client.ui.SimplePanel

- void setWidget(Widget w)

   Sets the lone widget allowed when the SimplePanel class is extended. Simple panels can have only one widget—that's why they are simple panels. If you call this method when a simple panel already has a widget, GWT removes that existing widget before adding the new one.

- void add(Widget w)

   Overrides the add method inherited when SimplePanel extends the Panel class. The SimplePanel add method calls setWidget(), but first add() checks to see if the simple panel has an existing widget; if so, it throws an IllegalStateException.

   Note the difference in behavior between add() and setWidget(): When you try to add a widget to a simple panel that already has a widget, add() throws an exception, whereas setWidget() quietly removes the existing widget.

Our use of pop-up panels here is pretty fundamental, except for one thing: We override the pop-up panel's default event handling behavior.

Overriding a Pop-Up Panel's Default Event Handling Behavior

By default, pop-up panels are modal, meaning you cannot manipulate any other GWT widgets in the page outside the pop-up when the pop-up is visible. That's appropriate for pop-up panels, but it's not appropriate for our simple windows. When a window is shown, we do not want to deny the use of other widgets in the application.

The PopupPanel class achieves modality by means of the EventPreview interface. When a pop-up is shown, the PopupPanel's show method adds itself to the event stack, and when the pop-up is hidden, the PopupPanel's hide method removes itself from the event stack. The PopupPanel implements the event preview like this:

```java
// The following code is from com.google.gwt.user.client.ui.PopupPanel.java:

public boolean onEventPreview(Event event) {
    int type = DOM.eventGetType(event);
    switch (type) {
      case Event.ONKEYDOWN: {
        return onKeyDownPreview((char) DOM.eventGetKeyCode(event),
          KeyboardListenerCollection.getKeyboardModifiers(event));
      }
      case Event.ONKEYUP: {
        return onKeyUpPreview((char) DOM.eventGetKeyCode(event),
          KeyboardListenerCollection.getKeyboardModifiers(event));
      }
      case Event.ONKEYPRESS: {
        return onKeyPressPreview((char) DOM.eventGetKeyCode(event),
          KeyboardListenerCollection.getKeyboardModifiers(event));
      }

      case Event.ONMOUSEDOWN:
      case Event.ONMOUSEUP:
      case Event.ONMOUSEMOVE:
      case Event.ONCLICK:
      case Event.ONDBLCLICK: {
        // Don't eat events if event capture is enabled, as this can interfere
        // with dialog dragging, for example.
        if (DOM.getCaptureElement() == null) {
          // Disallow mouse events outside of the popup.
          Element target = DOM.eventGetTarget(event);
          if (!DOM.isOrHasChild(getElement(), target)) {
            // If it's a click event, and auto-hide is enabled: hide the popup
            // and _don't_ eat the event.
            if (autoHide && (type == Event.ONCLICK)) {
              hide(true);
              return true;
            }
            return false;
          }
        }
        break;
      }
    }
    return true;
}
```

While a pop-up is shown, it inhibits all mouse events outside the pop-up by returning false from the pop-up's onEventPreview method. The only time the pop-up allows mouse events outside the pop-up to be handled by other widgets is when the pop-up's autohide feature is enabled, meaning a mouse click outside the pop-up hides the pop-up.

For our simple windows, we don't want either of those features. We don't want autohide because users couldn't click anything outside a window without closing it, nor do we want our windows to be modal. To defeat both of those features, therefore, we override the pop-up panel's onEventPreview method on line 122 of Listing 7.2 on page 204, like this:

```
...
public class SimpleWindow extends PopupPanel {
  ...
  // By default, PopupPanel eats mouse events outside of the
  // popup (unless it's a mouse click and autohide
  // enabled) by returning false from onEventPreview.
  // That's fine for a popup, but for our window,
  // we don't want to disallow mouse events outside of the
  // window, so we override onEventPreview to return true.
  public boolean onEventPreview(Event event) {
    return true;
  }
  ...
}
```

That simple override cancels the inherited event previewing and simply allows all mouse events to pass through to other widgets in the application.

com.google.gwt.user.client.EventPreview

- boolean onEventPreview(Event event)

  Returns a boolean to signify whether event should be handled (true), or whether it should be cancelled (false). If you add an event preview to the event preview stack with DOM.addEventPreview(), GWT calls your event preview's onEventPreview before anyone else gets a crack at the event.

  The more you use GWT, the more uses you will find for an event preview; it is an incredibly handy mechanism to have at your disposal. In the preceding code, we overrode PopupPanel.onEventPreview to enable mouse clicks outside our simple window. We use event previews in Solution 4 and Solution 6, when we discuss viewports and drag and drop.

`com.google.gwt.user.client.DOM`

- `static boolean isOrHasChild(Element parent, Element child)`

  Returns `true` if the child element is equal to, or is the child of, the parent element.

- `static int eventGetType(Event event)`

  Returns the type of an event. The integer value returned is a public constant defined in GWT's `Event` class, such as `Event.ONMOUSEOVER`, `Event.ONKEYUP`, and `Event.ONDBLCLICK`.

- `static int eventGetKeyCode(Event event)`

  Returns the key code for keyboard events. For `Event.ONKEYPRESS` events, this method returns the Unicode value of the key that was pressed; otherwise, for `Event.ONKEYUP` and `Event.ONKEYDOWN` events, the method returns the code associated with the physical key.

- `Element getCaptureElement()`

  Returns the DOM element, if any, that is currently capturing events.

Now that we've seen how `SimpleWindow` extends `PopupPanel`, let's see how it uses a GWT flex table.

Using a GWT Flex Table and Formatting Its Cells

The `SimpleWindow`'s `createAndPopulate` method creates the window's flex table on line 79 of Listing 7.2 on page 206, sets the table's width and height to 100% so that the table completely fills the pop-up panel, and sets the table's border width, cell padding, and cell spacing to zero so that all the table cells fit together without any gaps.

Subsequently, the `createAndPopuplateTable` method invokes nine private methods that create the individual widgets stored in the table's cells. Those nine methods take up a good deal of the `SimpleWindow` class, starting on line 139 and ending on line 208. For the most part, those methods create images, set their URLs to images contained in the `Components` module, and place the images in the appropriate table cell.

For example, the `createTopLeft` method, starting on line 139, creates an image, sets its URL to `images/topleft.png`, and places the image in the table at cell (0,0).

The `createContent` method, starting on line 204, places the content widget at table cell (1,1). Subsequently, that method uses a table *cell formatter* to format that cell's width and height to 100%. That formatting ensures that the cell always takes up all available space in the table, even after the window has been resized.

com.google.gwt.user.client.ui.HTMLTable

- `HTMLTable.CellFormatter getCellFormatter()`

    Returns a cell formatter, which formats cells in the table.

- `void setBorderWidth(int width)`

    Sets the width, in pixels, of the border inside table cells. GWT applies the border to all cells in the table.

- `void setCellPadding(int padding)`

    Sets the padding, in pixels, of the border inside table cells. GWT applies the padding to all cells in the table.

- `void setCellSpacing(int spacing)`

    Sets the spacing, in pixels, of the border inside table cells. GWT applies the spacing to all cells in the table.

com.google.gwt.user.client.ui.HTMLTable.CellFormatter

- `void setHeight(int row, int column, String height)`

    sets the height of a specified table cell in CSS units.

- `void setWidth(int row, int column, String width)`

    sets the width of a specified table cell in CSS units.

Sinking Events

As we saw in Table 1.2 (page 17), only four GWT widget classes source mouse events: `FocusPanel`, `HTML`, `Image`, and `Label`. That means that only those four widgets fire mouse events to interested listeners.

For our simple windows, we want to handle mouse clicks so that a mouse click anywhere in a window brings the window to the front of all other windows. But pop-up panels do not source mouse events, so we cannot attach a mouse listener to a pop-up panel and handle mouse clicks. How, then, can we handle mouse clicks in our simple windows?

The answer is sinking events. When you sink events, GWT calls the `Widget` method `onBrowserEvent` for the type of event(s) that you sank. Here's how we sink events in the `SimpleWindow` class, listed in Listing 7.2 on page 204:

```
...
public class SimpleWindow extends PopupPanel {
  ...
  private void createAndPopulateTable() {
    ...
    sinkEvents(Event.ONCLICK);
  }

  public void onBrowserEvent(Event event) {
    moveToFront();
  }

  public void moveToFront() { // Move this window to the front
    incrementZIndex(getElement());
  }
  ...
}
```

We sink mouse clicks for our simple window so that GWT will call our simple window's onBrowserEvent for mouse clicks in the window. In that method, we move the window to the front by incrementing the Z index for the window widget's DOM element.

The Event class defines many constants in addition to Event.ONCLICK. To specify more than one event, we use a bitwise OR; for example, we could specify that both mouse clicks and key up events bring windows to the front, like this:

```
sinkEvents(Event.ONCLICK | Event.ONKEYUP)
```

com.google.gwt.user.client.ui.UIObject

- void sinkEvents(int eventBitsToAdd)

  Specifies one or more events that are sunk for a particular widget. Once events are sunk for a particular widget, GWT invokes the widget's onBrowserEvent method when those events occur either in the widget itself or within any contained widgets.

  The integer value passed to the sinkEvents method is a bitwise OR of constants defined in GWT's Event class. There are many such constants; for example, ONCLICK, ONMOUSEOVER, ONKEYUP. See the Event class for more information.

com.google.gwt.user.client.ui.Widget

- void onBrowserEvent(Event event)

  Is called by GWT for sink events. See the preceding discussion of UIObject.sinkEvents() for more information.

Use Event.ONMOUSEOVER to Bring Windows to the Front Without Clicking

If you want to move windows to the front when the cursor enters the window, you could change the preceding code snippet to sink events like this:

sinkEvents(Event.ONMOUSEOVER).

Because GWT calls onBrowserEvent() for all events that you sink, you wouldn't need to change anything else in the SimpleWindow listing on page 206.

Manipulating the Z Index for a Widget's DOM Element

CSS specifies a Z-index property that you can set on HTML elements. That property controls whether one element is displayed above or below another element in the same HTML page. Elements with higher Z indexes are positioned above elements with lower Z indexes.

You can bring a simple window to the front of other windows by clicking anywhere inside the window, as we discussed in "Sinking Events" on page 215. That feature is shown in Figure 7.4.

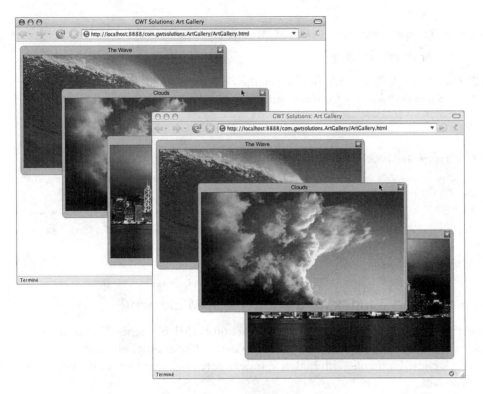

Figure 7.4   Bringing a window to the front by clicking inside it

For our simple windows, we move windows to the front of other windows by incrementing their Z indexes. The `SimpleWindow` class maintains a static integer representing the current Z index, and when a window is moved to the front with the `SimpleWindow`'s `moveToFront` method, we increment the window's Z index like this:

```
private void incrementZIndex(Element element) {
    DOM.setIntStyleAttribute(element, "zIndex", ++topZIndex);
}
```

com.google.gwt.user.client.DOM

- `static void setIntStyleAttribute(Element element, String attribute, int value)`

  Sets a CSS style attribute as an integer value. In the preceding code fragment, we used this method to set the `zIndex` attribute of our simple window's DOM element.

- `static void setStyleAttribute(Element element, String attribute, String value)`

  Sets a CSS attribute's value for the specified DOM element.

Resizing Pop-Up Panels

Users can resize our simple windows by dragging the lower-right corner of the window as shown in Figure 7.5.

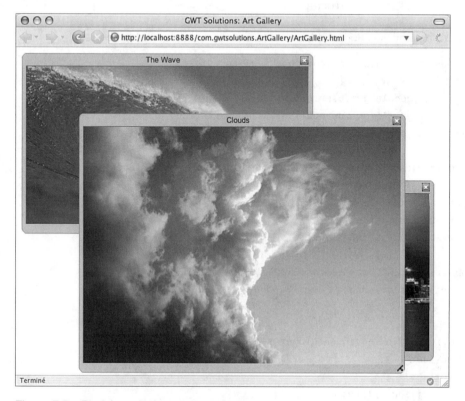

Figure 7.5   Resizing windows

When a user presses the mouse button in the lower-left corner of the window, we change the mouse cursor and monitor subsequent mouse movements. As the user drags the corner, we resize the window. Changing the mouse cursor and resizing the window is handled by an instance of SimpleWindowResizer. In the SimpleWindow's createBottomRight method, we add an instance of SimpleWindowResizer to the image in the bottom-right corner of the window, like this:

```
public class SimpleWindow extends PopupPanel {
  ...
  private void createBottomRight() {
    final Image bottomRight = new Image();
    ...
    bottomRight.addMouseListener(
        new SimpleWindowResizer(this));
  }
}
```

As you can see from the preceding code fragment, the SimpleWindowResizer class, listed in Listing 7.3, implements the MouseListener interface.

Also, as you can see from the preceding code fragment, we pass the simple window to the SimpleWindowResizer constructor.

Listing 7.3   com.gwtsolutions.components.client.ui.sw.SimpleWindowResizer

```
1. package com.gwtsolutions.components.client.ui.sw;
2.
3. import com.google.gwt.user.client.DOM;
4. import com.google.gwt.user.client.ui.MouseListener;
5. import com.google.gwt.user.client.ui.Widget;
6.
7.    public class SimpleWindowResizer implements MouseListener {
8.    private SimpleWindow simpleWindow;
9.    private int xoffset;
10.   private int yoffset;
11.   private boolean isResizing;
12.
13.   public SimpleWindowResizer(SimpleWindow simpleWindow) {
14.      this.simpleWindow = simpleWindow;
15.   }
16.
17.   public void onMouseDown(Widget sender, int x, int y) {
18.      xoffset = x;
19.      yoffset = y;
20.      isResizing = true;
21.   }
22.   public void onMouseMove(Widget sender, int x, int y) {
23.      if (isResizing) {
24.         // Calculate the new width and height of the window
25.         // and call the window's setPixelSize method. Also,
26.         // call the windowResized method to notify the window
27.         // that its size has changed.
28.         int newW = simpleWindow.getOffsetWidth() + x - xoffset;
29.         int newH = simpleWindow.getOffsetHeight() + y - yoffset;
30.         simpleWindow.setPixelSize(newW, newH);
31.         simpleWindow.windowResized(newW, newH);
32.      }
33.   }
34.   public void onMouseUp(Widget sender, int x, int y) {
35.      // Turn off resizing, and
```

```
36.    // release event capturing
37.    isResizing = false;
38.    DOM.releaseCapture(sender.getElement());
39.  }
40.  public void onMouseEnter(Widget sender) {
41.    // Add a CSS style to the window that changes the cursor,
42.    // turn on event capturing
43.    simpleWindow.addStyleName(
44.        "gwtsolutions-SimpleWindow-seResizeCursor");
45.    DOM.setCapture(sender.getElement());
46.  }
47.  public void onMouseLeave(Widget sender) {
48.    // Return the window's CSS styles to what they were
49.    // before the resize started
50.    simpleWindow.removeStyleName(
51.        "gwtsolutions-SimpleWindow-seResizeCursor");
52.  }
53.}
```

When the mouse enters the image in the bottom-left corner of a simple window, the window resizer changes the cursor by adding a CSS style to the window and turns on event capturing by calling DOM.setCapture(). We've already discussed DOM.setCapture() in "Capturing Events" (page 111), but briefly, calling that method sends all subsequent mouse events only to the specified DOM element until DOM.releaseCapture() is called.

When a user presses the mouse button, we record the x and y coordinates of the mouse press, offset from the top-left corner of the widget that sent the event. That widget, known as the *sender* widget, is the image in the bottom-left corner of the simple window. We also set a flag signifying that resizing is underway.

Subsequently, as the user drags the mouse, we calculate an updated width and height for the simple window and call the simple window's setPixelResize method to resize the window. We also call another SimpleWindow method—windowResized()—to notify the window that we are finished resizing the window for this particular movement of the mouse. That method does nothing in the SimpleWindow class, but subclasses can override it to react to window resizing.

When the user releases the mouse, we turn off resizing and release event capturing by calling DOM.releaseCapture().

Finally, when the mouse leaves the image in the bottom-left corner of the simple window, we remove the CSS class that sets the mouse cursor.

com.google.gwt.user.client.ui.UIObject

- void setWidth(String width)

  Sets a widget's width, in CSS units, such as "125px" or "10em".

- void setHeight(String height)

  Sets a widget's height, in CSS units, such as "125px" or "10em".

- int getOffsetWidth()

  Returns the total width of a widget, including any decorations, such as padding, margins, borders, and so on.

  Don't be confused by the use of *Offset* in this method's name. The width is not really offset from anything.

- int getOffsetHeight()

  Returns the total height of a widget, including decorations such as padding, margins, borders, and so on.

Preventing Unwanted Browser Effects

By default, browsers react to mouse dragging. For example, if you put an image in an HTML page and a user tries to drag the image, most browsers oblige by dragging an outline of the image.

We have seven images in the borders of our simple window, and therefore, by default, if users grab one of those images, the browser lets them drag an outline of the image, as shown in Figure 7.6.

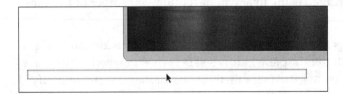

Figure 7.6   Unwanted browser effects

This dragging of images in the border of our simple window is an example of an unwanted browser effect. We don't want users to drag outlines of our images, so we defeat that browser feature by preventing the browser from reacting to mouse drags inside the window. We do that by adding a mouse listener to all the images contained in our simple window, like this:

```
public class SimpleWindow extends PopupPanel {
  ...
  // The following mouse listener adapter prevents the
  // browser from reacting to drag events. All pieces of
  // the window use this listener, except for the window's
  // content.
  private PreventDefaultDuringDragging
    preventDefaultDuringDragging =
      new PreventDefaultDuringDragging();
  ...
  private void createTopLeft() {
    Image topLeft = new Image();

    ...

    topLeft.addMouseListener(preventDefaultDuringDragging);
  }
  ...
  private void createTopRight() {
    Image topRight = new Image();

    ...

    topRight.addMouseListener(preventDefaultDuringDragging);
  }

  private void createLeftEdge() {
    Image leftEdge = new Image();

    ...

    leftEdge.addMouseListener(preventDefaultDuringDragging);
  }

  private void createRightEdge() {
    Image rightEdge = new Image();

    ...

    rightEdge.addMouseListener(preventDefaultDuringDragging);
  }

  private void createBottomLeft() {
    Image bottomLeft = new Image();

    ...

    bottomLeft.addMouseListener(preventDefaultDuringDragging);
  }

  private void createBottom() {
    Image bottom = new Image();

    ...
```

```
    bottom.addMouseListener(preventDefaultDuringDragging);
  }


  private void createBottomRight() {
    final Image bottomRight = new Image();
    ...
    bottomRight.addMouseListener(preventDefaultDuringDragging);
    ...
  }
  ...
}
```

Each instance of SimpleWindow contains a single instance of PreventDefaultDuringDragging, which is a mouse listener. That class is listed in Listing 7.4.

Listing 7.4   com.gwtsolutions.components.client.ui.sw.PreventDefaultDuringDragging

```
1. package com.gwtsolutions.components.client.ui.sw;
2.
3. import com.google.gwt.user.client.DOM;
4. import com.google.gwt.user.client.Event;
5. import com.google.gwt.user.client.EventPreview;
6. import com.google.gwt.user.client.ui.MouseListenerAdapter;
7. import com.google.gwt.user.client.ui.Widget;
8.
9. public class PreventDefaultDuringDragging extends
10.    MouseListenerAdapter {
11.   private final PreventEventPreview preview =
12.       new PreventEventPreview();
13.
14.   public void onMouseEnter(Widget sender) {
15.     // We don't want the browser to react to mouse drags,
16.     so we call
17.     // DOM.addEventPreview, passing it the event preview
18.     // we created at the top of this file.
19.     DOM.addEventPreview(preview);
20.   }
21.   public void onMouseLeave(Widget sender) {
22.     // After the mouse leaves the window bar, we remove
23.     // the event preview that we set in onMouseEnter()
24.     // from the event stack. That returns event handling
25.     // to normal so the browser can react to mouse events
26.     // once again.
27.     DOM.removeEventPreview(preview);
```

```
28.  }
29.
30.  public void removeEventPreview() {
31.    DOM.removeEventPreview(preview);
32.  }
33.
34.  private class PreventEventPreview implements EventPreview {
35.    public boolean onEventPreview(Event event) {
36.      switch (DOM.eventGetType(event)) {
37.        case Event.ONMOUSEDOWN:
38.        case Event.ONMOUSEMOVE:
39.          DOM.eventPreventDefault(event);
40.      }
41.      return true;
42.    }
43.  }
44.}
```

The preceding class implements a single instance of PreventEventPreview, which is a private class in SimpleWindow.java. That class implements the EventPreview interface and prevents the browser from reacting to mouse down and mouse move events by calling DOM.eventPreventDefault().

When the mouse enters the PreventEventPreview's associated widget, the PreventEventPreview instance adds its event preview to the event stack. When the mouse leaves the widget, the PreventEventPreview instance removes the preview from the event stack.

Notice that the PreventEventPreview class also contains a convenience method to explicitly remove the event preview from the event stack. We do not use that method in the SimpleWindow class, but we do use it when we prevent unwanted browser effects in the window's window bar. See "Preventing Unwanted Browser Effects" on page 222 for details.

The Window Bar

A simple window's window bar resides at row 0 and column 1 in the simple window's flex table, as shown in Figure 7.3 on page 203. Window bars consist of a title and a Close button, as illustrated in Figure 7.7.

Hong Kong	☒

Figure 7.7   A window bar

In addition to containing a title and a Close button, window bars have another note-worthy feature: Users can drag a window by dragging the mouse in the window bar's title.

The WindowBar class is listed in Listing 7.5.

Listing 7.5   com.gwtsolutions.components.client.ui.sw.WindowBar

```
1. package com.gwtsolutions.components.client.ui.sw;
2.
3. import com.google.gwt.user.client.DOM;
4. import com.google.gwt.user.client.ui.HTML;
5. import com.google.gwt.user.client.ui.HasHorizontalAlignment;
6. import com.google.gwt.user.client.ui.HasVerticalAlignment;
7. import com.google.gwt.user.client.ui.HorizontalPanel;
8. import com.google.gwt.user.client.ui.Image;
9. import com.google.gwt.user.client.ui.Label;
10.import com.google.gwt.user.client.ui.MouseListenerAdapter;
11.import com.google.gwt.user.client.ui.Widget;
12.
13.public class WindowBar extends HorizontalPanel {
14.   private static final int CLOSE_BUTTON_WIDTH = 14;
15.   private final SimpleWindow window;
16.   private final Image closeButton = new Image();
17.   private Label title = new Label();
18.
19.   private PreventDefaultDuringDragging
20.     preventDefaultDuringDragging =
21.       new PreventDefaultDuringDragging();
22.
23.   public WindowBar(SimpleWindow window,
24.       String bgUrl) {
25.     this.window = window;
26.
27.     addTitle();
28.     addCloseButton();
29.
30.     if (bgUrl != null) {
31.       DOM.setStyleAttribute(getElement(), "backgroundImage",
32.           "url(" + bgUrl + ")");
33.     }
```

```
34.
35.     setWidth("100%");
36.   }
37.
38.   public void setTitle(String titleString) {
39.     title.setText(titleString);
40.   }
41.
42.   // PRIVATE METHODS THAT INITIALIZE TITLE, BACKGROUND IMAGE,
43.   // AND CLOSE BUTTON, AND ADD THEM TO THE WINDOW BAR
44.
45.   private void addTitle() {
46.     title.addStyleName("gwtsolutions-WindowBar-Title");
47.
48.     add(title);
49.
50.     setCellHorizontalAlignment(title,
51.         HasHorizontalAlignment.ALIGN_CENTER);
52.     setCellVerticalAlignment(title,
53.         HasVerticalAlignment.ALIGN_MIDDLE);
54.
55.     // The title widget has two mouse listeners, one for
56.     // moving the window, and another to prevent the browser
57.     // from reacting to mouse dragging
58.     title.addMouseListener(new SimpleWindowMover(window));
59.     title.addMouseListener(preventDefaultDuringDragging);
60.   }
61.
62.   private void addCloseButton() {
63.     closeButton.setUrl("images/close.png");
64.
65.     add(closeButton);
66.
67.     // Prevent unwanted browser effects when dragging
68.     // the mouse in the close button
69.     closeButton.addMouseListener(preventDefaultDuringDragging);
70.
71.     // Set the width of the cell in which
72.     // the close button resides
73.     setCellWidth(closeButton, CLOSE_BUTTON_WIDTH + "px");
74.
75.     // Set cell alignments
76.     setCellHorizontalAlignment(closeButton,
```

continues

Listing 7.5   com.gwtsolutions.components.client.ui.sw.WindowBar   *continued*

```
77.          HasHorizontalAlignment.ALIGN_RIGHT);
78.     setCellVerticalAlignment(closeButton,
79.          HasVerticalAlignment.ALIGN_MIDDLE);
80.
81.     closeButton.addMouseListener(new MouseListenerAdapter() {
82.        public void onMouseEnter(Widget sender) {
83.           closeButton.setUrl("images/close-hover.png");
84.        }
85.        public void onMouseLeave(Widget sender) {
86.           closeButton.setUrl("images/close.png");
87.        }
88.        public void onMouseDown(Widget sender, int x, int y) {
89.           closeButton.setUrl("images/close-press.png");
90.        }
91.        public void onMouseUp(Widget sender, int x, int y) {
92.           window.hide();
93.           preventDefaultDuringDragging.removeEventPreview();
94.        }
95.     });
96.  }
97.}
```

The WindowBar class is a fairly simple extension of GWT's HorizontalPanel class. We add two widgets to the window bar. On line 48, we add the title widget, which is a label, and on line 65, we add the Close button, which is an image.

Like the SimpleWindow class, the WindowBar class illustrates some general GWT techniques:

- Aligning widgets within cells in a horizontal panel

- Simulating a 3-D button with a mouse listener and images

- Moving pop-up panels

- Preventing unwanted browser effects (redux)

Let's begin by discussing how we align the window bar's title and Close button in the horizontal panel.

Aligning Widgets Within Cells in a Horizontal Panel

The window bar, by virtue of extending HorizontalPanel, lays out its widgets horizontally. The HorizontalPanel class, in turn, extends the CellPanel class, so our window bar's DOM element is an HTML table with a single row and two columns. The left column contains the title and the right column contains the Close button—because horizontal panels lay out their widgets from left to right—and we add the title to the window bar first.

To align the title and Close button within their respective cells, we use the setCellHorizontalAlignment and setVerticalCellAlignment methods that HorizontalPanel inherits from CellPanel, starting on lines 50 and 76, respectively, in the preceding listing. We specify that both the title and the Close button are vertically aligned in the middle of the window bar, and horizontally, we align the title in the middle of its cell, and the Close button in the right of its cell.

`com.google.gwt.user.client.ui.CellPanel`

- `void setCellWidth(Widget w, String width)`

  Sets the width for the specified widget's table cell. The width is specified as a string in CSS units; for example, `"100px"` or `"2em"`.

- `void setCellHorizontalAlignment(Widget w,`
  `HasHorizontalAlignment.HorizontalAlignmentConstant alignment)`

  Sets the horizontal alignment for the specified widget's table cell. Valid values for the `alignment` parameter are `HasHorizontalAlignment.ALIGN_LEFT`, `HasHorizontalAlignment.ALIGN_CENTER`, and `HasHorizontalAlignment.ALIGN_RIGHT`.

- `void setCellVerticalAlignment(Widget w,`
  `HasVerticalAlignment.VerticalAlignmentConstant alignment)`

  Sets the vertical alignment for the specified widget's table cell. Valid values for the `alignment` parameter are `HasVerticalAlignment.ALIGN_TOP`, `HasVerticalAlignment.ALIGN_MIDDLE`, and `HasVerticalAlignment.ALIGN_BOTTOM`.

Simulating a 3-D Button with a Mouse Listener and Images

The Close button in the window bar is a simulation of a 3-D button, implemented with a mouse listener and images. Figure 7.8 shows the 3-D button effect. The middle picture shows the button when the mouse enters the image, and the bottom picture shows the image when the mouse button is pressed.

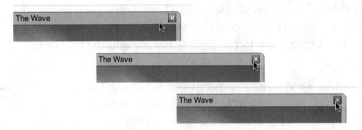

Figure 7.8   Simulating a 3-D button

On line 81 of the previous listing, we add a mouse listener to the Close button. When the mouse enters, leaves, or is pressed in the button, we simply change the Close button's image. That's all there is to simulating a 3-D button: Use a mouse listener and change the image's URL as appropriate.

Another interesting aspect of the window bar is its ability to drag the window to which it is attached.

Dragging the window is done by another object, which is an implementation of `SimpleWindowMover`. On line 58 of the previous listing, we add an instance of `SimpleWindowMover` to the window bar's title widget. Let's see how that class is implemented.

Moving Pop-Up Panels

In Figure 7.4 on page 218, we showed how users can click in a window to bring a window to the front of all other windows. Figure 7.9 shows how users can also move a window by dragging its window bar.

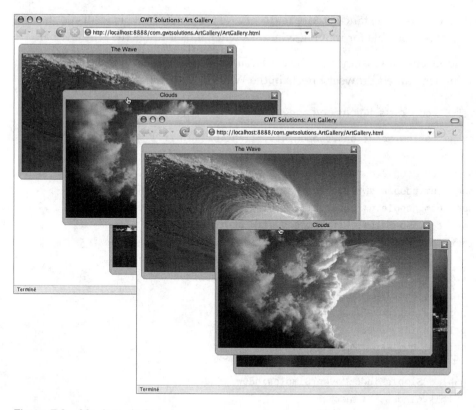

Figure 7.9   Moving windows

In Listing 7.5 on page 226, we added two mouse listeners to the window bar's title widget, like this:

```
...
public class WindowBar extends HorizontalPanel {
  ...
  private void addTitle() {
    ...
    // The title widget has two mouse listeners, one for
    // moving the window, and another to prevent the browser
    // from reacting to mouse dragging
    title.addMouseListener(new SimpleWindowMover(window));
    title.addMouseListener(preventDefaultDuringDragging);
  }
  ...
}
```

The first listener is an instance of `SimpleWindowMover`. That class, which is listed in Listing 7.6, is responsible for moving windows when a user drags the window bar.

The second listener, an instance of `PreventDefaultDuringDragging`, is discussed in "Preventing Unwanted Browser Effects in the Window Bar" on page 234.

Listing 7.6 com.gwtsolutions.components.client.ui.sw.SimpleWindowMover

```
1.package com.gwtsolutions.components.client.ui.sw;
2.
3.import com.google.gwt.user.client.DOM;
4.import com.google.gwt.user.client.ui.Image;
5.import com.google.gwt.user.client.ui.MouseListenerAdapter;
6.import com.google.gwt.user.client.ui.Widget;
7.import com.gwtsolutions.components.client.ui.StringHelpers;
8.
9.public class SimpleWindowMover extends MouseListenerAdapter {
10.    private SimpleWindow window;
11.    private int moveStartX;
12.    private int moveStartY;
13.    private boolean isMoving = false;
14.
15.    public SimpleWindowMover(SimpleWindow window) {
16.      this.window = window;
17.    }
18.
19.    public void onMouseDown(Widget sender, int x, int y) {
20.      window.removeStyleName(
21.          "gwtsolutions-SimpleWindow-MoveCursor");
22.      window.addStyleName("gwtsolutions-SimpleWindow-Pointer");
23.
24.      // Set variables that we'll use in onMouseMove()
25.      moveStartX = x;
26.      moveStartY = y;
27.      isMoving = true;
28.
29.      // When the user presses the mouse in the window bar
30.      // outside of the close button, we capture events,
31.      // meaning that until we call DOM.releaseCapture()
32.      // in onMouseUp, the window bar will be the only
33.      // widget that is notified of events. That will make
34.      // dragging the window more efficient.
35.      DOM.setCapture(sender.getElement());
36.    }
```

```
37.
38.  public void onMouseMove(Widget sender, int x, int y) {
39.     if (isMoving) {
40.        int deltaX = x - moveStartX;
41.        int deltaY = y - moveStartY;
42.
43.        // Move the window as the user is dragging the mouse
44.        window.setWindowPosition(window.getAbsoluteLeft()
45.           + deltaX, window.getAbsoluteTop() + deltaY);
46.     }
47.  }
48.
49.  public void onMouseUp(Widget sender, int x, int y) {
50.     if (isMoving) {
51.        window
52.           .removeStyleName("gwtsolutions-SimpleWindow-Pointer");
53.        isMoving = false;
54.     }
55.     // If the user releases the mouse in the window bar
56.     // outside of the close button, we release the capture
57.     // that we set in onMouseDown() by calling
58.     // DOM.setCapture(). That returns event handling to
59.     // normal and ends the window bar's exclusive rights
60.     // to all mouse events.
61.     DOM.releaseCapture(sender.getElement());
62.  }
63.
64.  public void onMouseEnter(Widget sender) {
65.     window
66.        .addStyleName("gwtsolutions-SimpleWindow-MoveCursor");
67.  }
68.
69.  public void onMouseLeave(Widget sender) {
70.     window.removeStyleName(
71.        "gwtsolutions-SimpleWindow-MoveCursor");
72.  }
73.}
```

The SimpleWindowMover class is a mouse listener that reacts to mouse events in the window bar's title. In many respects, this class is similar to the SimpleWindowResizer class we discussed in "Resizing Pop-Up Panels" on page 219.

Both SimpleWindowMover and SimpleWindowResizer implement the MouseListener interface, both change the mouse cursor when the cursor enters their associated widget,
and both use DOM.setCapture() to restrict mouse events to their associated widget
while the user is dragging the mouse.

There's one more interesting aspect of the window bar. Like the window itself, the
window bar must prevent unwanted browser effects, but there's a twist to how the
window bar prevents the browser from reacting to mouse events.

Preventing Unwanted Browser Effects in the Window Bar

The window bar contains an image—the Close button—so we must prevent the
browser from dragging that image, as shown in Figure 7.10, if the user happens to
drag the mouse while the mouse cursor is in the Close button.

Figure 7.10   Unwanted browser effects in the window bar

As we saw in "Moving Pop-Up Panels" on page 230, we add two mouse listeners
to the window bar's title widget. One of those listeners is an instance of
PreventDefaultDuringDragging, which we discussed in "Preventing Unwanted Browser
Effects" on page 222. That listener prevents the browser from reacting to mouse
dragging.

Here's the appropriate code from the WindowBar class:

```
public class WindowBar extends HorizontalPanel {
  ...
  private PreventDefaultDuringDragging
    preventDefaultDuringDragging =
      new PreventDefaultDuringDragging();
  ...
  private void addTitle() {
    ...
    title.addMouseListener(preventDefaultDuringDragging);
  }
  ...
  private void addCloseButton() {
```

```
    ...
    closeButton.addMouseListener(new MouseListenerAdapter() {
      ...
      public void onMouseUp(Widget sender, int x, int y) {
        window.hide();
        preventDefaultDuringDragging.removeEventPreview();
      }
    });
  }
}
```

Adding an instance of `PreventDefaultDuringDragging` to the title ensures that the browser stays out of the picture while a user drags a window. That's similar to how adding an instance of `PreventDefaultDuringDragging` to the window's bottom-right image prevented the browser from reacting to window resizing in "Preventing Unwanted Browser Effects" on page 222.

Here, however, is the window bar's twist. When a user enters the window bar, the `PreventDefaultDuringDragging` class adds to the event stack an event preview that prevents the browser from reacting to mouse events. When the user leaves the window bar, the `PreventDefaultDuringDragging` class removes that event preview. Removing the event preview is vital; without that removal, the browser will not react to mouse events, which means the user cannot click in a text field or activate buttons or links. Leaving that preview on the event stack when the mouse leaves the window bar effectively locks up our application.

Now, consider what happens when the user clicks a window's Close button. To click the Close button, the user must enter the window bar, which activates the event preview. But because clicking the Close button hides the window, *the mouse never leaves the window bar when the user clicks the Close button*. That means the `PreventDefaultDuringDragging` class *never removes the event preview from the event stack*, and the application locks up.

To straighten out the twist, we explicitly remove the event preview when the mouse is released in the Close button. We call the `PreventDefaultDuringDragging` class's `removeEventPreview` method, which removes the event preview from the event stack.

 Be Careful with Event Previews That Inhibit Browser Reactions to Events

Adding event previews to the event stack to inhibit the browser from reacting to events is vital for desktop applications that run in a browser, as we have seen in this solution. However, leaving that event preview on the event stack is asking for trouble because you can potentially lock up the browser. Make sure that you remove event previews from the event stack when you are through with them.

Stuff We Covered in This Solution

In this solution, we showed you a fish. We think simple windows are a nice addition to GWT, and we're confident that many readers will find uses for them in their own applications.

But mostly, in this solution, we talked a great deal about fishing. We explored two GWT staples that we haven't discussed so far—pop-up panels and flex tables—and we also explored many corners of GWT, such as sinking events, previewing events, and simulating 3-D buttons with a mouse listener and some images. We are certain that, even if you have no need for simple windows, you will find the techniques discussed in this solution to be useful in your own applications.

Before we move on to discussing and extending GWT tables in the next solution, we should note that we called our windows *simple* windows, not because they were simple to implement, but because they are pretty basic as far as windows go. Our windows are not part of a window manager, and our window bars do not have buttons for maximizing or minimizing windows, as is common for windows in a real windowing system.

Finally, we want to emphasize how much fun we had implementing simple windows. After the past few years of developing classic, form-based web applications, it was a blast to create something as graphic and responsive as simple windows. And, in the end, that is what GWT brings to the table that other web application frameworks do not.

Flex Tables

The application that many regard as the impetus for the personal computer revolution—VisiCalc[1] (which stands for Visible Calculator)—was a simple table that performed basic arithmetic calculations.

Much has changed in the software industry since VisiCalc was introduced in 1979, but tables, in various forms, are still an essential component of many applications, both desktop and web applications.

In this solution, we explore GWT's flex table widget, which, as its name implies, is a flexible table that you can dynamically manipulate at runtime. For example, you can add rows, columns, or cells to a table; you can edit a table's cells; and you can add cells that span more than one row or column. We see how to do all those things in this solution. We also create some classes of our own that encapsulate some of the more tedious aspects of flexible tables.

Stuff You're Going to Learn

This solution explores the following aspects of GWT:

- Using GWT's `FlexTable` (page 238)
- Formatting a table's rows, columns, and cells (page 245)
- Encapsulating low-level `FlexTable` details in a subclass (page 246)
- Placing GWT widgets in a table's cells (page 238)
- Creating table listeners to handle mouse clicks in table cells (page 257)
- Dynamically resizing table columns (page 257)
- Learning how GWT implements listeners and fires events (page 259)
- Implementing event sources and event listeners (page 259)
- Providing table data as needed (page 272)

---

[1] See http://en.wikipedia.org/wiki/VisiCalc for more information about VisiCalc.

- Paging through table data (page 272)

- Spanning multiple rows or columns with a single table cell (page 272)

This solution explores many facets of GWT's flex tables, but when we discuss dynamically resizing table columns and paging through data, we take some time to discover how GWT constructs event listeners and how it fires events to those listeners. Then we apply the same techniques to construct widgets that fire events for dynamically resizing columns and paging through table data.

Introduction to Flex Tables

GWT provides an abstract class for tables, `HTMLTable`, and two concrete extensions of that class: `Grid` and `FlexTable`. We have used the `Grid` class in a number of examples in this book. Now it's time to turn our attention to the `FlexTable` class.

As with GWT grids, you can put any kind of GWT widget in a flex table's cells, although you can also put plain text or HTML in a table cell with `HTMLTable.setText(int row, int column, String text)` or `HTMLTable.setHTML(int row, int col, String html)`, respectively. The ability to add any kind of widget to a flex table makes it easy to create tables with special capabilities; for example, you could add a Delete button to the first column of each row in a table to let users delete the associated row from the table. In fact, we show you how to do that in "Row Deletion in a Flex Table" on page 251.

Most tables have a fixed number of columns whose cells all span one column; however, the `FlexTable` class lets you add table cells that span more than one column. That feature is especially handy when you want to embed a widget such as a pager in a corner of a table, as shown in Figure 8.1.

First Name	Last Name	City	State
Gary	VanMatre	Castle Rock	CO
Derek	Roy	Buffalo	NY
Glenn	Miller	Atlanta	GA
Brian	Campbell	Burlington	VT
Claude	Loublier	Boston	MA
			◀▶

Figure 8.1   Spanning columns with a flex table

In "Data Page-Through in a Flex Table" on page 272, you will see how to implement the paging widget shown in Figure 8.1, but for now, let's start with the simple example shown in Figure 8.2.

Figure 8.2   Using a GWT flex table

The flex table application shown in Figure 8.2 is listed in Listing 8.1.

Listing 8.1   com.gwtsolutions.client.FlexTableByHand

```
1. package com.gwtsolutions.client;
2.
3. import com.google.gwt.core.client.EntryPoint;
4. import com.google.gwt.user.client.ui.Button;
5. import com.google.gwt.user.client.ui.FlexTable;
6. import com.google.gwt.user.client.ui.HTMLTable;
7. import com.google.gwt.user.client.ui.Label;
8. import com.google.gwt.user.client.ui.RootPanel;
9. import com.google.gwt.user.client.ui.Widget;
10.
11.public class FlexTableByHand implements EntryPoint {
12.   private static final int HEADER_ROW = 0;
13.   private static final int FIRST_DATA_ROW = 1;
14.   private static final int FIRST_COLUMN = 0;
15.   private static final int DATA_INDEX_ZERO = 0;
16.   private static final int DEFAULT_TABLE_CELL_SPACING = 0;
17.
18.   private static final Object[][] rowData = {
19.     { "Richard", "Tattersall", "New York", "NY"},
20.     { "Lynn", "Seckinger",  "Valhalla", "NY"},
```

continues

Listing 8.1   com.gwtsolutions.client.FlexTableByHand   *continued*

```
21.     { "Gabriella", "Sarantini", "Yonkers", "NY"},
22.     { "Homer", "Kenney", "Richmond", "VA"},
23.     { "Anna", "Richards", "Buffalo", "NY"},
24.     { "Gary", "VanMatre", "Castle Rock", "CO"},
25.     { "Derek", "Roy", "Buffalo", "NY"},
26.     { "Glenn", "Miller", "Atlanta", "GA"},
27.     { "Brian", "Campbell", "Burlington", "VT"},
28.     { "Claude", "Loublier", "Boston", "MA"},
29.     { "Gilbert", "Perrault", "Las Vegas", "NV"},
30.     { "Rene", "Robert", "Sacramento", "CA"},
31.     { "Daniel", "Briere", "Rochester", "NY"},
32.   };
33.
34.   private FlexTable flexTable = new FlexTable();
35.   private int nextRow = FIRST_DATA_ROW;
36.
37.   public void onModuleLoad() {
38.     flexTable.insertRow(HEADER_ROW);
39.     flexTable.getRowFormatter().addStyleName(HEADER_ROW,
40.     "gwtsolutions-FlexTable-Header");
41.
42.     addColumn("First Name");
43.     addColumn("Last Name");
44.     addColumn("City");
45.     addColumn("State");
46.
47.     for (int row = DATA_INDEX_ZERO;
48.         row < rowData.length; row++) {
49.       addRow(rowData[row]);
50.     }
51.
52.     applyDataRowStyles();
53.
54.     flexTable.setCellSpacing(DEFAULT_TABLE_CELL_SPACING);
55.     flexTable.addStyleName("gwtsolutions-FlexTable");
56.
57.     RootPanel.get().add(flexTable);
58.   }
59.
60.   private void addColumn(Object columnHeading) {
61.     Widget widget = createCellWidget(columnHeading);
62.     int cell = flexTable.getCellCount(HEADER_ROW);
```

```
63.
64.    widget.setWidth("100%");
65.    widget.addStyleName(
66.        "gwtsolutions-FlexTable-ColumnLabel");
67.
68.    flexTable.setWidget(HEADER_ROW, cell, widget);
69.
70.    flexTable.getCellFormatter().addStyleName(
71.        HEADER_ROW, cell,
72.        "gwtsolutions-FlexTable-ColumnLabelCell");
73.  }
74.
75.  private Widget createCellWidget(Object cellObject) {
76.    Widget widget = null;
77.
78.    if (cellObject instanceof Widget)
79.      widget = (Widget) cellObject;
80.    else
81.      widget = new Label(cellObject.toString());
82.
83.    return widget;
84.  }
85.
86.  private void addRow(Object[] cellObjects) {
87.    for (int cell = FIRST_COLUMN;
88.            cell < cellObjects.length; cell++) {
89.      Widget widget = createCellWidget(cellObjects[cell]);
90.      flexTable.setWidget(nextRow, cell, widget);
91.      flexTable.getCellFormatter().addStyleName(nextRow,
92.          cell,
93.          cell == 0 ? "gwtsolutions-FlexTable-Cell0"
94.                    : "gwtsolutions-FlexTable-Cell");
95.    }
96.    nextRow++;
97.  }
98.
99.  private void applyDataRowStyles() {
100.    HTMLTable.RowFormatter rf = flexTable.getRowFormatter();
101.
102.    for (int row = FIRST_DATA_ROW;
103.            row < flexTable.getRowCount(); ++row) {
104.      if ((row % 2) != 0) {
105.        rf.addStyleName(row, "gwtsolutions-FlexTable-OddRow");
```

continues

Listing 8.1   com.gwtsolutions.client.FlexTableByHand   *continued*

```
106.       }
107.       else {
108.          rf.addStyleName(row,
109.             "gwtsolutions-FlexTable-EvenRow");
110.       }
111.    }
112. }
113.}
```

As you can see in Figure 8.2 on page 239, the first row in our table is a header row, meaning it contains column headings, such as First Name, Last Name, and so on. The rest of the rows contain the table's data. We declare that data as an array of Object arrays, starting on line 18 of the preceding listing.

Although header rows are typical for most tables, you might not need a header row, so the FlexTable class does not contain any special methods or special treatment for the first row in a flex table.

After creating the table's data, we instantiate an instance of FlexTable on line 34. On line 38, we insert the header row into the table with the FlexTable's insertRow method, and using the table's row formatter, we apply a CSS style to the header row. Then we add column headings with a private addColumn method, starting on line 60.

The addColumn method takes an Object, which it wraps in a widget. That method subsequently places the widget in a table cell in the table's first row with the FlexTable setWidget method. The setWidget method takes a row, a column, and a widget. We transform the Object passed to addColumnHeading into a Widget suitable for the flex table's setWidget method with another private method, createCellWidget. The createCellWidget method simply returns the object it is passed if the object is a widget; otherwise, it creates a label widget whose text is the result of invoking toString() on the object that createCellWidget is passed. Notice that although we place label widgets only in header row cells in this example, we could have put any type of widget in those cells.

The addColumn method also adds CSS styles to the widget it places in header row cells and, using the table's cell formatter, adds a style to the header row cell itself.

After we've created and populated the header row, we iterate over the row data and add more rows to the table with the private addRow method, starting on line 86. The addRow method takes an array of objects that it places inside each subsequent row, where each object in the array is placed in a table cell in the specified row. One thing to notice here is that we do not invoke FlexTable.insertRow() for the data rows in our table, because FlexTable.setWidget() creates a row if no row corresponds to the specified row index.

Once we have created and populated the header row and data rows, we apply CSS styles to the data rows with the private `applyDataRowStyles` method, starting on line 99. That method uses the table's row formatter to add one of two styles to each row, depending on whether the row is an even or odd row in the table.

Finally, starting on line 54, we set the table's cell spacing to zero, apply a CSS style to the table as a whole, and add the table to the application's root panel. For completeness, we list the CSS classes used by our application in Listing 8.2.

Listing 8.2 gwtsolutions.css (truncated)

```
1....
2..gwtsolutions-EasyFlexTable {
3.   border-top: thin solid #666666;
4.   border-left: thin solid #666666;
5.   border-right: thin solid #000000;
6.   border-bottom: thin solid #000000;
7.   background-color:  #8080ff;
8.}
9.
10..gwtsolutions-EasyFlexTable-Header {
11.}
12.
13..gwtsolutions-EasyFlexTable-OddRow {
14.   background-color: #cccccc;
15.}
16.
17..gwtsolutions-EasyFlexTable-EvenRow {
18.   background-color:  #8080ff;
19.}
20.
21..gwtsolutions-EasyFlexTable-ColumnLabel {
22.   color: white;
23.   padding: 3px;
24.}
25.
26..gwtsolutions-EasyFlexTable-ColumnLabelCell {
27.   color: white;
28.   border-width: 0 0 0 1px;
29.   border-style: solid;
30.   border-color: white;
31.   margin: 0;
32.   padding: 0;
33.   text-align: center;
```

continues

Listing 8.2   gwtsolutions.css (truncated)   *continued*

```
34.}
35.
36..gwtsolutions-EasyFlexTable-Cell {
37.   border-width: 0px 0px 0px 1px;
38.   border-style: solid;
39.   color: white;
40.   border-color: white;
41.   padding: 5px;
42.}
43..gwtsolutions-EasyFlexTable-Cell0 {
44.   padding: 3px;
45.}
46.
47..gwtsolutions-EasyFlexTable-ColumnResizeCursor {
48.    cursor: col-resize;
49.}
50.
51..gwtsolutions-EasyFlexTable-PagerRow {
52.   border-width: 1px 0 0 0;
53.   border-style: solid;
54.   border-color: white;
55.   background-color: #cccccc;
56.}
57.
58..gwtsolutions-EasyFlexTable-ResizeCell {
59.}
60.
61..gwtsolutions-EasyFlexTable-Row {
62.    height: 32px;
63.    background-color: #ff0000;
64.}
```

com.google.gwt.user.client.ui.HTMLTable

- void setCellSpacing(int cellspacing)

  Sets the cell spacing for all cells in the table.

- `HTMLTable.CellFormatter getCellFormatter()`

  Returns a cell formatter. Cell formatters have a number of methods that let you add a CSS style to a cell, set a cell's horizontal and vertical alignments, set the width and height of a cell, set word wrap for a cell, and set a cell's visibility, among other things.

- `HTMLTable.RowFormatter getRowFormatter()`

  Returns a row formatter. Row formatters provide a number of methods for formatting table rows. You can use a row formatter to add a CSS style to a row, set a row's visibility and vertical alignment (note that it doesn't make sense to set a row's horizontal alignment), among other things.

- `void setWidget(int row, int cell, Widget widget)`

  Places the specified widget in the specified row and cell. If the cell does not exist, this method creates that cell. If the specified row does not exist, this method creates that row.

- `abstract int getCellCount(int row)`

  Returns the cell count for a specified row. If the specified row does not exist, this method throws an `IndexOutOfBounds` exception.

`com.google.gwt.user.client.ui.FlexTable`

- `void insertRow(int row)`

  Inserts a row at a specified index. If the row already exists, this method fails silently.

Flex Tables and Grids with Embedded Widgets Can Be Slow

When this book went to press, tables that embed widgets did not scale well to large numbers of rows. If you create a table with embedded widgets that contain hundreds or thousands of rows, your table's performance will almost certainly suffer.

Fortunately, the GWT team at Google is well aware of this performance problem, and is actively working to alleviate it by incorporating lightweight data binding to help developers sidestep performance issues.

FlexTable.setWidget() Creates Rows As Necessary

In the preceding example, we used the `FlexTable`'s `setWidget` method to place widgets in table cells. That method takes a row index, cell index, and a widget. If the specified row or cell does not exist, `setWidget` creates it automatically. That's part of the flex in flex table.

However, you may have noticed that in Listing 8.1, we explicitly created the header row with a call to `FlexTable.insertRow()` on line 38. Since we subsequently use `FlexTable.setWidget()` on line 68 to populate the header row, you may wonder why we need the call to `insertRow()` because `setWidget()` automatically creates the header row if it doesn't exist. The answer is that on line 62—before we call `setWidget()` for column headings—we call `FlexTable.getCellCount()` for the header row. If the header row doesn't exist, `getCellCount()` throws an exception. Since we call `getCellCount()` for the header row but not for data rows, we need to preallocate the header row but not the data rows.

An Easy Flex Table

In the preceding section, we covered the fundamentals of GWT's flex table: inserting and formatting rows, placing widgets in cells, adding CSS styles, and formatting cells. You can take that section's example and extrapolate it for your own needs.

However, we found it somewhat tedious to code that example, so we decided to encapsulate the low-level details in a base class so we wouldn't have to repeat that code every time we needed a table. That base class is listed in Listing 8.3.

Listing 8.3   com.gwtsolutions.components.client.ui.table.EasyFlexTable

```
1. package com.gwtsolutions.components.client.ui.table;
2.
3. import com.google.gwt.user.client.ui.FlexTable;
4. import com.google.gwt.user.client.ui.HTMLTable;
5. import com.google.gwt.user.client.ui.Label;
6. import com.google.gwt.user.client.ui.Widget;
7.
8. public class EasyFlexTable extends FlexTable {
9.    protected static final int HEADER_ROW = 0;
10.   protected static final int FIRST_DATA_ROW = 1;
11.   protected static final int FIRST_COLUMN = 0;
12.   protected static final int DATA_INDEX_ZERO = 0;
13.   protected static final int DEFAULT_TABLE_CELL_SPACING = 0;
14.
15.   private int nextRow = 1;
16.   private Object[][] rowData = null;
17.
18.   public EasyFlexTable(Object[][] rowData) {
```

```
19.    this();
20.    this.rowData = rowData;
21.    createRows(DATA_INDEX_ZERO);
22.    applyDataRowStyles();
23.  }
24.
25.  protected EasyFlexTable() {
26.    insertRow(HEADER_ROW);
27.    getRowFormatter().addStyleName(HEADER_ROW,
28.    "gwtsolutions-EasyFlexTable-Header");
29.    setCellSpacing(DEFAULT_TABLE_CELL_SPACING);
30.    addStyleName("gwtsolutions-EasyFlexTable");
31.  }
32.
33.  public void createRows(int rowIndex) {
34.    if (rowData == null)
35.      return;
36.
37.    for (int row = rowIndex; row < rowData.length; row++) {
38.      addRow(rowData[row]);
39.    }
40.  }
41.
42.  private void addRow(Object[] cellObjects) {
43.    for (int cell = FIRST_COLUMN;
44.            cell < cellObjects.length; cell++) {
45.      addCell(nextRow, cell, cellObjects[cell]);
46.    }
47.    nextRow++;
48.  }
49.
50.  public void addCell(int row, int cell, Object cellObject) {
51.    Widget widget = createCellWidget(cellObject);
52.    setWidget(row, cell, widget);
53.    getCellFormatter().addStyleName(row,
54.        cell,
55.        cell == 0 ? "gwtsolutions-EasyFlexTable-Cell0"
56.                  : "gwtsolutions-EasyFlexTable-Cell");
57.  }
58.
59.  public void applyDataRowStyles() {
60.    HTMLTable.RowFormatter rf = getRowFormatter();
61.
```

continues

Listing 8.3   com.gwtsolutions.components.client.ui.table.EasyFlexTable   *continued*

```
62.     for (int row = FIRST_DATA_ROW; row < getRowCount(); ++row) {
63.       if ((row % 2) != 0) {
64.         // Remove the even row style, just in case this used
65.         // to be an even row
66.         rf.removeStyleName(row,
67.             "gwtsolutions-EasyFlexTable-EvenRow");
68.         rf.addStyleName(row,
69.             "gwtsolutions-EasyFlexTable-OddRow");
70.       }
71.       else {
72.         // Remove the odd row style, just in case this used
73.         // to be an odd row
74.         rf.removeStyleName(row,
75.             "gwtsolutions-EasyFlexTable-OddRow");
76.         rf.addStyleName(row,
77.             "gwtsolutions-EasyFlexTable-EvenRow");
78.       }
79.     }
80.   }
81.
82.   public void addColumn(Object columnHeading) {
83.     Widget widget = createCellWidget(columnHeading);
84.     int columnIndex = getColumnCount();
85.
86.     widget.setWidth("100%");
87.     widget.addStyleName(
88.         "gwtsolutions-EasyFlexTable-ColumnLabel");
89.
90.     setWidget(HEADER_ROW, columnIndex, widget);
91.
92.     getCellFormatter().addStyleName(HEADER_ROW, columnIndex,
93.         "gwtsolutions-EasyFlexTable-ColumnLabelCell");
94.   }
95.
96.   public int getColumnCount() {
97.     return getCellCount(HEADER_ROW);
98.   }
99.
100.  protected Widget createCellWidget(Object cellObject) {
101.    Widget widget = null;
102.
103.    if (cellObject instanceof Widget)
```

```
104.        widget = (Widget) cellObject;
105.     else
106.        widget = new Label(cellObject.toString());
107.
108.     return widget;
109.   }
110.}
```

Listing 8.3 is similar to Listing 8.1 on page 239, except for the omission of the application itself. We merely encapsulated the methods that created a header row and data rows, added CSS styles, and formatted rows and cells.

Realize that the base class in Listing 8.3 is intended for tables that have a header row with column headings followed by data rows. We also expect that you will supply all the data for the table when you instantiate it, although we did include a protected no-argument constructor for subclasses that dynamically access data—we cover dynamic data in "Data Page-Through in a Flex Table" on page 272. Tables with column headings and data rows account for most of the tables you need to implement, so the base class will come in handy in most situations. If it does not, you can always fall back on creating your tables by hand.

Besides including the protected no-argument constructor, our `EasyFlexTable` base class differs from the implementation of Listing 8.1 on page 239 in one other respect. In `applyDataRowStyles()`, we remove even row styles before setting odd row styles, and vice versa. We do that in case users delete table rows, as discussed in the next section.

The application shown in Figure 8.2 is reimplemented in Listing 8.4, but with the aid of the base class listed in Listing 8.3.

Listing 8.4   com.gwtsolutions.client.EasyFlexTableExample

```
1. package com.gwtsolutions.client;
2.
3. import com.google.gwt.core.client.EntryPoint;
4. import com.google.gwt.user.client.Command;
5. import com.google.gwt.user.client.DeferredCommand;
6. import com.google.gwt.user.client.ui.Button;
7. import com.google.gwt.user.client.ui.KeyboardListener;
8. import com.google.gwt.user.client.ui.KeyboardListenerAdapter;
9. import com.google.gwt.user.client.ui.Label;
10.import com.google.gwt.user.client.ui.RootPanel;
11.import com.google.gwt.user.client.ui.SourcesTableEvents;
12.import com.google.gwt.user.client.ui.TableListener;
13.import com.google.gwt.user.client.ui.TextBox;
14.import com.google.gwt.user.client.ui.Widget;
```

continues

Listing 8.4   com.gwtsolutions.client.EasyFlexTableExample   *continues*

```
15.import com.gwtsolutions.components.client.ui.table.EasyFlexTable;
16.
17.public class EasyFlexTableExample implements EntryPoint {
18.   private static final Object[][] rowData = {
19.   { "Richard", "Tattersall", "New York", "NY"},
20.   { "Lynn", "Seckinger", "Valhalla", "NY"},
21.   { "Gabriella", "Sarantini", "Yonkers", "NY"},
22.   { "Homer", "Kenney", "Richmond", "VA"},
23.   { "Anna", "Richards", "Buffalo", "NY"},
24.   { "Gary", "VanMatre", "Castle Rock", "CO"},
25.   { "Derek", "Roy", "Buffalo", "NY"},
26.   { "Glenn", "Miller", "Atlanta", "GA"},
27.   { "Brian", "Campbell", "Burlington", "VT"},
28.   { "Claude", "Loublier", "Boston", "MA"},
29.   { "Gilbert", "Perrault", "Las Vegas", "NV"},
30.   { "Rene", "Robert", "Sacramento", "CA"},
31.   { "Daniel", "Briere", "Rochester", "NY"},
32.   };
33.
34.   public void onModuleLoad() {
35.     final EasyFlexTable table =
36.        new EasyFlexTable(rowData);
37.
38.     table.addColumn("First Name");
39.     table.addColumn("Last Name");
40.     table.addColumn("City");
41.     table.addColumn("State");
42.
43.     RootPanel.get().add(table);
44.   }
45.}
```

Notice that by using the EasyFlexTable base class, we made the preceding listing much simpler than the corresponding implementation in Listing 8.1 on page 239. That base class also simplifies the examples in the next two sections, where we explore row deletion and cell editing.

Row Deletion in a Flex Table

Flex tables are, as you might suspect, flexible. We can delete rows at runtime with the greatest of ease. Figure 8.3 shows an application that does just that.

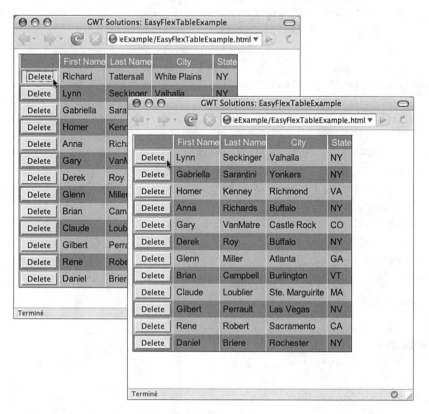

Figure 8.3   Deleting rows in a flex table

The application shown in Figure 8.3 is similar to the one shown in Listing 8.4 on page 249, except that we've added a Delete button to the first column. When a user clicks one of those buttons, we remove the corresponding row from the table. Here's the pertinent code from our updated application:

```
...
public class EasyFlexTableExample implements EntryPoint {
  private final Object[][] rowData = {
  { new DeleteButton("Delete"), "Richard", "Tattersall",
      "New York", "NY"},
  { new DeleteButton("Delete"), "Lynn", "Seckinger",
      "Valhalla", "NY"},
  { new DeleteButton("Delete"), "Gabriella", "Sarantini",
      "Yonkers", "NY"},
```

```
  { new DeleteButton("Delete"), "Homer", "Kenney",
      "Richmond", "VA"},
  { new DeleteButton("Delete"), "Anna", "Richards",
      "Buffalo", "NY"},
  { new DeleteButton("Delete"), "Gary", "VanMatre",
      "Castle Rock", "CO"},
  { new DeleteButton("Delete"), "Derek", "Roy",
      "Buffalo", "NY"},
  { new DeleteButton("Delete"), "Glenn", "Miller",
      "Atlanta", "GA"},
  { new DeleteButton("Delete"), "Brian", "Campbell",
      "Burlington", "VT"},
  { new DeleteButton("Delete"), "Claude", "Loublier",
      "Boston", "MA"},
  { new DeleteButton("Delete"), "Gilbert", "Perrault",
      "Las Vegas", "NV"},
  { new DeleteButton("Delete"), "Rene", "Robert",
      "Sacramento", "CA"},
  { new DeleteButton("Delete"), "Daniel", "Briere",
      "Rochester", "NY"},
  };
  ...
  public void onModuleLoad() {
    final EasyFlexTable table =
      new EasyFlexTable(rowData);
    ...
    RootPanel.get().add(table);
    ...
}
private class DeleteButton extends Button {
    public DeleteButton(String text) {
      super(text);
      addClickListener(new ClickListener() {
        public void onClick(Widget sender) {
          table.removeRow(getThisRow());
          table.applyDataRowStyles();
        }
      });
    }
    private int getThisRow() {
      int row = -1;
      for (int i=1; i < table.getRowCount(); ++i) {
        if (table.getWidget(i, 0) == this) {
```

```
        row = i;
        break;
      }
    }
    return row;
  }
}
}
```

The Delete buttons in the table are instances of a private DeleteButton class, which adds a click listener to its instances. That listener removes the table row in which the button resides by invoking HTMLTable.removeRow(). To find the row the button resides in, we iterate over the table rows and call HTMLTable.getWidget(int row, int column), passing the current row index and column zero, to see if the widget matches the button.

One other aspect of the preceding code deserves mention. Notice that we invoke our EasyFlexTable's applyDataRowStyles() after removing a row. We do that because our EasyFlexTable applies different styles to odd and even rows. If we do not update the data row CSS styles after deleting a row, we wind up with two previously even rows, or two previously odd rows, next to each other, which will ruin our even and odd styling.

com.google.gwt.user.client.ui.HTMLTable

- void removeRow(int row)

  Removes a row from a table. If the specified row does not exist, this method throws an IndexOutOfBoundsException.

- Widget getWidget(int row, int column)

  Returns the widget that resides at the specified cell in the table.

Flex Table Cell Editing

Now that we've seen how to delete rows in a table, let's see how to edit a table cell. Editing is a little more involved than deleting because editing requires two steps, and deletions only one, but cell editing is still simple to implement.

Figure 8.4 shows an application that lets users edit the text contained in a table's data rows.

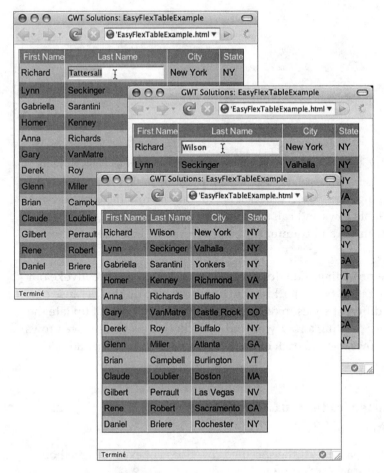

Figure 8.4   Editing cells in a flex table

The application shown in Figure 8.4 is the same as the one in Listing 8.4 on page 249, except for the following changes.

```
...
  public void onModuleLoad() {
    final EasyFlexTable table =
      new EasyFlexTable(rowData);
    ...
    RootPanel.get().add(table);

    table.addTableListener(new TableListener() {
      public void onCellClicked(SourcesTableEvents sender,
          final int row, final int cell) {
        // If the click was not in a column header...
        if (row != 0) {
```

```
// ...get the cell's widget
final Widget widget = table.getWidget(row, cell);

// If the widget is a label...
if (widget instanceof Label) {
  // .cast the widget to a Label, and create
  // a text box
  final Label label = (Label)widget;
  final TextBox textBox = new TextBox();

  // Copy the text in the cell to the text box,
  // and replace the label with the text box
  textBox.setText(table.getText(row, cell));
  table.setWidget(row, cell, textBox);

  // Give the text box focus and select all
  // of its text, in a deferred command
  DeferredCommand.addCommand(new Command() {
    public void execute() {
      textBox.setFocus(true);
      textBox.selectAll();
    }
  });

  // Add a focus listener that copies the text box's
  // text into the label and replaces the text box
  // with the label when the text box loses focus
  textBox.addFocusListener(
      new FocusListenerAdapter() {
    public void onLostFocus(Widget sender) {
      label.setText(textBox.getText());
      table.setWidget(row, cell, label);
    }
  });

  // Add a keyboard listener to the text box that
  // reacts to the ENTER and ESC keys
  textBox.addKeyboardListener(
      new KeyboardListenerAdapter() {
        public void onKeyPress(Widget sender,
            char keyCode, int modifiers) {
          // If the key pressed was ENTER, copy
          // the text box's text to the label and
```

```
                              // replace the text box with the label
                              if (keyCode == KeyboardListener.KEY_ENTER) {
                                label.setText(textBox.getText());
                                table.setWidget(row, cell, label);
                              }
                              // If the key pressed was ESC, replace the
                              // text box with the label. Because we're
                              // not changing the label's text, any
                              // edits are automatically cancelled
                              else if (keyCode ==
                                KeyboardListener.KEY_ESCAPE) {
                                table.setWidget(row, cell, label);
                              }
                          }
                      });
                }
              }
            }
          });
      }
}
```

When the user clicks a label in a data row—meaning a row other than the column heading row—we copy the label's text into a text box, replace the label widget with the text box, give the text box focus, and select all the text in the text box. Notice that we give the text box focus and select its text in a deferred command because those two operations do not work unless they are deferred until the text box's DOM element is added to the DOM tree.

We also add a focus listener to the text box, so that when the text box loses focus, we copy the text box's text into the label and replace the text box with the label.

Finally, we add to the text box a keyboard listener that detects the ENTER and ESCAPE keys. When the user presses ENTER in a table cell, we replace the text box with the original label widget and copy the text box's text to the label. Instead of implementing the KeyboardListener interface directly, we extend the KeyboardListenerAdapter class so that we don't have to implement all the KeyboardListener methods.

When the user presses ESCAPE, we simply replace the text box with the label. Because we don't modify the label's original text, any modifications to the text in the text box are automatically cancelled when the user presses the ESCAPE key.

com.google.gwt.user.client.ui.TableListener

- void onCellClicked(SourcesTableEvents sender, int row, int cell)

  Is called by GWT when a user clicks in a table cell. GWT calls this method for each table listener attached to a table. The sender widget is the table, and the row and cell represent the row and cell that the user clicked in.

com.google.gwt.user.client.ui.SourcesTableEvents

- void addTableListener(TableListener listener)

  Lets you add table listeners to any subclass of HTMLTable because the HTMLTable class implements SourcesTableEvents. The table invokes the onCellClicked method for each of its registered listeners when a user clicks in a cell.

- void removeTableListener(TableListener listener)

  Removes a table listener from a table.

com.google.gwt.user.client.ui.TextBoxBase

- void selectAll()

  Selects all the text in a text box.

  Note that this method does not work if the text box's DOM element is not attached to the DOM tree when the method is invoked. If you need to select text in a text box that hasn't yet been displayed, wrap the call to selectAll() in a deferred command, as we did in the preceding example.

You've now seen how to use flex tables, how to encapsulate low-level, table-building details in a convenient base class, and how to delete rows and edit cells. So next, let's see how to extend the EasyFlexTable base class, introduced in "An Easy Flex Table" on page 246, to dynamically resize a table's columns and to dynamically page through data.

Dynamic Resizing of a Flex Table's Columns

Flex tables, as we have seen, are indeed flexible. You can insert and remove rows and cells, and you can insert widgets or remove widgets from cells. You can also format cells to span more than one row or one column with an instance of FlexTable.CellFormatter.

You can even set the width of a cell with an instance of `HTMLTable.CellFormatter` by calling its `setWidth(int row, int column, String width)` method. GWT, however, does not provide an out-of-the-box widget that lets you dynamically resize columns. In this section, we remedy that oversight by extending the `EasyFlexTable` class, implemented in "An Easy Flex Table" on page 246, to build a widget that accomplishes dynamic column resizing.

Figure 8.5 shows a user in the act of dynamically resizing a table's columns. The user resizes a column by placing the cursor to the left of the column to be resized in the table's header row and dragging the mouse to the left or right to resize the cell.

The top two pictures in Figure 8.5 show the user resizing the `Last Name` column, and the bottom two pictures show the user resizing the `City` column.

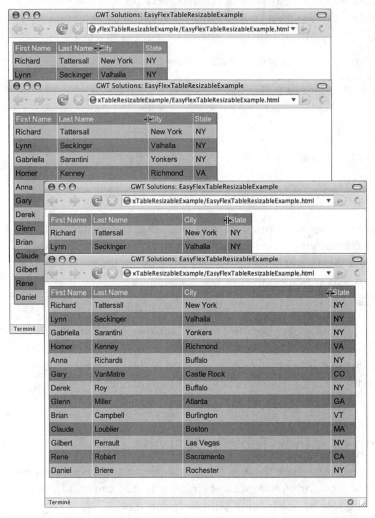

Figure 8.5   Resizing columns in a flex table

To accommodate dynamic resizing as shown in Figure 8.5, we follow the recipe that GWT uses internally for implementing event listeners and firing events to those listeners. Before we discuss our approach to dynamic resizing, let's look at how GWT follows that recipe to implement event listeners and fire events.

Constructing Event Listeners and Firing Events with GWT

In "Row Deletion in a Flex Table" on page 251 we showed you how to implement the TableListener interface to handle mouse clicks in table cells. Let's see how GWT internally handles event firing to table listeners.

First, GWT defines a ClickListener interface, listed in Listing 8.5.

Listing 8.5   com.google.gwt.user.client.ui.TableListener (truncated)

```
1./*
2. * Copyright 2006 Google Inc.
3. * ...
4. */
5.package com.google.gwt.user.client.ui;
6.
7./**
8. * Event listener interface for table events.
9. */
10.public interface TableListener {
11.
12.  /**
13.   * Fired when a cell is clicked.
14.   *
15.   * @param sender the widget sending the event
16.   * @param row the row of the cell being clicked
17.   * @param cell the index of the cell being clicked
18.   */
19.  void onCellClicked(SourcesTableEvents sender,
20.                     int row, int cell);
21.}
```

The preceding interface is the interface we implemented in "Row Deletion in a Flex Table" on page 251 to delete rows from a table.

Next, GWT defines a SourcesTableEvents interface, shown in Listing 8.6.

Listing 8.6   com.google.gwt.user.client.ui.SourcesTableEvents (truncated)

```
1./*
2. * Copyright 2006 Google Inc.
3. * ...
4. */
5.package com.google.gwt.user.client.ui;
6.
7./**
8. * A widget that implements this interface
9. * sources the events defined by the
10. * {@link com.google.gwt.user.client.ui.TableListener}
11. * interface.
12. */
13.public interface SourcesTableEvents {
14.
15.   /**
16.    * Adds a listener interface to receive click events.
17.    *
18.    * @param listener the listener interface to add
19.    */
20.   public void addTableListener(TableListener listener);
21.
22.   /**
23.    * Removes a previously added listener interface.
24.    *
25.    * @param listener the listener interface to remove
26.    */
27.   public void removeTableListener(TableListener listener);
28.}
```

The SourcesTableEvents interface, which specifies how table listeners are added to and removed from a table, is implemented by HTMLTable, the base class for GWT table classes. Listing 8.7 shows how HTMLTable implements the SourcesTableEvents interface and how it fires events to its table listeners.

Listing 8.7   com.google.gwt.user.client.ui.HTMLTable (truncated)

```
1./*
2. * Copyright 2006 Google Inc.
3. * ...
4. */
5.
6.package com.google.gwt.user.client.ui;
```

```
7.
8....
9.
10./**
11. * HTMLTable contains the common table algorithms for
12. * {@link com.google.gwt.user.client.ui.Grid} and
13. * {@link com.google.gwt.user.client.ui.FlexTable}.
14. * <p>
15. * <img class='gallery' src='Table.png'/>
16. * </p>
17. */
18.public abstract class HTMLTable
19. extends Panel implements SourcesTableEvents {
20.  ...
21.  private TableListenerCollection tableListeners;
22.  ...
23.  /**
24.   * Adds a listener to the current table.
25.   *
26.   * @param listener listener to add
27.   */
28.  public void addTableListener(TableListener listener) {
29.    if (tableListeners == null) {
30.      tableListeners = new TableListenerCollection();
31.    }
32.    tableListeners.add(listener);
33.  }
34.  ...
35.  /**
36.   * Removes the specified table listener.
37.   *
38.   * @param listener listener to remove
39.   */
40.  public void removeTableListener(TableListener listener) {
41.    if (tableListeners != null) {
42.      tableListeners.remove(listener);
43.    }
44.  }
45.  ...
46.  /**
47.   * Method to process events generated from the browser.
48.   *
49.   * @param event the generated event
```

continues

Listing 8.7   com.google.gwt.user.client.ui.HTMLTable (truncated)   *continued*

```
50.    */
51.    public void onBrowserEvent(Event event) {
52.      switch (DOM.eventGetType(event)) {
53.        case Event.ONCLICK: {
54.          if (tableListeners != null) {
55.            // Find out which cell was actually clicked.
56.            Element td = getEventTargetCell(event);
57.            if (td == null) {
58.              return;
59.            }
60.            Element tr = DOM.getParent(td);
61.            Element body = DOM.getParent(tr);
62.            int row = DOM.getChildIndex(body, tr);
63.            int column = DOM.getChildIndex(tr, td);
64.            // Fire the event.
65.            tableListeners.fireCellClicked(this, row, column);
66.          }
67.          break;
68.        }
69.        default: {
70.          // Do nothing
71.        }
72.      }
73.    }
74.}
```

HTMLTable maintains a collection of table listeners. That collection is an instance of
TableListenerCollection, shown in Listing 8.8.

Listing 8.8   com.google.gwt.user.client.ui.TableListenerCollection (truncated)

```
1./*
2. * Copyright 2006 Google Inc.
3. * ...
4. */
5.package com.google.gwt.user.client.ui;
6.
7.import java.util.Iterator;
8.import java.util.Vector;
9.
10./**
```

```
11. * A helper class for implementers of the
12. * {@link com.google.gwt.user.client.ui.SourcesTableEvents}
13. * interface. This subclass of Vector assumes that all
14. * objects added to it will be of type
15. * {@link com.google.gwt.user.client.ui.TableListener}.
16. */
17.public class TableListenerCollection extends Vector {
18.
19.   /**
20.    * Fires a cellClicked event to all listeners.
21.    *
22.    * @param sender the widget sending the event
23.    * @param row the row of the cell being clicked
24.    * @param cell the index of the cell being clicked
25.    */
26.   public void fireCellClicked(SourcesTableEvents sender,
27.                                int row, int cell) {
28.     for (Iterator it = iterator(); it.hasNext();) {
29.       TableListener listener = (TableListener) it.next();
30.       listener.onCellClicked(sender, row, cell);
31.     }
32.   }
33.}
```

Table listener collections are a vector of table listeners. The `TableListenerCollection` class implements a `fireCellClicked` method that invokes `onCellClicked()` on all table listeners in the collection when a user clicks in a table cell.

Now we know how GWT maintains a collection of table listeners and how it fires events to those listeners when a user clicks in a table cell. To summarize, GWT does the following:

- Defines a `TableListener` interface

- Implements a `TableListenerCollection` class

- Defines a `SourcesTableEvents` interface

- Implements `SourcesTableEvents` in `HTMLTable` with an instance of `TableListenerCollection` that maintains the table's list of table listeners

We do something similar to build a widget that fires resize events to its associated table to achieve dynamic column resizing, as shown in Figure 8.5 on page 258.

Building the ResizableCellPanel Widget

To create dynamically resizing table columns by dragging column headings, as shown in Figure 8.5 on page 258, we replace column heading widgets with a resizable cell panel, as shown in Figure 8.6.

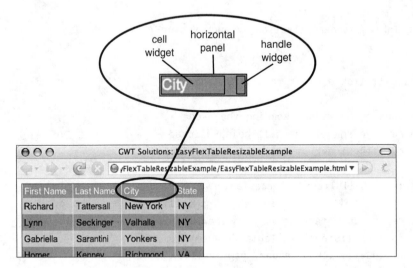

Figure 8.6   A resizable cell panel

Our `ResizableCellPanel` class extends `HorizontalPanel` to contain two widgets: the column heading widget, which is left-justified in the panel, and a handle widget, which is right-justified in the panel.

The handle widget enables mouse dragging. When the cursor enters the handle widget, we add to the handle widget a CSS style that specifies a resize cursor. As the user subsequently drags the mouse, the resizable cell panel *fires resize events to a collection of resize listeners*.

We implement resize listeners similarly to the way in which GWT implements table listeners. We do that like this:

- Define a `ResizeListener` interface.

- Implement a `ResizeListenerCollection` class.

- Define a `SourcesResizeEvents` interface.

- Implement `SourcesResizeEvents` in `ResizableCellPanel` with an instance of `ResizeListenerCollection` that maintains the resizable cell panel's list of resize listeners.

The `ResizeListener` interface is listed in Listing 8.9.

Listing 8.9   com.gwtsolutions.components.client.ui.ResizeListener

```
1.package com.gwtsolutions.components.client.ui;
2.
3.public interface ResizeListener {
4.   public void onResize(SourcesResizeEvents sender,
5.      int width, int height);
6.}
```

Resize listeners react to resize events. They are passed the sender of the resize event—which implements `SourcesResizeEvents`—and the new width and height of the widget after the resize.

The `ResizeListenerCollection` class is listed in Listing 8.10.

Listing 8.10   com.gwtsolutions.components.client.ui.ResizeListenerCollection

```
1.package com.gwtsolutions.components.client.ui;
2.
3.import java.util.Iterator;
4.import java.util.Vector;
5.import com.google.gwt.user.client.ui.Widget;
6.
7.public class ResizeListenerCollection extends Vector {
8.   public void fireResize(SourcesResizeEvents sender, int width,
9.       int height) {
10.    Iterator it = iterator();
11.    while (it.hasNext()) {
12.       ResizeListener rl = (ResizeListener) it.next();
13.       rl.onResize(sender, width, height);
14.    }
15.  }
16.}
```

Like GWT's `TableListenerCollection` class, our `ResizeListenerCollection` class extends `Vector` and implements one method that fires events to registered listeners.

Next, we define a `SourcesResizeEvents` interface, listed in Listing 8.11.

Listing 8.11   com.gwtsolutions.components.client.ui.SourcesResizeEvents

```
1.package com.gwtsolutions.components.client.ui;
2.
```

continues

Listing 8.11   com.gwtsolutions.components.client.ui.SourcesResizeEvents   *continued*

```
3.public interface SourcesResizeEvents {
4.  public void addResizeListener(ResizeListener listener);
5.  public void removeResizeListener(ResizeListener listener);
6.}
```

Finally, we create the ResizableCellPanel class, which implements
SourcesResizeEvents, in Listing 8.12.

Listing 8.12   com.gwtsolutions.components.client.ui.table.ResizableCellPanel

```
1. package com.gwtsolutions.components.client.ui.table;
2.
3. import com.google.gwt.user.client.DOM;
4. import com.google.gwt.user.client.Event;
5. import com.google.gwt.user.client.EventPreview;
6. import com.google.gwt.user.client.ui.HTML;
7. import com.google.gwt.user.client.ui.HasHorizontalAlignment;
8. import com.google.gwt.user.client.ui.HorizontalPanel;
9. import com.google.gwt.user.client.ui.MouseListener;
10.import com.google.gwt.user.client.ui.Widget;
11.import com.gwtsolutions.components.client.ui.ResizeListener;
12.import com.gwtsolutions.components.client.ui.ResizeListenerCollection;
13.import com.gwtsolutions.components.client.ui.SourcesResizeEvents;
14.
15.public class ResizableCellPanel extends HorizontalPanel
16.    implements SourcesResizeEvents, MouseListener {
17.  private static final String CURSOR_STYLE =
18.    "gwtsolutions-EasyFlexTable-ColumnResizeCursor";
19.
20.  private String RESIZE_HANDLE_WIDTH = "8px";
21.
22.  private EventPreview eventPreview = new EventPreview() {
23.    public boolean onEventPreview(Event event) {
24.        switch (DOM.eventGetType(event)) {
25.          case Event.ONMOUSEDOWN:
26.          case Event.ONMOUSEMOVE:
27.            DOM.eventPreventDefault(event);
28.        }
29.        return true;
30.    }
31.  };
32.
```

```
33.   private Widget cellWidget;
34.   private boolean isResizing;
35.   private int startX;
36.   private ResizeListenerCollection resizeListeners =
37.     new ResizeListenerCollection();
38.
39.   public ResizableCellPanel(Widget cellWidget) {
40.     setWidgets(cellWidget, new HTML(" "));
41.     setBorderWidth(0);
42.   }
43.
44.   protected void setWidgets(Widget cellWidget,
45.                                 HTML handleWidget) {
46.     this.cellWidget = cellWidget;
47.     handleWidget.setHeight("100%");
48.     handleWidget.setWidth(RESIZE_HANDLE_WIDTH);
49.
50.     handleWidget.addMouseListener(this);
51.
52.     add(cellWidget);
53.     add(handleWidget);
54.
55.     setCellHorizontalAlignment(cellWidget,
56.         HasHorizontalAlignment.ALIGN_LEFT);
57.
58.     setCellHorizontalAlignment(handleWidget,
59.         HasHorizontalAlignment.ALIGN_RIGHT);
60.
61.     setWidth("100%");
62.   }
63.
64.   public void onMouseEnter(Widget sender) {
65.     sender.addStyleName(CURSOR_STYLE);
66.     DOM.addEventPreview(eventPreview);
67.   }
68.
69.   public void onMouseLeave(Widget sender) {
70.     if ( ! isResizing) {
71.       sender.removeStyleName(CURSOR_STYLE);
72.       DOM.removeEventPreview(eventPreview);
73.     }
74.   }
75.
```

continues

```
76.   public void onMouseDown(Widget sender, int x, int y) {
77.     DOM.setCapture(sender.getElement());
78.
79.     isResizing = true;
80.     startX = x;
81.   }
82.
83.   public void onMouseUp(Widget sender, int x, int y) {
84.     if (isResizing) {
85.       DOM.releaseCapture(sender.getElement());
86.       DOM.removeEventPreview(eventPreview);
87.       sender.removeStyleName(CURSOR_STYLE);
88.       isResizing = false;
89.     }
90.   }
91.
92.   public void onMouseMove(Widget sender, int x, int y) {
93.     if (isResizing) {
94.       int width = Math.min(0, getOffsetWidth() + (x - startX));
95.       resizeListeners.fireResize(this, width,
96.           cellWidget.getOffsetHeight());
97.     }
98.   }
99.
100.  public void addResizeListener(ResizeListener listener) {
101.    resizeListeners.add(listener);
102.  }
103.
104.  public void removeResizeListener(ResizeListener listener) {
105.    resizeListeners.remove(listener);
106.  }
107.}
```

The preceding class is a simple extension of HorizontalPanel that contains two widgets. The handle widget, which is right-justified in the panel, enables mouse dragging. When the user drags the mouse in the handle widget, the ResizableCellPanel's onMouseMove method, starting on line 92, fires resize events to all registered resize listeners.

At this point, only one question remains: What resize listeners listen to the resizable cell panel? As it turns out, you can attach a collection of resize listeners to a resizable cell panel, but for our purposes, we attach only one listener: an instance of

`ColumnResizeListener`. Column resize listeners are resize listeners that keep track of the table column to which they are attached. Column resize listeners work in concert with an extension of `EasyFlexTable` that places instances of `ResizableCellPanel` in column headings.

> **Array Lists vs. Vectors**
>
> Like GWT's built-in collection classes, our `ResizeListenerCollection` class, listed on page 265, uses a vector to store listeners. There was a time when GWT's vectors were slightly faster than array lists because of an implementation detail. That's no longer true, so in GWT 1.4, built-in collections will use array lists instead of vectors because array lists will be a bit faster than vectors. If you implement your own collection classes, you should also prefer array lists to vectors.

Incorporating the ResizableCellPanel into a Flex Table

The `EasyFlexTableResizable` class, listed in Listing 8.13, extends the `EasyFlexTable` class.

Listing 8.13   com.gwtsolutions.components.client.ui.table.EasyFlexTableResizable

```
1. package com.gwtsolutions.components.client.ui.table;
2.
3. import com.google.gwt.user.client.ui.Widget;
4.
5. public class EasyFlexTableResizable
6.     extends EasyFlexTable implements HasResizableColumns {
7.
8.   public EasyFlexTableResizable(Object[][] rowData) {
9.     super(rowData);
10.  }
11.
12.  protected EasyFlexTableResizable() {
13.     super();
14.  }
15.
16.  public void addColumn(Object columnHeading) {
17.    Widget widget = createCellWidget(columnHeading);
18.    int columnIndex = getColumnCount();
19.
20.    widget.setWidth("100%");
21.    widget.addStyleName(
22.        "gwtsolutions-EasyFlexTable-ColumnLabel");
23.
24.    getCellFormatter().addStyleName(HEADER_ROW,
```

continues

Listing 8.13   com.gwtsolutions.components.client.ui.table.
EasyFlexTableResizable   *continued*

```
25.          columnIndex,
26.          "gwtsolutions-EasyFlexTable-ColumnLabelCell");
27.
28.      setWidget(HEADER_ROW, columnIndex,
29.          wrapCellWidgetInResizablePanel(widget, columnIndex));
30.  }
31.
32.  private Widget wrapCellWidgetInResizablePanel(Widget wrapMe,
33.      int column) {
34.      ResizableCellPanel rcp = new ResizableCellPanel(wrapMe);
35.      rcp.addResizeListener(
36.          new ColumnResizeListener(this, column));
37.
38.      return rcp;
39.  }
40.
41.  public void setColumnWidth(int column, int width) {
42.      getColumnFormatter().setWidth(column,
43.          width + "px");
44.  }
45.}
```

The preceding listing extends `EasyFlexTable` and overrides the `addColumn` method. The overridden method is just like the original method, except that on line 29 we wrap the widget placed in the header row in an instance of `ResizableCellPanel` by calling a private method named `wrapCellWidgetInResizableCellPanel`.

The `wrapCellWidgetInResizableCellPanel` method creates an instance of `ResizableCellPanel`, passing it the widget to wrap. Then, on line 36, we add an instance of `ColumnResizeListener` to the resizable cell panel. Subsequently, when the user drags the mouse in a column heading to resize a column, the resizable cell panel notifies that listener. The `ColumnResizeListener` class is listed in Listing 8.14.

Listing 8.14   com.gwtsolutions.components.client.ui.table.ColumnResizeListener

```
1.package com.gwtsolutions.components.client.ui.table;
2.
3.import com.gwtsolutions.components.client.ui.ResizeListener;
4.import com.gwtsolutions.components.client.ui.SourcesResizeEvents;
5.
```

```
6.public class ColumnResizeListener implements ResizeListener {
7.   private HasResizableColumns hasResizableColumns;
8.   private int columnIndex;
9.
10.   public ColumnResizeListener(
11.       HasResizableColumns hasResizableColumns,
12.       int columnIndex) {
13.     this.hasResizableColumns = hasResizableColumns;
14.     this.columnIndex = columnIndex;
15.   }
16.
17.   public void onResize(SourcesResizeEvents sender,
18.       int width, int height) {
19.     hasResizableColumns.setColumnWidth(columnIndex, width);
20.   }
21.}
```

Notice that column resize listeners are passed an instance of HasResizableColumns in their constructor. That interface, listed in Listing 8.15, is implemented by EasyFlexTableResizable, listed in Listing 8.13.

Listing 8.15   com.gwtsolutions.components.client.ui.table.HasResizableColumns

```
1.package com.gwtsolutions.components.client.ui.table;
2.
3.public interface HasResizableColumns {
4.   public void setColumnWidth(int columnIndex, int width);
5.}
```

Here's a recap of how EasyFlexTableResizable works with ResizableCellPanel to dynamically resize columns. When you add a column to the table, the table's addColumn method creates an instance of ResizableCellPanel on line 34 of Listing 8.13 and subsequently adds the resizable cell panel to the column heading. On line 35, the table adds an instance of ColumnResizeListener to the resizable cell panel, passing to the column resize listener a reference to the table and the index of the column.

Subsequently, when a user drags the mouse in the resizable cell panel's handle widget, the resizable cell panel notifies its column resize listener of the mouse drag. The column resize listener calls the table's setColumnWidth method on line 19 of Listing 8.14, and on line 42 of Listing 8.13, the table reacts by using a column formatter to reset the width of the column.

com.google.gwt.user.client.ui.HTMLTable.ColumnFormatter

- void setWidth(int column, String width)

  Sets the width of a table column. The width is specified as a string representing CSS units; for example "25px" or "100%".

com.google.gwt.user.client.ui.CellPanel

- void setCellHorizontalAlignment(Widget widget,
  HasHorizontalAlignment.HorizontalAlignmentConstant align)

  Sets the horizontal alignment of a widget inside its cell. The CellPanel class is the superclass of DockPanel, HorizontalPanel, and VerticalPanel, all of which inherit this method.

Data Page-Through in a Flex Table

Now we know how GWT implements event listeners and fires events internally, and now we also know how to create similar functionality for custom widgets. So let's explore how to do the same thing to page through data in a flex table.

Up to now, we've passed table data to our tables' constructors. In practice, that's likely to be unrealistic because web applications often access data dynamically. For example, for a large amount of data stored in a database, you might not even know how much data your table is ultimately going to display, let alone know exactly what that data is.

In this section, we extend EasyFlexTableResizable, discussed in "Dynamic Resizing of a Flex Table's Columns" on page 257. In addition to letting users dynamically resize columns, we also adorn the table with a pager widget that lets users page through data, as shown in Figure 8.7.

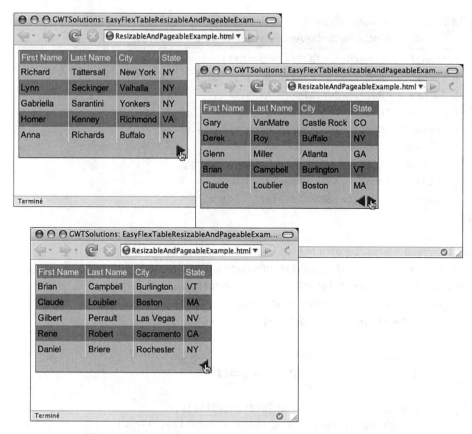

Figure 8.7   Paging through data in a flex table

The application shown in Figure 8.7 is listed in Listing 8.16.

Listing 8.16   com.gwtsolutions.client.EasyFlexTableResizableAndPageableExample

```
1.package com.gwtsolutions.client;
2.
3.import com.google.gwt.core.client.EntryPoint;
4.import com.google.gwt.user.client.ui.RootPanel;
5.import
âcom.gwtsolutions.components.client.ui.table.EasyFlexTableResizableAndPageable;
6.
7.public class EasyFlexTableResizableAndPageableExample
8.    implements EntryPoint {
9.    private static Object[][] rowData = {
10.    { "Richard", "Tattersall", "New York", "NY"},
11.    { "Lynn", "Seckinger",  "Valhalla", "NY"},
12.    { "Gabriella", "Sarantini", "Yonkers", "NY"},
13.    { "Homer", "Kenney", "Richmond", "VA"},
```

continues

```
14.    { "Anna", "Richards", "Buffalo", "NY"},
15.    { "Gary", "VanMatre", "Castle Rock", "CO"},
16.    { "Derek", "Roy", "Buffalo", "NY"},
17.    { "Glenn", "Miller", "Atlanta", "GA"},
18.    { "Brian", "Campbell", "Burlington", "VT"},
19.    { "Claude", "Loublier", "Boston", "MA"},
20.    { "Gilbert", "Perrault", "Las Vegas", "NV"},
21.    { "Rene", "Robert", "Sacramento", "CA"},
22.    { "Daniel", "Briere", "Rochester", "NY"},
23.  };
24.
25.  public void onModuleLoad() {
26.    final EasyFlexTableResizableAndPageable
27.    table = new EasyFlexTableResizableAndPageable(5) {
28.      public Object[][] getData(int index) {
29.        int pageSize = getPageSize();
30.
31.        if (isLastPage(index))
32.          index = rowData.length - pageSize;
33.
34.        Object[][] array = new Object[pageSize][];
35.        for (int row=index; row < index + pageSize; ++row) {
36.          array[row-index] = rowData[row];
37.        }
38.        return array;
39.      }
40.      public boolean isLastPage(int topOfPageIndex) {
41.        return
42.          topOfPageIndex + getPageSize() >= rowData.length;
43.      }
44.    };
45.
46.    table.addColumn("First Name");
47.    table.addColumn("Last Name");
48.    table.addColumn("City");
49.    table.addColumn("State");
50.
51.    RootPanel.get().add(table);
52.  }
53.}
```

Instead of specifying the table's data when we construct the table, we create a table with no initial data. We instantiate the table on line 27 of the preceding listing, and the only thing we pass the constructor is the size of a page of data; in our case, that's five rows.

To populate the table with data, we use the table's abstract getData method, starting on line 28. The table passes that method the starting index, and it's up to getData to supply the corresponding data. In the preceding listing, we carve out an array of Object arrays from our fixed set of data. Notice that our fixed set of data need not be fixed at all—we could have read data from a database, for example—but for illustration, it's simpler to use a fixed array of data.

The getData method on line 31 checks to see if the index passed to getData() corresponds to the last page of data; if so, it adjusts the starting index to supply the last page of data.

The table calls getData() under two circumstances: once when the table is constructed, and subsequently every time the user clicks one of the arrows in the pager widget. The table is implemented in Listing 8.17.

Listing 8.17   com.gwtsolutions.components.client.ui.table.
                EasyFlexTableResizableAndPageable

```
1.package com.gwtsolutions.components.client.ui.table;
2.
3.import com.google.gwt.user.client.ui.HasHorizontalAlignment;
4.import com.gwtsolutions.components.client.ui.CanPage;
5.import com.gwtsolutions.components.client.ui.Pager;
6.import com.gwtsolutions.components.client.ui.PagerListener;
7.import com.gwtsolutions.components.client.ui.SourcesPagerEvents;
8.
9.public abstract class EasyFlexTableResizableAndPageable extends
10.    EasyFlexTableResizable implements CanPage, PagerListener {
11.    private static final int DEFAULT_PAGE_SIZE = 6;
12.
13.    private Pager pager = null;
14.    private int pageSize = DEFAULT_PAGE_SIZE;
15.
16.    public abstract Object[][] getData(int startIndex);
17.    public abstract boolean isLastPage(int index);
18.
19.    public EasyFlexTableResizableAndPageable(int pageSize) {
20.      super();
21.      this.pageSize = pageSize;
22.
```

continues

Listing 8.17   com.gwtsolutions.components.client.ui.table.
            EasyFlexTableResizableAndPageable   *continued*

```
23.    createDataRows();
24.    populateDataRows(getData(DATA_INDEX_ZERO));
25.    applyDataRowStyles();
26.    addPager();
27. }
28.
29. private void createDataRows() {
30.    for (int row = FIRST_DATA_ROW; row < pageSize; ++row)
31.      insertRow(row);
32. }
33.
34. private void populateDataRows(Object[][] data) {
35.    for (int row = FIRST_DATA_ROW; row <= pageSize; ++row) {
36.      Object[] rowData = data[row-1];
37.      for (int cell = 0; cell < rowData.length; ++cell)
38.        addCell(row, cell, rowData[cell]);
39.    }
40. }
41.
42. private void addPager() {
43.    pager = new Pager(this);
44.    pager.addPagerListener(this);
45.
46.    int row = getRowCount();
47.    setWidget(row, FIRST_COLUMN, pager);
48.
49.    getRowFormatter().addStyleName(row,
50.        "gwtsolutions-EasyFlexTable-PagerRow");
51.
52.    getCellFormatter().setHorizontalAlignment(row,
53.        FIRST_COLUMN, HasHorizontalAlignment.ALIGN_RIGHT);
54.
55.    ((FlexCellFormatter) getCellFormatter()).setColSpan(row,
56.        FIRST_COLUMN, getCellCount(FIRST_DATA_ROW));
57. }
58.
59. public void onPage(SourcesPagerEvents sender, int index) {
60.    clearDataRows();
61.    populateDataRows(getData(index));
62. }
```

```
63.
64.   private void clearDataRows() {
65.     for (int row = FIRST_DATA_ROW; row <= pageSize; ++row) {
66.       for (int cell = 0; cell < getCellCount(row); ++cell) {
67.         clearCell(row, cell);
68.       }
69.     }
70.   }
71.
72.   public int getPageSize() {
73.     return pageSize;
74.   }
75.}
```

On line 26 of the preceding listing, after populating the table's data rows, we add the pager widget to the table. On line 43, we instantiate an instance of the Pager class and add the table to it as a listener on line 44.

When the user clicks the arrows in the pager, the pager invokes the table's onPage method, starting on line 59 of the preceding listing. That method clears the widgets from the data rows and repopulates those rows with data returned from the abstract getData method. The onPage method is defined by the PagerListener interface, which is listed in Listing 8.18.

Listing 8.18   com.gwtsolutions.components.client.ui.PagerListener

```
1.package com.gwtsolutions.components.client.ui;
2.
3.public interface PagerListener {
4.   public void onPage(SourcesPagerEvents sender, int index);
5.}
```

The EasyFlexTableResizableAndPageable class, listed in Listing 8.17, implements the PagerListener interface. It also implements the CanPage interface, listed in Listing 8.19.

Listing 8.19   com.gwtsolutions.components.client.ui.CanPage

```
1.package com.gwtsolutions.components.client.ui;
2.
3.public interface CanPage {
4.   public int getPageSize();
5.   public boolean isLastPage(int topOfPageIndex);
6.}
```

The CanPage interface signifies that an object can page through data, requiring the interface to provide the getPageSize and isLastPage methods. The EasyFlexTableResizableAndPageable class implements getPageSize() on line 72 of Listing 8.17, but since the table itself does not know what constitutes the last page, it leaves isLastPage() for subclasses to implement.

com.google.gwt.user.client.ui.HTMLTable

- void clearCell(int row, int cell)

  Removes any one of the three things you can place in a table cell: HTML, text, or a GWT widget.

com.google.gwt.user.client.ui.FlexTable

- FlexTable.CellFormatter getFlexCellFormatter()

  Obviates the need for casting an HTMLTable.CellFormatter to a FlexTable.CellFormatter. That is, when you call getCellFormatter() on a flex table, GWT actually returns an instance of FlexTable.CellFormatter. You can cast the HTMLTable.CellFormatter that is returned, or you can use getFlexCellFormatter() and so do away with the cast.

com.google.gwt.user.client.ui.FlexTable.CellFormatter

- void setColSpan(int row, int column, int colspan)

  Sets the column span for the specified cell. Being able to set column spans is one reason to use a FlexTable.CellFormatter instead of an HTMLTable.CellFormatter. The other reason is to set row spans with the setRowSpan(int row, int column, int rowSpan) method.

 Use Flex Table Cell Formatters to Span Multiple Rows or Columns

On line 55 of the EasyFlexTableResizableAndPageable class, we use an instance of FlexTable.CellFormatter to make the pager's table row span the number of columns in the table, thereby putting the pager in the lower-right corner of the table. The capability to span multiple rows and columns is unique to flex table cell formatters.

Now that we've seen how the EasyFlexTableResizableAndPageable class is defined and extended, let's look at the pager widget.

Using the Pager Widget

The final piece of our paging table implementation is the Pager class, which is listed in Listing 8.20.

Listing 8.20   com.gwtsolutions.components.client.ui.Pager

```
1.package com.gwtsolutions.components.client.ui;
2.
3.import com.google.gwt.user.client.ui.*;
4.
5.public class Pager extends Composite
6.   implements ClickListener, SourcesPagerEvents {
7.   public static final String NEXT_TOOLTIP = "Next";
8.   public static final String PREVIOUS_TOOLTIP = "Previous";
9.   public static final String PREVIOUS_IMAGE =
10.      "images/previous-arrow.gif";
11.   public static final String NEXT_IMAGE =
12.      "images/next-arrow.gif";
13.
14.   private static final int PAGE_ARROW_SPACING = 2;
15.   private static final int ARROW_WIDTH = 18;
16.
17.   private int currentIndex = 0;
18.   private Image forward;
19.   private Image back;
20.   private CanPage pageableData;
21.   private PagerListenerCollection pagerListeners =
22.      new PagerListenerCollection();
23.
24.   public Pager(CanPage pageableData) {
25.      this.pageableData = pageableData;
26.      HorizontalPanel pagerPanel = new HorizontalPanel();
27.      initWidget(pagerPanel);
28.      pagerPanel.setSpacing(PAGE_ARROW_SPACING);
29.      pagerPanel.setHorizontalAlignment(
30.            HasHorizontalAlignment.ALIGN_RIGHT);
31.
32.      back = new Image();
33.      back.setTitle(PREVIOUS_TOOLTIP);
34.      back.setUrl(PREVIOUS_IMAGE);
35.      back.setWidth(ARROW_WIDTH + "px");
36.      pagerPanel.add(back);
37.      back.addClickListener(this);
```

continues

Listing 8.20   com.gwtsolutions.components.client.ui.Pager   *continued*

```
38.
39.    forward = new Image();
40.    forward.setTitle(NEXT_TOOLTIP);
41.    forward.setUrl(NEXT_IMAGE);
42.    forward.setWidth(ARROW_WIDTH + "px");
43.    pagerPanel.add(forward);
44.    forward.addClickListener(this);
45.  }
46.
47.  public void reset() {
48.    currentIndex = 0;
49.  }
50.
51.  public void onClick(Widget sender) {
52.    if (sender == forward) {
53.      currentIndex = currentIndex + pageableData.getPageSize();
54.    }
55.    if (sender == back) {
56.      currentIndex = Math.max(currentIndex
57.          - pageableData.getPageSize(), 0);
58.    }
59.    setArrowVisibility();
60.    pagerListeners.firePage(this, currentIndex);
61.  }
62.
63.  public void onLoad() {
64.    setArrowVisibility();
65.  }
66.
67.  private void setArrowVisibility() {
68.    back.setVisible(currentIndex == 0 ? false : true);
69.    forward
70.        .setVisible(pageableData.isLastPage(currentIndex)
71.            ? false : true);
72.  }
73.  public int getCurrentIndex() {
74.    return currentIndex;
75.  }
76.
77.  public void setCurrentIndex(int index) {
78.    currentIndex = index;
```

```
79.  }
80.
81.  public void addPagerListener(PagerListener listener) {
82.    pagerListeners.add(listener);
83.  }
84.
85.  public void removePagerListener(PagerListener listener) {
86.    pagerListeners.remove(listener);
87.  }
88.}
```

The pager widget is a composite widget that consists of two images inside a horizontal panel. The Pager class implements GWT's ClickListener interface to handle mouse clicks on its arrow images.

The Pager class also implements the SourcesPagerEvents interface, which is listed in Listing 8.21.

Listing 8.21   com.gwtsolutions.components.client.ui.SourcesPagerEvents

```
1.package com.gwtsolutions.components.client.ui;
2.
3.public interface SourcesPagerEvents {
4.   public void addPagerListener(PagerListener listener);
5.   public void removePagerListener(PagerListener listener);
6.}
```

The Pager class implements the SourcesPagerEvents interface by maintaining a collection of pager listeners and by firing events to those listeners when a user clicks one of the pager's arrows, on line 60 of Listing 8.20.

The PagerListenerCollection interface is listed in Listing 8.22.

Listing 8.22   com.gwtsolutions.components.client.ui.PagerListenerCollection

```
1.package com.gwtsolutions.components.client.ui;
2.
3.import java.util.Iterator;
4.import java.util.Vector;
5.
6.public class PagerListenerCollection extends Vector {
7.   public void firePage(SourcesPagerEvents sender, int index) {
8.     Iterator it = iterator();
9.     while (it.hasNext()) {
```

Solution 8: Flex Tables

Listing 8.22   com.gwtsolutions.components.client.ui.PagerListenerCollection   *continued*

```
10.        PagerListener rl = (PagerListener) it.next();
11.        rl.onPage(sender, index);
12.    }
13.  }
14.}
```

Stuff We Covered in This Solution

We covered a good deal of ground in this solution, from flex table basics, to extending the `FlexTable` class, to building helper widgets that let us dynamically resize columns and page through table data. Additionally, we looked at how GWT implements listeners and how it fires events to those listeners, and then we applied those same techniques to widgets that resized columns and paged through data.

So far in this book, we've covered many aspects of GWT: GWT fundamentals and beyond in the first solution; incorporating JavaScript into GWT applications; implementing custom widgets and viewports complete with user gestures; using online web services in GWT applications; implementing a drag-and-drop framework; and using and extending pop-up panels to achieve a useful simple window class.

From here on out, we shift gears a bit and cover topics that are peripheral to GWT proper. We start by exploring how you can incorporate server-side functionality with GWT's client-side classes to accomplish file uploads and to incorporate database access with Hibernate. Then we follow with a solution on deploying your applications to external servers such as Tomcat, Resin, or WebSphere, and finally, we show you how to easily incorporate GWT widgets into legacy code such as Struts or JavaServer Faces applications.

File Uploads

GWT is a user-interface framework with hooks, in the form of remote procedure calls (RPCs), to the server. But generally, when you get to the server, you're on your own. So you will undoubtedly need to build a good deal of server-side functionality yourself. Fortunately, in most cases, you can do that by taking advantage of existing open-source projects that can do the heavy lifting for you on the server.

A case in point is GWT's support for file uploads. GWT provides a file upload widget that generates an HTML input field whose type is file, but provides no support for actually uploading the file on the server side.

Therefore, to actually upload files on the server, we turn to the Apache Commons FileUpload, from the Apache Software Foundation. In this solution, we see how to use Commons FileUpload in combination with GWT's file upload widget to provide a complete file upload solution.

Stuff You're Going to Learn

This solution explores the following aspects of GWT:

- Using GWT's FileUpload widget (page 284)

- Using GWT's FormPanel widget to submit an HTML form (page 293)

- Using JavaScript Object Notation (JSON) to send data from the server to the client (page 301)

- Using CSS to differentiate between error and success messages (page 292)

- Using Apache Commons fileUpload on the server (page 297)

- Restricting uploads by file size (page 284)

- Restricting uploads by file type (page 284)

In addition to GWT's file upload widget and Apache Commons FileUpload, we also look at some peripheral topics, such as GWT's form panel widget and the use of CSS styles to customize the message widget we discussed in Solution 3.

GWT's File Upload Widget

Let's start on the client and see how to use GWT's file upload widget. Figure 9.1 shows our file upload application in action.

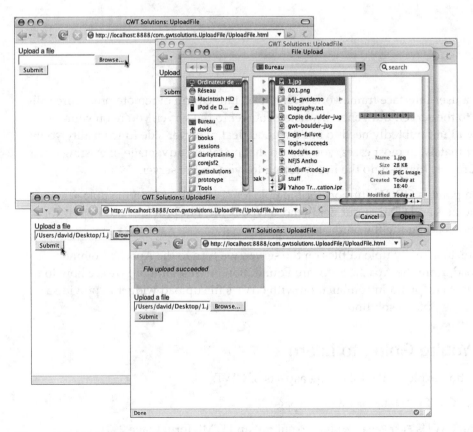

Figure 9.1   Using GWT's file upload widget

The file upload widget is platform dependent. In Figure 9.1, we show the application running in web mode in Firefox. If you run the application in a different browser, the file upload widget may look different but it works similarly across browsers.

When you click the Browse button, Firefox displays a File Upload dialog box that lets you select a file. When you select the file, the file's name is displayed in the file upload widget's corresponding text box. When you click the Submit button, which is not part of the file upload widget, GWT submits a form to the server because the file upload widget resides in a GWT form panel widget. More about GWT's form panel later.

When the file upload is completed on the server, we display a message indicating that the upload succeeded. But file uploads should not always succeed, because of security restrictions. There are plenty of reasons to disallow file uploads—perhaps you want to limit the file's type or size; we enforce both of those restrictions in our example, by restricting uploads to JPEG files in addition to an arbitrary cap on file sizes. Figure 9.2 shows the result when a user tries to upload something other than a JPEG file.

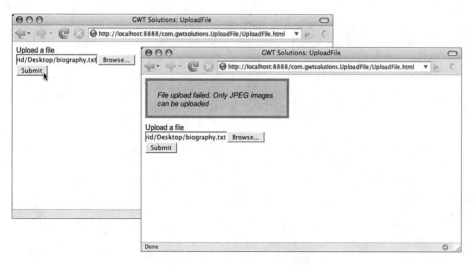

Figure 9.2   Restricting file types

Notice a subtle difference between Figure 9.1, which shows a successful upload, and Figure 9.2 and Figure 9.3, which show failed attempts. For a successful upload, our message has a thin, dark gray border, whereas failed attempts adorn the message with a thick red border. We implement that adornment by setting CSS styles for our message custom widget. We discuss that customization shortly.

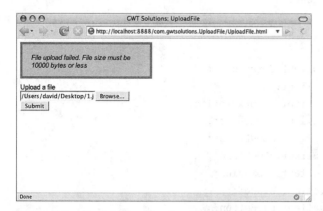

Figure 9.3   Restricting the size of uploaded files

One thing that none of the preceding figures illustrates is the shake effect for the message. Every time the message is shown, it shakes for half a second, thanks to the Script.aculo.us effect that's baked into the widget. See Solution 3 for details of the message custom widget.

Figure 9.4 shows the file upload application's associated files and directories.

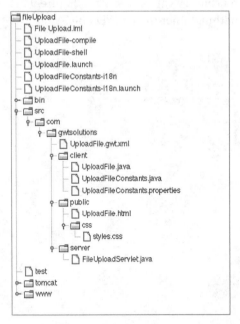

Figure 9.4   The upload file application's files and directories

Listing 9.1 lists the UploadFile application class.

Listing 9.1   com.gwtsolutions.client.UploadFile.java

```
1. package com.gwtsolutions.client;
2.
3. import java.util.Set;
4.
5. import com.google.gwt.core.client.EntryPoint;
6. import com.google.gwt.core.client.GWT;
7. import com.google.gwt.json.client.JSONException;
8. import com.google.gwt.json.client.JSONObject;
9. import com.google.gwt.json.client.JSONParser;
10.import com.google.gwt.json.client.JSONString;
11.import com.google.gwt.json.client.JSONValue;
12.import com.google.gwt.user.client.Window;
13.import com.google.gwt.user.client.ui.Button;
14.import com.google.gwt.user.client.ui.ClickListener;
15.import com.google.gwt.user.client.ui.FileUpload;
16.import com.google.gwt.user.client.ui.FormHandler;
17.import com.google.gwt.user.client.ui.FormPanel;
18.import com.google.gwt.user.client.ui.FormSubmitCompleteEvent;
```

```
19.import com.google.gwt.user.client.ui.FormSubmitEvent;
20.import com.google.gwt.user.client.ui.Label;
21.import com.google.gwt.user.client.ui.RootPanel;
22.import com.google.gwt.user.client.ui.VerticalPanel;
23.import com.google.gwt.user.client.ui.Widget;
24.import com.gwtsolutions.components.client.ui.Message;
25.
26.public class UploadFile implements EntryPoint {
27.    // The Message widget is a GWT Solutions widget. See
28.    // the GWTSolutions Components module for details.
29.    private final Message statusMessage = new Message(
30.        null, Message.SHAKE, 0.5);
31.
32.    public void onModuleLoad() {
33.        final UploadFileConstants constants =
34.            (UploadFileConstants) GWT
35.                .create(UploadFileConstants.class);
36.
37.        // Create a GWT FileUpload widget and set its name.
38.        // GWT will send the name in the request when the
39.        // surrounding form is submitted
40.        final FileUpload fileUpload = new FileUpload();
41.        fileUpload.setName("uploadFormElement");
42.
43.        // Create a GWT FormPanel, which submits an HTML form.
44.        // Set the encoding, method, and action associated with
45.        // file uploads, and set the form panel's widget to the
46.        // file upload widget created above.
47.        final FormPanel formPanel = new FormPanel();
48.        formPanel.setEncoding(FormPanel.ENCODING_MULTIPART);
49.        formPanel.setMethod(FormPanel.METHOD_POST);
50.        formPanel.setAction(GWT.getModuleBaseURL()
51.            + "/fileupload");
52.        formPanel.setWidget(fileUpload);
53.
54.        // Now create the user interface, wrapped in a
55.        // vertical panel
56.        VerticalPanel verticalPanel = new VerticalPanel();
57.        Label label = new Label(constants.uploadPrompt());
58.        Button button =
59.            new Button(constants.uploadSubmitPrompt());
60.
61.        verticalPanel.add(statusMessage);
```

continues

Listing 9.1   com.gwtsolutions.client.UploadFile.java   *continued*

```
62.      verticalPanel.add(label);
63.      verticalPanel.add(formPanel);
64.      verticalPanel.add(button);
65.
66.      // Since there is no status initially, hide the
67.      // status message
68.      statusMessage.setVisible(false);
69.
70.      // Add the vertical panel, which contains all the
71.      // other widgets, to the root panel
72.      RootPanel.get().add(verticalPanel);
73.
74.      // When the user clicks on the button, we submit
75.      // the surrounding form
76.      button.addClickListener(new ClickListener() {
77.        public void onClick(Widget sender) {
78.          formPanel.submit();
79.        }
80.      });
81.
82.      // GWT calls this form handler after the form
83.      // is submitted in the button click listener implemented
84.      // above.
85.      formPanel.addFormHandler(new FormHandler() {
86.        // When the submit starts, make sure the user
87.        // selected a file to upload
88.        public void onSubmit(FormSubmitEvent event) {
89.          if (fileUpload.getFilename().length() == 0) {
90.            Window.alert("You must select a file!");
91.            event.setCancelled(true);
92.          }
93.        }
94.
95.        // After the submit, get the JSON result and parse it.
96.        // NOTE: The removePreTags method is a workaround for
97.        // a bug in GWT 1.3.3 that wraps the response in
98.        // a PRE tag, like this: <pre>JSON response</pre>
99.        public void onSubmitComplete(
100.           FormSubmitCompleteEvent event) {
101.           // For a successful file upload, the JSON response
102.           // looks like this:
103.           //
```

```
104.        // <pre>{message: 'File upload succeeded'}</pre>
105.        //
106.        // For a failed file upload, the response looks
107.        // like this:
108.        //
109.        // <pre>{error: [error message]}</pre>
110.        //
111.        // The <pre> tag is a bug in GWT 1.3.3
112.        String jsonResult = removePreTags(event.getResults());
113.
114.        // JSONObject, JSONValue, and JSONString are all
115.        // part of the GWT's JSON parsing package
116.        JSONObject jso = null;
117.        JSONValue jsv = null;
118.        jsv = JSONParser.parse(jsonResult);
119.        jso = jsv.isObject();
120.
121.        if (jso != null) {
122.          Set keySet = jso.keySet();
123.          Object[] keys = keySet.toArray();
124.
125.          if (keys.length == 1) { // expect only one object
126.            String status = (String)keys[0];
127.            JSONValue v = jso.get(status);
128.            JSONString message = v.isString();
129.
130.            if (message != null) {
131.              statusMessage.removeStyleName("successBorder");
132.              statusMessage.removeStyleName("failureBorder");
133.              statusMessage.setText(message.stringValue());
134.
135.              // Add a border style in accordance with
136.              // whether the file upload failed or succeeded
137.              // on the server. That status is included
138.              // in the JSON response.
139.              if("error".equals(status))
140.                statusMessage.addStyleName("failureBorder");
141.              else
142.                statusMessage.addStyleName("successBorder");
143.
144.              statusMessage.setVisible(true);
145.            }
146.          }
```

continues

Listing 9.1   **com.gwtsolutions.client.UploadFile.java**   *continued*

```
147.           }
148.         }
149.         // This method strips the <pre> tag out of the response.
150.         // That <pre> tag in the response is because of a
151.         // GWT 1.3.3 bug.
152.         private String removePreTags(String response) {
153.           if (response.startsWith("<pre>")) {
154.             return response.substring("<pre>".length(),
155.               response.length() - "</pre>".length());
156.           }
157.           else {
158.             return response;
159.           }
160.         }
161.     });
162.   }
163.}
```

The preceding listing covers a fair bit of ground, so let's look at the two major aspects of that class: creating the user interface and submitting the form; and parsing the JavaScript Object Notation (JSON) returned from the server.

Creating the User Interface

To begin, we instantiate an instance of the Message widget, specifying null for the message's text, and a shake effect that lasts for half a second. In the application's onModuleLoad method, we create five other widgets:

- A file upload widget on line 40

- A form panel on line 47

- A vertical panel on line 56

- A label on line 57, whose text is Upload a file

- A submit button on line 58 to submit our form

On line 41, we set the name of the file upload widget to a name we pulled out of a hat: uploadFormElement. The name itself is inconsequential, but *you must give the file upload widget a name* because that ultimately becomes the name of the HTML file input element. If you don't give the file upload widget a name, you will get a NullPointerException when you use Commons fileUpload to extract the file name on the server side.

Starting on line 48, we set the encoding, method, and action for the form panel: Those settings are crucial for the form panel's enclosed file upload widget to work properly. The action, as you might guess, corresponds to a servlet, which we declare in our application's configuration file, which is listed in Listing 9.3 on page 296. On line 52, we set the file upload widget as the form panel's lone widget.

Finally, starting on line 61, we add the message, label, form panel, and button to a vertical panel. On line 68, we set the message widget's visibility to `false` because initially there is no status message to show, and then we add the vertical panel, which contains all the other widgets, to the root panel.

That's it for constructing our simplistic user interface and submitting the form with a click listener attached to our button. Now let's look at how we deal with the JSON returned from the form submit.

After we've created our user interface, we define two event handlers: one for the button that submits the form and another attached to the form panel that reacts to the form submit.

The form handler, starting on line 85, implements two methods: `onSubmit()` and `onSubmitComplete()`. GWT calls the former immediately after we call `formPanel.submit()` on line 78 and calls the latter when that form submission is complete.

The form handler's `onSubmit` method checks to see that the user has selected a file with a call to `fileUpload.getFilename()`. If that method returns a zero-length string, then we know that the user has been negligent, so we display an alert, telling the user to select a file, and we cancel the submit event. Otherwise, if the user selected a file, we do nothing, which lets the form submit go through to the server.

Parsing JavaScript Object Notation (JSON)

The `onSubmitComplete` method of the form handler, which starts on line 99, gets the result of the form submit on line 112 from the event object that the method is passed. That result is a string whose format is *JavaScript Object Notation* (JSON).

Unfortunately, the latest stable version of GWT as we went to press—1.3.3—has a bug that embeds an HTML `pre` tag in the response, even though we explicitly specified a response content type of `text/plain` on the server. The `removePreTags` method, starting on line 152, checks to see if the response starts with `<pre>`; if so, we strip the tags from the response; otherwise, we return the response as is. That approach guarantees that our code will work after the bug is fixed.

After working around the embedded `<pre>` tag, we parse the JSON string. That string is one of three possible values, as you will see when we discuss the `FileUploadServlet`. Here are the three possible strings:

- {message: 'File upload succeeded'}

- {error: 'File upload failed. Only JPEG images can be uploaded'}

- {error: 'File upload failed. File size must be 50000 bytes or less'}

JSON notation is similar to a Java properties file: You define key/value pairs that correspond to object properties. Each of our JSON strings listed above defines one JavaScript object with exactly one property. In the first case, the property is named message, and in the last two cases, the property is named error. The values after the colons are the values of the properties, which in this case are all strings but could be other types of JavaScript objects: a boolean, a null value, a number, another JSON object, or an array of JSON objects.

The first thing we do is call JSONParser.parse() on line 118, which turns the JSON string into a JSONValue object. Then we invoke JSONObject.isObject(), which, although its name implies that it returns a boolean value, actually returns either an instance of JSONObject if the JSONValue contains a bona fide JSON object, or null if it does not.

Once we have the JSON object, we get the set of keys from the object on line 122 with a call to JSONObject.keySet(), and we subsequently turn that set into an array.

Because we always return a JSON object with exactly one property, we know there must be only one key, which we check on line 125. If that's the case, we continue by getting the status from the first item in the array and using that key to get the corresponding value with JSONObject.get() on line 127. Finally, on line 128, we essentially cast our JSON object to a JSONString with the JSONValue.isString method, and on line 133, we invoke JSONString.stringValue() to get a Java representation of the string. Whew.

From here on out, we do three things.

First, on line 131 and 132, we remove both the successBorder and failureBorder CSS styles from our message widget. Our widget will actually have only one of those styles, but UIObject.removeStyleName() fails silently if you try to remove a CSS style that's not applied to an object. That handy feature lets us avoid checking to see whether the styles are currently applied to the message widget.

Second, we set the message widget's text to the string that we dug out of the JSON response.

Finally, if the key from the JSON response was error, we add the failureBorder CSS style to the message widget; otherwise, we add the successBorder CSS style. Adding the appropriate CSS style to the message widget gives us the effect shown in Figure 9.1 on page 284 and Figure 9.2 on page 285.

com.google.gwt.user.client.ui.FormPanel

- void setAction(String url)

  Sets the action, meaning the URL, to which the form is submitted when you call the submit method.

- void setEncoding(String encodingType)

  Sets the encoding for the form submit. The string passed to this method must be either FormPanel.ENCODING_URLENCODED or FormPanel.ENCODING_MULTIPART. The latter encoding is required for forms that perform file uploads.

- void setMethod(String method)

  Sets the HTTP method for the ensuing form request triggered by a call to submit(). The string passed to this method must be either FormPanel.METHOD_GET or FormPanel.METHOD_POST. The latter method is required for forms that perform file uploads.

- void submit()

  Submits the form. The form submit is handled by an instance of FormHandler, which can cancel the form submit in its onSubmit method.

- void addFormHandler(FormHandler handler)

  Adds a form handler to the form panel. When you call the form panel's submit method, GWT invokes the handler's onSubmit method. When the form submit is complete, GWT invokes the handler's onSubmitComplete method.

com.google.gwt.user.client.ui.FormHandler

- void onSubmit(FormSubmitEvent event)

  Is called when GWT submits a form. You can cancel the form submit by passing true to the event's setCancelled method.

- void onSubmitComplete(FormSubmitEvent event)

  Is called by GWT after the form has been successfully submitted and the response is returned from the server.

com.google.gwt.user.client.ui.FormSubmitCompleteEvent

- `String getResults()`

Returns the result of a form submit. GWT passes an instance of `FormSubmitCompleteEvent` to a form handler's `onSubmitComplete` method.

com.google.gwt.user.client.ui.FormSubmitEvent

- `boolean isCancelled()`

Returns a `boolean` indicating whether a form submit has been cancelled.

- `void setCancelled(boolean cancelled)`

Cancels a form submit. GWT passes an instance of `FormSubmitEvent` to a form handler's `onSubmit` method.

com.google.gwt.json.client.JSONObject

- `JSONValue get(String key)`

Returns the JSON value associated with the specified key. The key is the name of a property associated with a JSON object, and the value returned by this method is the value of that property. If the specified key doesn't exist for this JSON object, this method returns `null`.

- `java.util.Set keySet()`

Returns the set of keys for a given JSON object. Those keys are names of properties of the JSON object. Use the `get` method to get the values corresponding to the names of the properties in the set returned by this method.

com.google.gwt.json.client.JSONParser

- `JSONValue parse(String jsonString)`

Parses a string that's encoded in JSON format and returns a corresponding JSON value. Once you have a JSON value, you can turn it into the object that it actually represents—a boolean, a null value, a number, a string, or an array of JSON objects—by invoking `JSONValue` methods such as `isArray()` or `isString()`.

com.google.gwt.json.client.JSONValue

- JSONString isString()

Returns an instance of JSONString if the JSON object is a JSON string; otherwise, returns null.

com.google.gwt.json.client.JSONValue

- JSONObject isObject()

Returns an instance of JSONObject if this object is a JSON object; otherwise, returns null.

> **Prefer JSON**
>
> JSON is the preferred format for returning data from the server because it's easy to construct on the server side, and on the client side, GWT provides extensive support for parsing JSON.
>
> If you are using GWT's RPC mechanism to return values from server-side calls, you won't use JSON, but if you are using a lower-level protocol, such as a form submit generated by calling FormPanel.submit(), or are using GWT's HttpRequest class to make an Ajax call, then, all other things being equal, you should prefer JSON.

Before we discuss the file upload servlet on the server, we have two things to show you. First is our CSS stylesheet, listed in Listing 9.2.

Listing 9.2   styles.css

```
1.body,td,a,div,.p{font-family:arial,sans-serif}
2.div,td{color:#000000}
3.a:link,.w,.w a:link{color:#0000cc}
4.a:visited{color:#551a8b}
5.a:active{color:#ff0000}
6.
7..gwtsolutions-Message {
8.    padding: 20px;
9.    margin-bottom: 10px;
10.    font-style: italic;
11.    background: lightGray;
12.    width: 250px;
13.    height: 2em;
14.}
```

continues

Listing 9.2   styles.css   *continued*

```
15.
16..successBorder {
17.    border: thin solid darkGray;
18.}
19.
20..failureBorder {
21.    border: thick solid red;
22.}
```

Next is our module configuration file, listed in Listing 9.3.

Listing 9.3   UploadFile.gwt.xml

```
1.<module>
2.    <!— Inherit the core Web Toolkit stuff.                —>
3.    <inherits name='com.google.gwt.user.User'/>
4.    <inherits name='com.google.gwt.i18n.I18N'/>
5.    <inherits name='com.gwtsolutions.components.Components'/>
6.
7.    <!— Include the stylesheet for this application. —>
8.    <stylesheet src="css/styles.css"/>
9.
10.    <!— Specify the app entry point class.                —>
11.    <entry-point class='com.gwtsolutions.client.UploadFile'/>
12.
13.    <!— Specify the servlet that handles file uploads.     —>
14.    <servlet path="/fileupload"
15.        class="com.gwtsolutions.server.FileUploadServlet"/>
16.</module>
```

We discuss the `FileUploadServlet` class in "Now that we've seen what's happening on the client, let's turn to the server."

FileUpload Widget Recipe
When you use GWT's file upload widget, you must do the following:

1. Create a form panel widget and a file upload widget.

2. Set the name of the file upload widget with the setName method.

3. Set the form panel widget's action, encoding, and method.

4. Add the file upload widget to the form panel widget.

5. Call the form panel's submit method, typically by implementing an event handler on a button or link.

6. Create a form handler for the form widget that handles the result of the file upload.

Now that we've seen what's happening on the client, let's turn to the server.

Apache Commons fileUpload

GWT, as we've seen, includes `FormPanel` and `FileUpload` classes that you can combine to upload files. However, once you're on the server, GWT doesn't offer a mechanism to actually perform the file upload.

To perform the actual file upload, we use the Apache Jakarta Commons FileUpload. Figure 9.5 shows the homepage for Commons FileUpload.

Figure 9.5   Apache Commons fileUpload homepage

Before we can use Commons FileUpload, we need to add the required JAR files to our application's build path. Figure 9.6 shows how to do that in Eclipse.

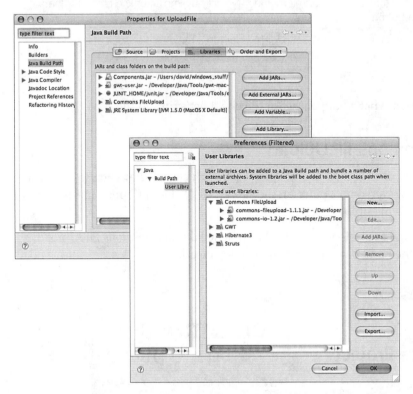

Figure 9.6   Adding a user library for Commons fileUpload to the Eclipse project

Notice that we create a user library in Eclipse, and we add the Commons FileUpload JAR and the Commons IO JAR, both of which are required for Commons FileUpload.

Once we've added the requisite JARs to our build path, we're ready to implement our file upload servlet, which is listed in Listing 9.4.

Listing 9.4   com.gwtsolutions.server.FileUploadServlet.java

```
1. package com.gwtsolutions.server;
2.
3. import java.io.File;
4. import java.io.IOException;
5. import java.util.Iterator;
6. import java.util.List;
7.
8. import javax.servlet.ServletException;
9. import javax.servlet.http.HttpServlet;
10.import javax.servlet.http.HttpServletRequest;
```

```
11.import javax.servlet.http.HttpServletResponse;
12.
13.import org.apache.commons.fileupload.FileItem;
14.import org.apache.commons.fileupload.FileItemFactory;
15.import org.apache.commons.fileupload.FileUploadException;
16.import org.apache.commons.fileupload.disk.DiskFileItemFactory;
17.import org.apache.commons.fileupload.servlet.ServletFileUpload;
18.
19.public class FileUploadServlet extends HttpServlet {
20.   private static final long
21.        serialVersionUID = 6098745782027999297L;
22.
23.   private static final String
24.        UPLOAD_DIRECTORY = "/Users/david/Desktop/";
25.
26.   private static final long MAX_SIZE = 50000;
27.   private static final String ACCEPTABLE_CONTENT_TYPE =
28.        "image/jpeg";
29.   private static final String CONTENT_TYPE_UNACCEPTABLE =
30.        "{error: 'File upload failed. "
31.        + " Only JPEG images can be uploaded'}";
32.
33.   private static final String SIZE_UNACCEPTABLE =
34.        "{error: 'File upload failed. File size must be "
35.        + MAX_SIZE + " bytes or less'}";
36.
37.   private static final String SUCCESS_MESSAGE =
38.      "{message: 'File upload succeeded'}";
39.
40.   public void doPost(HttpServletRequest request,
41.      HttpServletResponse response) throws ServletException,
42.      IOException {
43.     FileItemFactory factory = new DiskFileItemFactory();
44.     ServletFileUpload upload = new ServletFileUpload(factory);
45.     List items = null;
46.     String json = null;
47.
48.     try {
49.       items = upload.parseRequest(request);
50.     }
51.     catch (FileUploadException e) {
52.       e.printStackTrace();
53.     }
```

continues

Listing 9.4   com.gwtsolutions.server.FileUploadServlet.java   *continued*

```
54.    Iterator it = items.iterator();
55.    while (it.hasNext()) {
56.      FileItem item = (FileItem) it.next();
57.      json = processFile(item);
58.    }
59.    response.setContentType("text/plain");
60.    response.getWriter().write(json);
61.  }
62.  private String processFile(FileItem item) {
63.    if (!isContentTypeAcceptable(item))
64.      return CONTENT_TYPE_UNACCEPTABLE;
65.
66.    if (!isSizeAcceptable(item))
67.      return SIZE_UNACCEPTABLE;
68.
69.    File uploadedFile =
70.        new File(UPLOAD_DIRECTORY + item.getName());
71.
72.    String message = null;
73.    try {
74.      item.write(uploadedFile);
75.      message = SUCCESS_MESSAGE;
76.    }
77.    catch (Exception e) {
78.      e.printStackTrace();
79.    }
80.    return message;
81.  }
82.  private boolean isSizeAcceptable(FileItem item) {
83.    return item.getSize() <= MAX_SIZE;
84.  }
85.  private boolean isContentTypeAcceptable(FileItem item) {
86.    return item.getContentType().equals(
87.        ACCEPTABLE_CONTENT_TYPE);
88.  }
89.}
```

In GWT, form submissions are a different animal than regular RPCs. Instead of extending `RemoteServiceServlet`, as is the case for regular RPCs, you extend `HttpServlet` to handle form submissions on the server side and implement the servlet's `doPost` method.

Ultimately, we need an instance of `ServletFileUpload` so that we can invoke its `parseRequest` method, which parses the HTTP request, yielding a list of `FileItem` instances. Instances of `ServletFileUpload` are created by a factory, which is an instance of `DiskFileItemFactory`. The factory pattern is perhaps one of the most overused patterns in Java, providing ultimate flexibility at the cost of usability. It would be simpler if you could just create a servlet file upload object directly, but if necessary you can create different kinds of factories that create servlet file upload objects with specific configurations. Of course, you can implement your own factory—that's where the ultimate flexibility comes in—but in practice, most folks just stick to disk file item factories.

Once we've parsed the request, we iterate over our list of file items, of which we always have exactly one, and process the item by creating a file and subsequently reading the uploaded content into that file.

In our opinion, this is a lot of code for something that in other languages such as PHP or Ruby would be condensed into a handful of lines of code, but that's the price we pay for static type checking and overengineered factories. Fortunately, once you've written the servlet, you never have to write another one to subsequently upload other files.

Another thing worth mentioning about our servlet is that it uploads only JPEG images and files that are less than 50 Kbytes. Our example, because it doesn't exist in the Real World, doesn't have security restraints other than those that we arbitrarily chose for illustration, but of course your code will most likely have security considerations that must be adhered to.

Why Doesn't the GWT Use RPCs for Form Submits and File Uploads?

You may have noticed that when we submit a form by invoking the `FormPanel`'s `submit` method, we are submitting an HTML form to the server and subsequently handling the response on the client. That, of course, is similar to what we do when we implement remote procedure calls (RPCs). Why then, doesn't GWT use RPCs to implement form submissions and file uploads?

The answer is that GWT prefers to be as close to the metal as possible to ensure maximum flexibility, and RPCs are a level of abstraction above form submissions.

Don't Forget to Add the Commons IO JAR File to Your Build Path

Apache Commons projects often have dependencies on one another; for example, the fileUpload project uses Commons IO. Therefore, you must include both Commons fileUpload and Commons IO JAR files on your build path for Commons fileUpload to work properly.

A "class not found" exception when you are using Commons fileUpload most likely means that you've forgotten to add the Commons IO JAR to your build path.

Use Libraries for Software That Requires Multiple JAR Files

In Figure 9.6, we showed you how to create a user library in Eclipse that contains the Commons fileUpload and Commons IO JAR files. User libraries are a convenient reuse mechanism because you can subsequently just include a library instead of adding multiple JAR files to your build path.

Most IDEs, including IntelliJ's IDEA, have similar constructs.

Stuff We Covered in This Solution

Because GWT is a UI framework, it provides little direct support for server-side code, other than its built-in RPC mechanism. In this solution, we showed you how to ease your pain on the server by integrating a freely available open-source solution for uploading files. We also provided a complete solution for file uploads that you can modify to suit your own needs.

Before we move on to another server-side topic—integrating Hibernate on the server for database access—we should note that the fact that GWT sticks primarily to the client side is both a drawback and one of GWT's major strengths. It's a drawback because you must implement server-side functionality such as file uploads and database access; but it's a major strength because you can easily combine GWT widgets with existing frameworks like Struts, JavaServer Faces, or Tapestry, which provide extensive server-side support. In fact, in Solution 12, we show you how you can incorporate GWT widgets with your legacy applications written with those frameworks.

Hibernate Integration

Unless you're writing a trivial application—or perhaps a non-trivial application that's off the beaten path—you're probably going to want to store data in a database. Java technology provides many ways to do that, both open-source and proprietary, but ostensibly the most popular is Hibernate.

Hibernate is an object-to-relational mapping (ORM) tool that maps Java classes to database tables and manages storage and retrieval of Java objects to and from the database. Hibernate is popular because it lets you use plain old Java objects (POJOs) that contain no knowledge of your database schema whatsoever. That gives you a great deal of flexibility and simplifies the coding of your model layer.

Stuff You're Going to Learn

This solution explores the following aspects using GWT and using GWT with Hibernate:

- Dynamically updating Hibernate Query Language *where* clauses (page 314)
- Using a tab bar and pop-up panels (page 314)
- Repopulating a grid widget using Ajax (page 314)
- Using POJOs with Hibernate (page 316)
- Defining a Hibernate mapping file (page 316)
- Integrating Hibernate with remote procedure calls (RPCs) (page 319)
- Configuring Eclipse for Hibernate (page 323)

In this solution, our first priority is to show you how to integrate Hibernate into your GWT applications. By necessity, we show you an example that illustrates the basics of using Hibernate, but teaching you Hibernate is not our primary goal. Good books and other references on Hibernate abound, and if you are unfamiliar with Hibernate, we encourage you to use those resources in addition to this book.

In addition to Hibernate integration, we also cover quite a bit of ancillary ground, including how to use pop-up panels, how to repopulate a grid widget with Ajax, and how to use deferred commands, as you can see from the preceding list of stuff you're going to learn.

The Hibernate Example Application

Our exploration of Hibernate integration takes place within the confines of a Rolodex application, shown in Figure 10.1. The Rolodex application is a Create/Read/Update/Delete (CRUD) implementation that uses GWT to work its Ajaxian magic on the front end and the venerable Hibernate ORM tool on the back end.

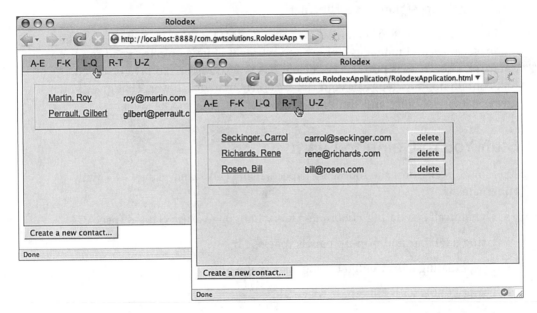

Figure 10.1   The Rolodex example application

The Rolodex contains a tab bar at the top that lets users manipulate contacts within certain alphabetical ranges and a panel underneath that displays contacts for the chosen range. At the bottom of the application is a button by which users can create a new contact and store it in the database. Figure 10.2 shows the steps involved in editing a contact.

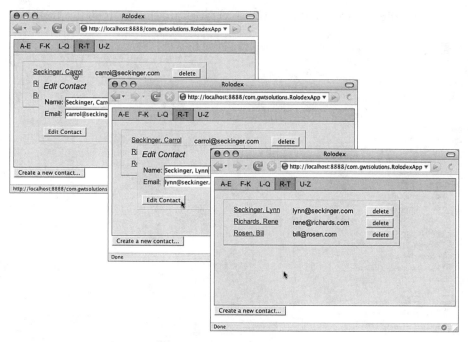

Figure 10.2   Editing a contact in the Rolodex

Figure 10.3 shows how to create a new contact in the database.

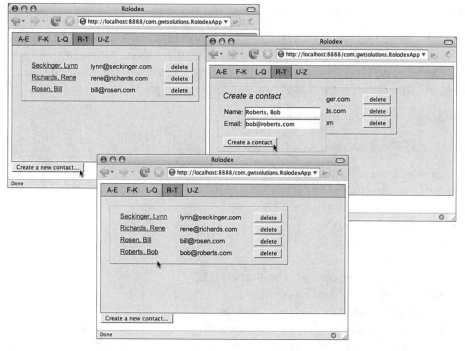

Figure 10.3   Creating a contact in the Rolodex

The Rolodex application's associated files and directories are shown in Figure 10.4.

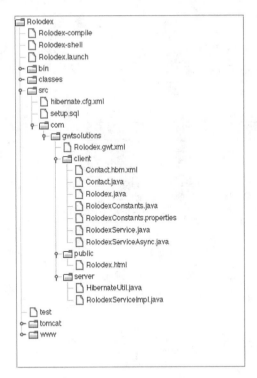

Figure 10.4   The Rolodex's files and directories

Notice that we have a few files in the Rolodex application that we normally do not have in a typical GWT application: an SQL file that initializes the database, a Hibernate configuration file, and a Hibernate mapping file. We discuss those files in more detail in "Hibernate on the Server" on page 316.

Listing 10.1 lists the Rolodex application.

Listing 10.1   com.gwtsolutions.client.Rolodex

```
1. package com.gwtsolutions.client;
2.
3. import java.util.HashMap;
4. import java.util.Iterator;
5. import java.util.List;
6.
7. import com.google.gwt.core.client.EntryPoint;
8. import com.google.gwt.core.client.GWT;
9. import com.google.gwt.user.client.Command;
10.import com.google.gwt.user.client.DeferredCommand;
11.import com.google.gwt.user.client.rpc.AsyncCallback;
```

```
12. import com.google.gwt.user.client.rpc.ServiceDefTarget;
13. import com.google.gwt.user.client.ui.Button;
14. import com.google.gwt.user.client.ui.ClickListener;
15. import com.google.gwt.user.client.ui.Grid;
16. import com.google.gwt.user.client.ui.HTML;
17. import com.google.gwt.user.client.ui.Hyperlink;
18. import com.google.gwt.user.client.ui.Label;
19. import com.google.gwt.user.client.ui.Panel;
20. import com.google.gwt.user.client.ui.PopupPanel;
21. import com.google.gwt.user.client.ui.RootPanel;
22. import com.google.gwt.user.client.ui.SourcesTabEvents;
23. import com.google.gwt.user.client.ui.TabBar;
24. import com.google.gwt.user.client.ui.TabListener;
25. import com.google.gwt.user.client.ui.TextBox;
26. import com.google.gwt.user.client.ui.VerticalPanel;
27. import com.google.gwt.user.client.ui.Widget;
28.
29. public class Rolodex implements EntryPoint {
30.   private final RolodexConstants constants =
31.       (RolodexConstants) GWT.create(RolodexConstants.class);
32.
33.   private final RolodexServiceAsync rolodexService =
34.       (RolodexServiceAsync) GWT.create(RolodexService.class);
35.
36.   private final Grid grid = new Grid();
37.
38.   // We must use a StringBuffer here instead of a String
39.   // because lastWhereClause has to be final because we
40.   // access it in an anonymous inner class below
41.   private final StringBuffer lastWhereClause =
42.       new StringBuffer();
43.
44.   public void onModuleLoad() {
45.     final Panel rolodex = createRolodex(createTabBar());
46.     initializeGrid();
47.
48.     final ServiceDefTarget target =
49.         (ServiceDefTarget) rolodexService;
50.
51.     target.setServiceEntryPoint(GWT.getModuleBaseURL()
52.         + "/rolodexService");
53.
54.     Button createButton =
```

continues

Listing 10.1   com.gwtsolutions.client.Rolodex   *continued*

```
55.          new Button(constants.createNewContactButtonText());
56.
57.    createButton.addClickListener(new ClickListener() {
58.      public void onClick(Widget sender) {
59.        createContact(sender);
60.      }
61.    });
62.
63.    RootPanel.get().add(rolodex);
64.    RootPanel.get().add(createButton);
65.  }
66.
67.  // CREATE THE USER INTERFACE
68.
69.  private Panel createRolodex(TabBar tabBar) {
70.    VerticalPanel rolodex = new VerticalPanel();
71.    rolodex.addStyleName("rolodex");
72.    rolodex.add(tabBar);
73.    rolodex.add(grid);
74.    return rolodex;
75.  }
76.
77.  private TabBar createTabBar() {
78.    final TabBar tabBar = new TabBar();
79.    final HashMap hashMap = new HashMap();
80.
81.    final String[] tabs = {
82.      constants.alphabeticalRangeOne(),
83.      constants.alphabeticalRangeTwo(),
84.      constants.alphabeticalRangeThree(),
85.      constants.alphabeticalRangeFour(),
86.      constants.alphabeticalRangeFive()
87.    };
88.
89.    final String[] whereClauses = {
90.      "where contact.name between 'A' and 'E'",
91.      "where contact.name between 'F' and 'K'",
92.      "where contact.name between 'L' and 'Q'",
93.      "where contact.name between 'R' and 'T'",
94.      "where contact.name between 'U' and 'Z'"
95.    };
96.
```

```
97.     for (int i = 0; i < tabs.length; ++i) {
98.       tabBar.addTab(tabs[i]);
99.       hashMap.put(tabs[i], whereClauses[i]);
100.    }
101.
102.    tabBar.addTabListener(new TabListener() {
103.      public boolean onBeforeTabSelected(
104.          SourcesTabEvents sender, int tabIndex) {
105.        // Return true to allow tab selection. The GWT will
106.        // not call onTabSelected() if this method returns
107.        // false
108.        return true;
109.      }
110.
111.      public void onTabSelected(SourcesTabEvents sender,
112.          int tabIndex) {
113.        if (!grid.isVisible())
114.          grid.setVisible(true);
115.
116.        // Get the text from the selected tab
117.        String whereClause =
118.            (String) hashMap.get(tabBar.getTabHTML(tabIndex));
119.
120.        // If the lastWhereClause doesn't contain any text,
121.        // insert the whereClause; otherwise, replace the
122.        // previous contents of lastWhereClause with the
123.        // current where clause
124.        if (lastWhereClause.length() == 0)
125.          lastWhereClause.insert(0, whereClause);
126.        else
127.          lastWhereClause.replace(0, lastWhereClause.length(),
128.              whereClause);
129.
130.        // Reload the rolodex every time a user selects
131.        // a tab from the tab bar
132.        loadRolodex();
133.      }
134.    });
135.    return tabBar;
136.  }
137.
138.  private void initializeGrid() {
139.    // The grid is initially invisible until the user clicks
```

continues

Listing 10.1   com.gwtsolutions.client.Rolodex   *continued*

```
140.    // on a tab in the tab bar
141.    grid.addStyleName("contactsTable");
142.    grid.setVisible(false);
143.  }
144.
145.  // CREATE AND EDIT CONTACTS WITH POPUP PANELS
146.
147.  private void createContact(Widget sender) {
148.    PopupPanel popup = new PopupPanel(true);
149.    popup.addStyleName("createContactPopup");
150.    popup.setPopupPosition(grid.getAbsoluteLeft() + 20, grid
151.        .getAbsoluteTop() + 20);
152.    Panel p =
153.        createContactPanel(popup, null, constants
154.            .createContactHeading());
155.    popup.add(p);
156.    popup.show();
157.  }
158.
159.  private void editContact(Widget sender, Contact contact) {
160.    PopupPanel popup = new PopupPanel(true);
161.    popup.addStyleName("createContactPopup");
162.    popup.setPopupPosition(sender.getAbsoluteLeft() + 25,
163.        sender.getAbsoluteTop() + sender.getOffsetHeight());
164.    Panel p =
165.        createContactPanel(popup, contact, constants
166.            .editContactHeading());
167.    popup.add(p);
168.    popup.show();
169.  }
170.
171.  private Panel createContactPanel(final PopupPanel panel,
172.      final Contact contact, final String headingText) {
173.
174.    final VerticalPanel vp = new VerticalPanel();
175.    final Grid grid = new Grid(5, 2);
176.    final Label heading = new Label(headingText);
177.    final Label namePrompt = new Label(constants.namePrompt());
178.    final TextBox nameTextBox = new TextBox();
179.    final TextBox emailTextBox = new TextBox();
180.    final Label emailPrompt =
181.        new Label(constants.emailPrompt());
```

```
182.    final Button button = new Button(headingText);
183.

184.    heading.addStyleName("heading");
185.

186.    DeferredCommand.addCommand(new Command() {
187.      public void execute() {
188.        // Make this method call "stick" by putting it
189.        // in a deferred command
190.        nameTextBox.setFocus(true);
191.      }
192.    });
193.

194.    if (contact != null) {
195.      nameTextBox.setText(contact.getName());
196.      emailTextBox.setText(contact.getEmail());
197.    }
198.

199.    button.addClickListener(new ClickListener() {
200.      public void onClick(Widget sender) {
201.        String name = nameTextBox.getText();
202.        String email = emailTextBox.getText();
203.

204.        if (contact != null) {
205.          contact.setName(name);
206.          contact.setEmail(email);
207.          updateContact(contact);
208.        }
209.        else
210.          saveContact(new Contact(null, name, email));
211.

212.        panel.hide();
213.      }
214.    });
215.

216.    grid.setWidget(0, 0, namePrompt);
217.    grid.setWidget(0, 1, nameTextBox);
218.    grid.setWidget(1, 0, emailPrompt);
219.    grid.setWidget(1, 1, emailTextBox);
220.

221.    vp.add(heading);
222.    vp.add(grid);
223.    vp.add(button);
224.    return vp;
```

Solution 10: Hibernate Integration

continues

Listing 10.1   com.gwtsolutions.client.Rolodex   *continued*

```
225.  }
226.
227.  // CRUD OPERATIONS
228.
229.  private void deleteContact(Contact contact) {
230.    rolodexService.deleteContact(contact, new AsyncCallback() {
231.      public void onSuccess(Object result) {
232.        loadRolodex();
233.      }
234.
235.      public void onFailure(Throwable t) {
236.        t.printStackTrace();
237.      }
238.    });
239.  }
240.
241.  private void updateContact(Contact contact) {
242.    rolodexService.updateContact(contact, new AsyncCallback() {
243.      public void onSuccess(Object result) {
244.        loadRolodex();
245.      }
246.
247.      public void onFailure(Throwable t) {
248.        t.printStackTrace();
249.      }
250.    });
251.  }
252.
253.  private void saveContact(Contact contact) {
254.    rolodexService.saveContact(contact, new AsyncCallback() {
255.      public void onSuccess(Object result) {
256.        loadRolodex();
257.      }
258.
259.      public void onFailure(Throwable t) {
260.        t.printStackTrace();
261.      }
262.    });
263.  }
264.
265.  private void loadRolodex() {
266.    String whereClause = lastWhereClause.toString();
```

```
267.    rolodexService.getContacts(whereClause,
268.        new AsyncCallback() {
269.          public void onSuccess(Object result) {
270.            List contacts = (List) result;
271.            Iterator it = contacts.iterator();
272.
273.            grid.clear();
274.
275.            if (contacts.size() == 0) {
276.              grid.setVisible(false);
277.              return;
278.            }
279.
280.            grid.resize(contacts.size(), 3);
281.
282.            for (int row = 0; it.hasNext(); ++row) {
283.              final Contact c = (Contact) it.next();
284.
285.              Button deleteButton =
286.                  new Button(constants.deleteButtonText());
287.
288.              Hyperlink nameLink =
289.                  new Hyperlink(c.getName(), c.getName());
290.
291.              HTML emailAddress = new HTML(c.getEmail());
292.
293.              nameLink.addStyleName("nameLink");
294.              emailAddress.addStyleName("emailAddress");
295.              deleteButton.addStyleName("deleteButton");
296.
297.              grid.setWidget(row, 0, nameLink);
298.              grid.setWidget(row, 1, emailAddress);
299.              grid.setWidget(row, 2, deleteButton);
300.
301.              nameLink.addClickListener(new ClickListener() {
302.                public void onClick(Widget sender) {
303.                  editContact(sender, c);
304.                }
305.              });
306.
307.              deleteButton
308.                  .addClickListener(new ClickListener() {
309.                    public void onClick(Widget sender) {
```

continues

Listing 10.1   com.gwtsolutions.client.Rolodex   *continued*

```
310.                      deleteContact(c);
311.                   }
312.                });
313.             }
314.          }
315.
316.          public void onFailure(Throwable t) {
317.             t.printStackTrace();
318.          }
319.       });
320.   }
321.}
```

This listing is rather long, so we've partitioned it into three sections, marked by comments. The first section, starting on line 67, contains methods that create the user interface; the second section, starting on line 145, creates contacts by using pop-up panels; and the last section, starting on line 227, performs CRUD operations and loads the Rolodex's Grid component, which displays contacts for the selected alphabetical range.

The Rolodex is an instance of VerticalPanel that contains two widgets: a tab bar and a grid. The tab bar has a listener that updates our database query's *where clause* to match the tab that was selected; for example, if a user clicks the R-T tab, the tab bar's listener updates the lastWhereClause class member variable—which is a string buffer—so that it contains this text: where contact.name between 'R' and 'T'. That *where clause* is not SQL, as you might expect, but instead is HQL, which stands for Hibernate Query Language. (Notice that we cannot use a string for the lastWhereClause variable because that variable must be final for us to use it in an anonymous inner class, meaning we could not assign to it once it was created. Because of that restriction, we make the lastWhereClause variable a string buffer, which we modify accordingly.)

The grid is initially invisible, by virtue of a call to grid.setVisible(false) on line 142. We make it visible by calling grid.setVisible(true) in the tab bar's listener. We populate the grid in loadRolodex(), which begins on line 265.

Our methods—createContact(), editContact(), and createContactPanel(), which create and edit contacts by means of pop-up panels—start on line 147. Those methods create and display the pop-up panels you see in Figure 10.2 on page 305 and Figure 10.3 on page 305.

The last four methods in our application—deleteContact(), updateContact(), saveContact(), and updateRolodex()—are the CRUD methods. Each of the first three methods calls updateRolodex(), which makes an RPC to the server. That RPC returns a list of contacts. Looking at that code, you would see no indication that we're using

Hibernate on the server or, indeed, even using a database, although the fact that we're constructing a where clause is a strong indication.

Now that we've seen how the application is implemented and how it invokes RPCs on the server, let's look at the most interesting aspect of the Rolodex application, from the standpoint of this solution: using Hibernate to access the database.

com.google.gwt.user.client.ui.TabBar

- void addTab(String tabText)

  Adds a tab, with the specified text, to a tab bar.

- void addTab(String tabText, boolean asHTML)

  Like add(String tabText), adds a tab to the tab bar, but you can also specify HTML for the tab text; if you specify true for the asHTML argument, GWT treats the text as HTML.

  For instance, in our example, we could have done this: addTab("" + tabs[i] + "", true). Had we done so, the browser would display our tab text in a bold font. If instead we did addTab("" + tabs[i] + "", false), then the first tab would contain the string "A-E".

- String getTabHTML(int tabIndex)

  Returns the HTML in the tab with the associated index. If you created the tab with plain text by using addTab(String tabText) or addTab(String tabText, false), this method returns that text.

com.google.gwt.user.client.ui.TabListener

- boolean onBeforeTabSelected(SourcesTabEvents sender, int tabIndex)

  Might be better named onTabClicked, because GWT calls this method after a user clicks a tab but before GWT selects the tab.

  Notice that unlike most event handler methods, this method returns a boolean value instead of void. That boolean value tells GWT whether to actually select the tab. If you return true from this method, GWT selects the tab the user clicked. If you return false, GWT cancels the tab selection.

- void onTabSelected(SourcesTabEvents sender, int tabIndex)

  Is called by GWT immediately after it calls onBeforeTabSelected() if that method returned true. This is the method you implement to handle tab selections.

Hibernate on the Server

Fundamentally, using Hibernate requires three artifacts:

- Hibernate configuration file

- Java class representing persistent objects

- Mapping file

The configuration file tells Hibernate about our database. The Java class is a plain old Java object (POJO) that knows nothing of the fact that its objects are stored in a database. The mapping file tells Hibernate how to map Java objects to rows in a database. Let's look at each of those artifacts for our Rolodex application.

The Hibernate Configuration File

Our Rolodex application's Hibernate configuration file is listed in Listing 10.2.

Listing 10.2   hibernate.cfg.xml

```
1.<?xml version='1.0' encoding='utf-8'?>
2.<!DOCTYPE hibernate-configuration
3.    PUBLIC "-//Hibernate/Hibernate Configuration DTD 3.0//EN"
4.    "http://hibernate.sourceforge.net/hibernate-configuration-3.0.dtd">
5.
6.<hibernate-configuration>
7.   <session-factory>
8.     <property name="connection.driver_class">
9.       com.mysql.jdbc.Driver
10.    </property>
11.
12.    <property name="connection.url">
13.      jdbc:mysql://localhost/test
14.    </property>
15.
16.    <property name="show_sql">true</property>
17.
18.    <property name="dialect">
19.      org.hibernate.dialect.MySQLDialect
20.    </property>
21.
22.    <!— Enable Hibernate's automatic session management —>
23.    <property name="current_session_context_class">
24.      thread
25.    </property>
```

```
26.
27.     <!— Disable the second-level cache —>
28.     <property name="cache.provider_class">
29.        org.hibernate.cache.NoCacheProvider
30.     </property>
31.
32.     <mapping
33.        resource="com/gwtsolutions/client/Contact.hbm.xml"/>
34.   </session-factory>
35.</hibernate-configuration>
```

We're using the MySQL database in our example, so in the preceding configuration file, we set the database dialect, our connection's driver, and our database url accordingly. The database url points to a test database, which is MySQL's default database. We set Hibernate's session management to `thread` so that we don't have to bother with closing database connections, and we turn off the second-level cache because we don't need it in our simple Rolodex example.[1]

Notice that we've also set the `show_sql` property to `true` in the configuration file, which means that Hibernate will print SQL to stdout as it executes queries. In Eclipse, those printouts appear in the console window, as shown in Figure 10.5.

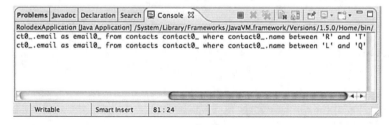

Figure 10.5   Hibernate SQL in Eclipse

That's all we need in our configuration file, so now let's look at our POJO.

The POJO Java Class

We're storing contacts in the database, so we have a corresponding `Contact` class, listed in Listing 10.3.

---

[1] The second-level cache can boost performance for applications with heavy database access. See the Hibernate documentation for more information about thread management and second-level caches.

Listing 10.3   com.gwtsolutions.client.Contact.java

```
1.package com.gwtsolutions.client;
2.
3.import com.google.gwt.user.client.rpc.IsSerializable;
4.
5.public class Contact implements IsSerializable {
6.   private Long id;
7.
8.   private String name, email;
9.
10.   public Contact() {
11.     // you must implement a no-arg constructor
12.   }
13.
14.   public Contact(Long id, String name, String email) {
15.     this.name = name;
16.     this.email = email;
17.   }
18.
19.   public void setId(Long id) {
20.     this.id = id;
21.   }
22.
23.   public Long getId() {
24.     return id;
25.   }
26.
27.   public String getName() {
28.     return name;
29.   }
30.
31.   public void setName(String name) {
32.     this.name = name;
33.   }
34.
35.   public String getEmail() {
36.     return email;
37.   }
38.
39.   public void setEmail(String email) {
40.     this.email = email;
41.   }
42.}
```

With Hibernate, classes that represent persistent objects are POJOs, but they must also be JavaBeans components, which means that they must implement a no-argument constructor and adhere to a naming convention for setters and getters. Our `Contact` class fits the bill.

Notice that our `Contact` class also implements GWT's `isSerializable` interface because GWT sends `Contact` objects from the server to the client as a result of our RPC call.

Now that we've seen the Hibernate configuration file and our POJO, let's look at our mapping file.

The Contact Mapping File

The mapping file is listed in Listing 10.4.

Listing 10.4   com.gwtsolutions.client.Contact.hbm.xml

```
1.<?xml version="1.0"?>
2.<!DOCTYPE hibernate-mapping
3.   PUBLIC "-//Hibernate/Hibernate Mapping DTD 3.0//EN"
4.   "http://hibernate.sourceforge.net/hibernate-mapping-3.0.dtd">
5.
6.<hibernate-mapping>
7.   <class name="com.gwtsolutions.client.Contact"
8.          table="contacts">
9.     <id name="id" column="id" >
10.       <generator class="native"/>
11.     </id>
12.
13.     <property name="name"/>
14.     <property name="email"/>
15.   </class>
16.</hibernate-mapping>
```

The mapping file maps our POJO class, `com.gwtsolutions.client.Contact`, to a database table named `contacts`. The `id` element declares the primary key in our table, and the `generator` property of the primary key specifies how Hibernate generates primary keys; in this case, we let MySQL generate the keys by specifying a native generator. Then we declare each property that we want saved to the database, and we're done.

We've seen the three artifacts necessary for Hibernate to store and retrieve our contacts to and from the database, but we still must do two more things to connect everything: Implement our RPC servlet and add the appropriate libraries to our project in Eclipse.

RPC Servlet Implementation

The remote servlet for CRUD operations is listed in Listing 10.5.

Listing 10.5   com.gwtsolutions.server.RolodexServiceImpl.java

```
1. package com.gwtsolutions.server;
2.
3. import java.util.List;
4.
5. import org.hibernate.HibernateException;
6. import org.hibernate.Session;
7.
8. import com.gwtsolutions.client.RolodexService;
9. import com.gwtsolutions.client.Contact;
10.import com.google.gwt.user.server.rpc.RemoteServiceServlet;
11.
12.public class RolodexServiceImpl extends RemoteServiceServlet
13.   implements RolodexService {
14.   private static final long serialVersionUID = 1L;
15.
16.   public List getContacts(String whereClause) {
17.     List contacts = null;
18.     try {
19.       Session session = HibernateUtil.getSessionFactory()
20.          .getCurrentSession();
21.       session.beginTransaction();
22.       contacts = session.createQuery("from Contact contact " +
23.         whereClause).list();
24.       session.getTransaction().commit();
25.     } catch (HibernateException e) {
26.       e.printStackTrace();
27.     }
28.     return contacts;
29.   }
30.   public void saveContact(Contact saveMe) {
31.     try {
32.       Session session = HibernateUtil.getSessionFactory()
33.          .getCurrentSession();
34.       session.beginTransaction();
35.       session.save(saveMe);
36.       session.getTransaction().commit();
37.     } catch (HibernateException e) {
38.       e.printStackTrace();
```

```
39.    }
40.  }
41.  public void updateContact(Contact updateMe) {
42.    try {
43.      Session session = HibernateUtil.getSessionFactory()
44.        .getCurrentSession();
45.      session.beginTransaction();
46.      session.update(updateMe);
47.      session.getTransaction().commit();
48.    } catch (HibernateException e) {
49.      e.printStackTrace();
50.    }
51.  }
52.  public void deleteContact(Contact deleteMe) {
53.    try {
54.      Session session = HibernateUtil.getSessionFactory()
55.        .getCurrentSession();
56.      session.beginTransaction();
57.      session.delete(deleteMe);
58.      session.getTransaction().commit();
59.    } catch (HibernateException e) {
60.      e.printStackTrace();
61.    }
62.  }
63.}
```

The four methods in the preceding class are pretty simplistic. Each one gets the Hibernate session, and within a transaction, creates, reads, updates, or deletes contacts from the database. Notice the use of the HibernateUtil class. That class, listed in Listing 10.6, is straight out of the documentation for Hibernate3.

Listing 10.6   com.gwtsolutions.server.HibernateUtil.java

```
1.package com.gwtsolutions.server;
2.
3.import org.hibernate.*;
4.import org.hibernate.cfg.*;
5.
6.public class HibernateUtil {
7.  private static final SessionFactory sessionFactory;
8.
9.  static {
10.    try {
```

continues

Listing 10.6   com.gwtsolutions.server.HibernateUtil.java   *continued*

```
11.         // Create the SessionFactory from hibernate.cfg.xml
12.         sessionFactory = new Configuration().configure()
13.            .buildSessionFactory();
14.      } catch (Throwable ex) {
15.         System.err.println(
16.            "Initial SessionFactory creation failed." + ex);
17.
18.         throw new ExceptionInInitializerError(ex);
19.      }
20.   }
21.
22.   public static SessionFactory getSessionFactory() {
23.      return sessionFactory;
24.   }
25.}
```

Like all remote servlets, our remote servlet class extends a remote interface, listed in Listing 10.7.

Listing 10.7   com.gwtsolutions.client.RolodexService.java

```
1.package com.gwtsolutions.client;
2.
3.import java.util.List;
4.
5.import com.google.gwt.user.client.rpc.RemoteService;
6.
7.public interface RolodexService extends RemoteService {
8.   public List getContacts(String range);
9.   public void deleteContact(Contact saveMe);
10. public void saveContact(Contact saveMe);
11. public void updateContact(Contact updateMe);
12.}
```

On the client, we use the asynchronous remote-service interface to make RPCs to the server that use Hibernate to update the database. That asynchronous interface is listed in Listing 10.8.

Listing 10.8   com.gwtsolutions.client.RolodexServiceAsync.java

```
1.package com.gwtsolutions.client;
2.
3.import com.google.gwt.user.client.rpc.AsyncCallback;
4.
5.public interface RolodexServiceAsync {
6.   public void getContacts(String range, AsyncCallback callback);
7.
8.   public void deleteContact(Contact saveMe,
9.       AsyncCallback callback);
10.
11.  public void saveContact(Contact saveMe,
12.       AsyncCallback callback);
13.
14.  public void updateContact(Contact updateMe,
15.       AsyncCallback callback);
16.}
```

And that's it for integrating Hibernate into our GWT applications, except for one thing: We must configure Eclipse to include our database driver and Hibernate itself.

Eclipse Configuration

Figure 10.6 shows the Java Build Path portion of the project preferences dialog box for our Rolodex project in Eclipse, where we've added an entry for the JAR file that contains our database driver.

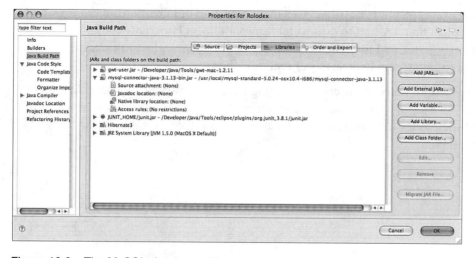

Figure 10.6   The MySQL database driver

Figure 10.7 shows the same dialog box, with a user library that contains the Hibernate3 JAR file (located in the top-level directory of the Hibernate distribution) and all the JAR files from the `lib` directory of the Hibernate distribution.

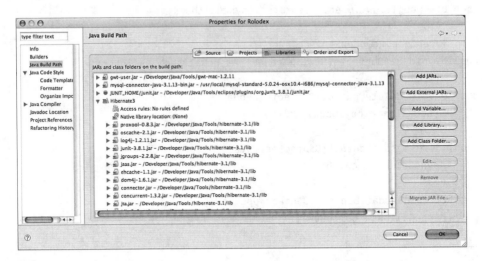

Figure 10.7   The Hibernate user library

Stuff We Covered in This Solution

Our Rolodex application covered a fair bit of ground in this solution. From strictly a UI perspective, we used a vertical panel containing a tab bar and a grid. With an RPC and subsequent updating of a grid panel, we easily achieved an Ajaxian updating of our Rolodex.

The meat of this solution, however, was the integration of Hibernate on the back end. To accomplish that, we had to do several things: define a Hibernate configuration file, implement a POJO, and map the POJO to our database table. In addition, we included the required libraries in Eclipse to put it all together.

In the real world, however, users aren't going to run your application in Eclipse, so this solution is somewhat incomplete. In our next solution, we show you how to deploy the Rolodex in an external servlet container so that you can take the Rolodex live on the Web.

Deployment to an External Server

In both hosted mode and web mode, GWT applications run in a version of Tomcat internal to GWT. In hosted mode, your application runs in the Google browser, which Google specifically implemented for GWT applications, whereas in web mode, GWT runs your application in your default browser. But regardless of whether you run your application in hosted or web mode, your application runs in the same internal version of Tomcat that's bundled with GWT.

GWT's internal version of Tomcat is fine for development, but eventually you will need to deploy your application to an external server. In fact, it's a good idea to periodically run your application in the server you plan to deploy on so that you can make sure the application behaves the same as it does in hosted mode.

Stuff You're Going to Learn

This solution explores the following aspects of deploying to an external server:

- Knowing what files and directories are required by servlet containers (page 326)

- Using Apache Ant to deploy applications to an external server (page 330)

- Running your applications in an external server (page 326)

- Using the -noserver option (page 340)

- Debugging your applications while they run in an external server (page 340)

Deploying to an external server is not rocket science, but it does require an understanding of the additional files needed by your application server to host your application. You must package your application in a directory structure suitable for deployment, along with the additional configuration and JAR files your servlet container needs. You can do that by hand, but it's not an experience that you will likely be eager to repeat, so in this solution we discuss automating that process with Apache Ant so that you can deploy your application with a simple command from your command line.

You may also want to debug your application when it's running in an external server, so we show you how to do that, too, with the -noserver option, which lets you do the seemingly impossible: debug your application as Java in a Java Virtual Machine (JVM) *after* it's been compiled to JavaScript and deployed to an external server.

External Server Directory Structure

For this solution, we explore deployment of the Rolodex application discussed in Solution 10 to Apache Tomcat, which is the official reference implementation for the Servlet specification and is also a popular choice for hosting Java-based web applications. Because servlet containers are implemented according to a single specification, you can take what you learn in this solution and apply it to any other servlet container, such as JBoss or Resin.[1] Figure 11.1 shows the Rolodex application running in the Google browser under GWT's internal version of Tomcat and also running in an external version of Tomcat.

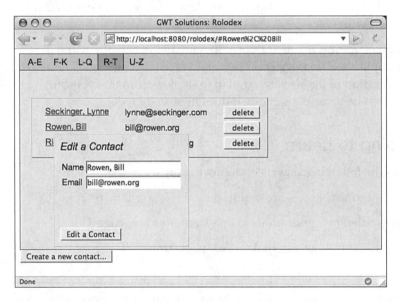

Figure 11.1 The Rolodex application running in Google's browser (left) and an external version of Tomcat (right)

ⓘ *The Compile/Browse Button in the Google Browser*

You can run your application in an external *browser*, so to speak (meaning outside the Google browser), by clicking the Compile/Browse button in the Google browser. When you click that button, GWT launches your application in your default browser. But notice the URL in the browser's address bar: You are still running on port 8888. That port points back to GWT's internal version of Tomcat, so although you are running outside the Google browser in web mode, you are not running in an external server.

---

[1] For the most part. Some things, like XML files that point the servlet container to your application, are server specific and are not defined in the Servlet specification.

When your applications are running in hosted mode, they are running in a Java Virtual Machine (JVM), which is why you can debug your Java code in an IDE like Eclipse or IDEA. However, when you click the Compile/Browse button, GWT compiles your Java code to JavaScript code. You may have noticed that GWT stores that JavaScript code in a www/[application module] subdirectory, where [application module] represents your application's module name. For example, when you click the Compile/Browse button for our Rolodex application, GWT creates a directory named www/com.gwtsolutions.Rolodex, and in that directory are the HTML files that contain the compiled JavaScript code.

When you deploy to an external server, you want to augment that generated directory with directories and files that an external servlet container will need to host your application. Figure 11.2 shows before and after pictures of the www/com.gwtsolutions.Rolodex directory for our Rolodex application.

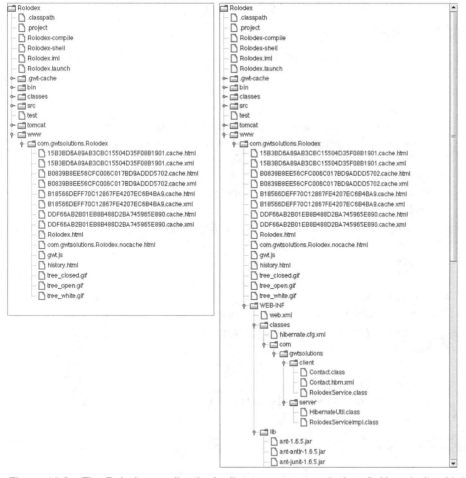

Figure 11.2   The Rolodex application's directory structure before (left) and after (right) deployment

In general, deploying to an external server requires the addition of the following directories and files (directories are prefixed with a /):

```
/WEB-INF
    web.xml (deployment descriptor)
    /classes
        /com
            (.class files for server-side Java code)
    /lib
        (required JAR files)
```

Everything your external server needs is contained in a directory named WEB-INF, which stands for web information. In that directory, you must have an XML configuration file named web.xml, otherwise known as your deployment descriptor. The deployment descriptor for the Rolodex application is listed in Listing 11.1.

Listing 11.1   Rolodex/src/web.xml

```
1.<?xml version="1.0" encoding="UTF-8"?>
2.
3.<web-app version="2.4"
4.          xmlns="http://java.sun.com/xml/ns/j2ee"
5.          xmlns:xsi="http://www.w3.org/2001/XMLSchema-instance"
6.          xsi:schemaLocation="http://java.sun.com/xml/ns/j2ee
Âhttp://java.sun.com/xml/ns/j2ee/web-app_2_4.xsd" >
7.     <servlet>
8.        <servlet-name>Rolodex Service</servlet-name>
9.        <servlet-class>
10.           com.gwtsolutions.server.RolodexServiceImpl
11.        </servlet-class>
12.     </servlet>
13.
14.     <servlet-mapping>
15.        <servlet-name>Rolodex Service</servlet-name>
16.        <url-pattern>/rolodexService</url-pattern>
17.     </servlet-mapping>
18.
19.     <welcome-file-list>
20.        <welcome-file>Rolodex.html</welcome-file>
21.     </welcome-file-list>
22.</web-app>
```

The preceding deployment descriptor describes two pieces of deployment information: the Rolodex's remote servlet that accesses a database via Hibernate (see Solution 10 for more about that servlet) and the application's welcome file, which is loaded by your servlet container when someone first accesses your application.

Besides a deployment descriptor, you need a few more things to satisfy your external server: Java class files for your server-side code; required configuration files for third-party software such as Hibernate (thus the `hibernate.cfg.xml` file listed in Figure 11.2); and requisite JAR files that contain compiled Java classes and other assorted sundries for your third-party software.

In all, here are the required steps to get from the left-hand picture in Figure 11.2 to the right-hand picture:

- Create a `WEB-INF` directory in `www/com.gwtsolutions.Rolodex`.

- Create a `WEB-INF/web.xml` file, known as a deployment descriptor.

- Create a `WEB-INF/classes` directory to contain server-side class files.

- Copy to `WEB-INF/classes` those files, such as Hibernate configuration files, that need to be on your classpath.

- Compile all server-side Java classes and copy the corresponding `.class` files to `WEB-INF/classes`.

- Create a `WEB-INF/lib` directory to contain application-specific JAR files.

- Copy the `gwt-servlet.jar` file to `WEB-INF/lib`.

- Copy other JAR files required by third-party software to `WEB-INF/lib`.

Performing those steps by hand is a real chore, so our next order of business is to automate that process.

 What JAR Files Go in the WEB-INF/lib Directory?
Exactly what JAR files are required in `/WEB-INF/lib` depends on the needs of your application. For example, the Rolodex application, because it uses Hibernate, requires the `hibernate3.jar` file found in `$HIBERNATE_HOME` and all the JAR files in `$HIBERNATE_HOME/lib`.

Use of Ant to Automate the Build Process

Apache's Ant is, in many respects, a make utility for Java programs, but it's ostensibly much friendlier than make. Figure 11.3 shows the homepage for Ant.

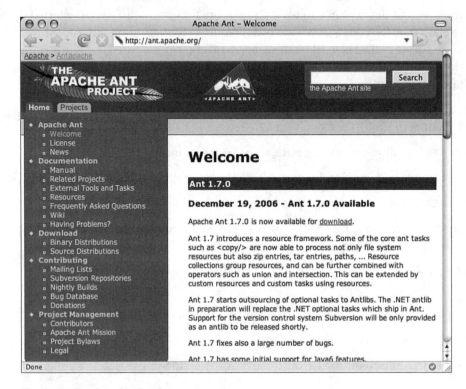

Figure 11.3   Apache Ant homepage

Using Ant is pretty simple. You create a build file, typically named build.xml, and then run the ant command from a command-line window. Figure 11.4 catches us in the act of using Ant to deploy the Rolodex application.

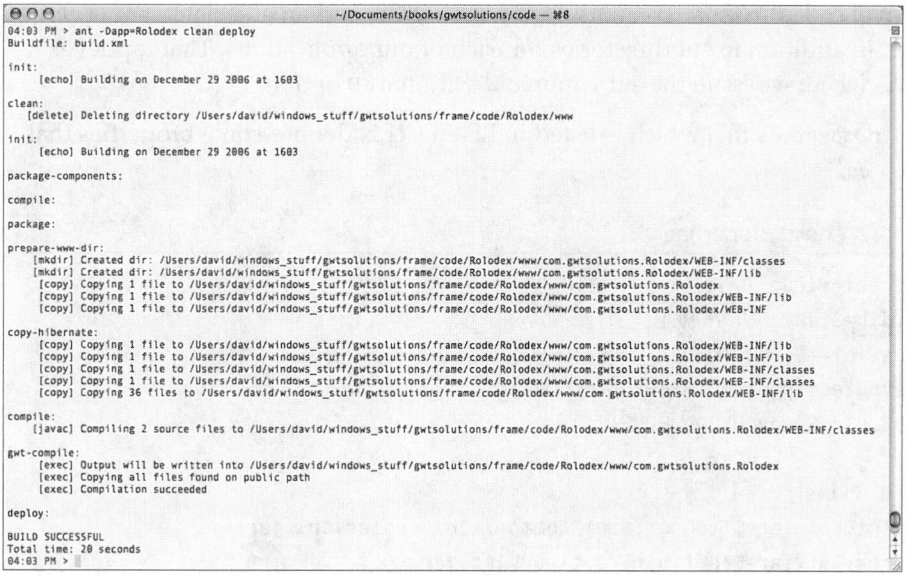

```
●○○                              ~/Documents/books/gwtsolutions/code — ⌘8
04:03 PM > ant -Dapp=Rolodex clean deploy
Buildfile: build.xml

init:
     [echo] Building on December 29 2006 at 1603

clean:
   [delete] Deleting directory /Users/david/windows_stuff/gwtsolutions/frame/code/Rolodex/www

init:
     [echo] Building on December 29 2006 at 1603

package-components:

compile:

package:

prepare-www-dir:
    [mkdir] Created dir: /Users/david/windows_stuff/gwtsolutions/frame/code/Rolodex/www/com.gwtsolutions.Rolodex/WEB-INF/classes
    [mkdir] Created dir: /Users/david/windows_stuff/gwtsolutions/frame/code/Rolodex/www/com.gwtsolutions.Rolodex/WEB-INF/lib
     [copy] Copying 1 file to /Users/david/windows_stuff/gwtsolutions/frame/code/Rolodex/www/com.gwtsolutions.Rolodex
     [copy] Copying 1 file to /Users/david/windows_stuff/gwtsolutions/frame/code/Rolodex/www/com.gwtsolutions.Rolodex/WEB-INF/lib
     [copy] Copying 1 file to /Users/david/windows_stuff/gwtsolutions/frame/code/Rolodex/www/com.gwtsolutions.Rolodex/WEB-INF

copy-hibernate:
     [copy] Copying 1 file to /Users/david/windows_stuff/gwtsolutions/frame/code/Rolodex/www/com.gwtsolutions.Rolodex/WEB-INF/lib
     [copy] Copying 1 file to /Users/david/windows_stuff/gwtsolutions/frame/code/Rolodex/www/com.gwtsolutions.Rolodex/WEB-INF/lib
     [copy] Copying 1 file to /Users/david/windows_stuff/gwtsolutions/frame/code/Rolodex/www/com.gwtsolutions.Rolodex/WEB-INF/classes
     [copy] Copying 1 file to /Users/david/windows_stuff/gwtsolutions/frame/code/Rolodex/www/com.gwtsolutions.Rolodex/WEB-INF/classes
     [copy] Copying 36 files to /Users/david/windows_stuff/gwtsolutions/frame/code/Rolodex/www/com.gwtsolutions.Rolodex/WEB-INF/lib

compile:
    [javac] Compiling 2 source files to /Users/david/windows_stuff/gwtsolutions/frame/code/Rolodex/www/com.gwtsolutions.Rolodex/WEB-INF/classes

gwt-compile:
     [exec] Output will be written into /Users/david/windows_stuff/gwtsolutions/frame/code/Rolodex/www/com.gwtsolutions.Rolodex
     [exec] Copying all files found on public path
     [exec] Compilation succeeded

deploy:

BUILD SUCCESSFUL
Total time: 20 seconds
04:03 PM >
```

Figure 11.4   Deploying the Rolodex application

In Figure 11.4, we executed the ant command like this:

```
ant -Dapp=Rolodex clean deploy
```

The -D specifies a command-line argument—app=Rolodex—that we use in our build file to determine which application from GWT Solutions source code to deploy. We do that because we have multiple applications and we typically only deploy one at a time. Figure 11.5 shows (an incomplete version of) the directory structure for GWT Solutions applications.

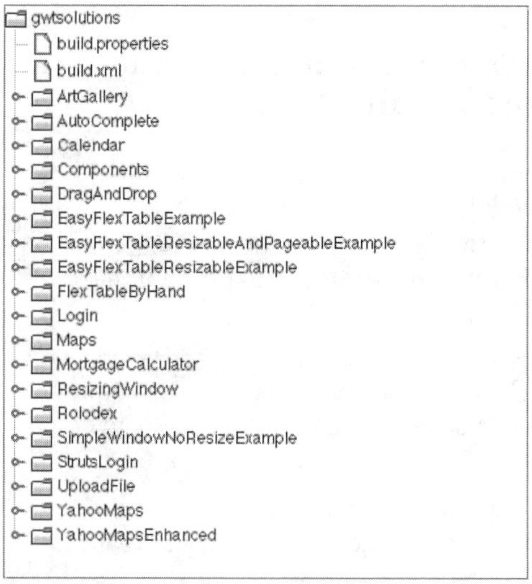

```
gwtsolutions
    build.properties
    build.xml
  ○ ArtGallery
  ○ AutoComplete
  ○ Calendar
  ○ Components
  ○ DragAndDrop
  ○ EasyFlexTableExample
  ○ EasyFlexTableResizableAndPageableExample
  ○ EasyFlexTableResizableExample
  ○ FlexTableByHand
  ○ Login
  ○ Maps
  ○ MortgageCalculator
  ○ ResizingWindow
  ○ Rolodex
  ○ SimpleWindowNoResizeExample
  ○ StrutsLogin
  ○ UploadFile
  ○ YahooMaps
  ○ YahooMapsEnhanced
```

Figure 11.5   Directory structure for GWT Solutions source code

Our top-level code directory contains our `build.xml` file and an associated `build.prop-erties` file, in addition to subdirectories for each of our applications. That top-level directory is where we issue the `ant` command with the `-D` option.

The `build.properties` file, which is listed in Listing 11.2, defines some properties that are used in `build.xml`.

Listing 11.2   build.properties

```
1. # Directories
2. gwt.dir=${env.GWT_HOME}
3. tomcat.dir=${env.TOMCAT_HOME}
4. hibernate.dir=${env.HIBERNATE_HOME}
5. mysql.dir=${env.MYSQL_HOME}
6.
7. # JAR files
8. servlet.api.jar=${tomcat.dir}/common/lib/servlet-api.jar
9. gwt.servlet.jar=${gwt.dir}/gwt-servlet.jar
10.hibernate3.jar=${hibernate.dir}/hibernate3.jar
11.mysql.driver.jar=${mysql.dir}/mysql-connector-java-3.1.13/
Âmysql-connector-java-3.1.13-bin.jar
```

Our build file needs to access the following JAR files:

- The `servlet-api` JAR

- The `gwt-servlet` JAR

- The `hibernate3` JAR

- The JAR file for the MySQL database driver

Additionally, our build file must know where Hibernate is located on our hard drive so that it can access all the JAR files in `$HIBERNATE_HOME/lib`.

Choose the Correct GWT JAR File for Deployment

The GWT JAR file for *hosted mode* is `gwt-user.jar`, but when you run your application in an *external server*, you must use `gwt-servlet.jar` (both files reside in the `$GWT_HOME` directory).

The `gwt-user.jar` file contains servlet classes, so if you try to load it in a servlet container, the servlet container will refuse to load the classes in the JAR. That's because the servlet container has its own servlet classes and is understandably loath to let them be overwritten.

If you get an error message in your servlet container's log file that says `com.google.gwt.user.server.rpc.RemoteServiceServlet couldn't be loaded`, check to make sure you're using the correct JAR file.

All information concerning JAR files and the Hibernate directory is specified in `build.properties`. Directories are all accessed through *environment variables*, specified by `${env.NAME_OF_ENVIRONMENT_VARIABLE}`. Setting environment variables is operating system specific, so if you're not familiar with environment variables, consult your operating system's documentation.

Listing 11.3 shows our `build.xml` file. We discuss it in more detail on the other side of the listing, but before we go there, look at line 6 of Listing 11.3. That's where we define the environment property as env, which lets us do the `${env.NAME_OF_ENVIRONMENT_VARIABLE}` business in `build.properties`. We could have picked any name for that property as long as we used the name in the corresponding `build.properties`. On line 10 is where we actually read the `build.properties` file. Of course, line 6 must come before line 10, or we couldn't access environment variables in `build.properties`.

Also, notice that the default *target* is specified on line 1 as deploy. Ant build files consist mostly of targets, each of which does something specific. Recall that in Figure 11.4 on page 331, we ran the ant command like this:

```
ant -Dapp=Rolodex clean deploy
```

In that case, clean and deploy are targets; first we ran the clean target and then the deploy target. If instead, we did this...

```
ant -Dapp=Rolodex
```

...then Ant would run the default target, which is deploy. To see what targets are defined in our build file, you can run the ant command with the -projecthelp option, like this:

```
> ant -projecthelp
Buildfile: build.xml

Main targets:

clean               Clean everything
compile             Compile server-side Java code
copy-hibernate      Copy Hibernate files
deploy              Deploy the application
gwt-compile         Execute the GWT compiler
init                Initialize before building
package-components  Create GWT Solutions components JAR
prepare-www-dir     Copy files to ${www.subdir} directory

Default target: deploy
```

Now let's look at the build file.

Listing 11.3   build.xml

```
1.<project default="deploy">
2.
3.    <!— ///////////////// PROPERTIES \\\\\\\\\\\\\\\\\ —>
4.
5.    <!— Define the environment variable —>
6.    <property environment="env"/>
7.
8.    <!— Include properties defined in build.properties,
9.         which uses the env property defined above —>
10.   <property file="build.properties"/>
11.
12.   <!— Define pertinent directories —>
13.   <property name="app.dir" value="${basedir}/${app}"/>
14.   <property name="src.dir" value="${app.dir}/src"/>
15.   <property name="www.subdir"
16.        value="${app.dir}/www/com.gwtsolutions.${app}"/>
17.
18.   <!— Define a property that indicates whether this
19.        application uses Hibernate. That property is
20.        used in an "if" attribute of the copy-hibernate
21.        task, meaning Ant will only execute that task
22.        if the using.hibernate property is true —>
23.   <available property="using.hibernate"
24.                   file="${src.dir}/hibernate.cfg.xml"/>
25.
26.   <!— ///////////////// CLASS PATH \\\\\\\\\\\\\\\\\ —>
27.
28.   <!— The classpath is used in the compile task —>
29.   <path id="classpath">
30.
31.       <pathelement location="${servlet.api.jar}"/>
32.       <pathelement location="${gwt.servlet.jar}"/>
33.
34.       <fileset dir="${www.subdir}/WEB-INF/lib">
35.           <include name="*.jar"/>
36.       </fileset>
37.
38.   </path>
39.
40.   <!— ///////////////// TARGETS \\\\\\\\\\\\\\\\\\ —>
41.
```

```
42.    <!— Make sure this buildfile is used correctly —>
43.    <target name="init"
44.       description="Initialize before building">
45.
46.       <fail unless="app" message="Run ant -Dapp=..."/>
47.       <tstamp/>
48.       <echo message="Building on ${TODAY} at ${TSTAMP}"/>
49.
50.    </target>
51.
52.    <!— Delete the target directory and the www directory —>
53.    <target name="clean" depends="init"
54.       description="Clean everything.">
55.
56.       <delete dir="${app.dir}/www"/>
57.
58.    </target>
59.
60.    <!— Create files to www directory —>
61.    <target name="prepare-www-dir" depends="init"
62.       description="Copy files to ${www.subdir} directory">
63.
64.       <!— Create WEB-INF/classes and WEB-INF/lib dirs —>
65.       <mkdir dir="${www.subdir}/WEB-INF/classes"/>
66.       <mkdir dir="${www.subdir}/WEB-INF/lib"/>
67.
68.       <!— Copy all public files to ${www.subdir} —>
69.       <copy todir="${www.subdir}">
70.          <fileset dir="${src.dir}/com/gwtsolutions/public"/>
71.       </copy>
72.
73.       <!— Copy the GWT servlet JAR to /WEB-INF/lib —>
74.       <copy todir="${www.subdir}/WEB-INF/lib"
75.             file="${gwt.servlet.jar}"/>
76.
77.       <!— Copy web.xml to /WEB-INF —>
78.       <copy todir="${www.subdir}/WEB-INF"
79.             file="${src.dir}/web.xml"/>
80.
81.    </target>
82.
83.    <!— Copy pertinent files for Hibernate —>
84.    <target name="copy-hibernate" depends="prepare-www-dir"
```

continues

Listing 11.3   build.xml   *continued*

```
85.                if="using.hibernate"
86.      description="Copy Hibernate files">
87.
88.        <!— Copy MySQL driver JAR to WEB-INF/lib —>
89.        <copy todir="${www.subdir}/WEB-INF/lib"
90.              file="${mysql.driver.jar}"/>
91.
92.        <!— Copy Hibernate3 JAR to WEB-INF/lib —>
93.        <copy todir="${www.subdir}/WEB-INF/lib"
94.              file="${hibernate3.jar}"/>
95.
96.        <!— Copy Mapping files to target's client directory—>
97.        <copy todir="${www.subdir}/WEB-INF/classes">
98.           <fileset dir="${src.dir}"
99.              includes="**/*.hbm.xml"/>
100.        </copy>
101.
102.        <!— Copy Hibernate config file —>
103.        <copy todir="${www.subdir}/WEB-INF/classes"
104.              file="${src.dir}/hibernate.cfg.xml"/>
105.
106.        <!— Copy all Hibernate JARs to WEB-INF/lib —>
107.        <copy todir="${www.subdir}/WEB-INF/lib">
108.           <fileset dir="${hibernate.dir}/lib"
109.              includes="*.jar"/>
110.        </copy>
111.
112.    </target>
113.
114.    <!— Execute the Java compiler for server-side code —>
115.    <target name="compile" depends="copy-hibernate"
116.        description="Compile server-side Java code">
117.
118.        <javac
119.           srcdir="${src.dir}"
120.           destdir="${www.subdir}/WEB-INF/classes"
121.           debug="true"
122.           deprecation="true"
123.           excludes="**/client/*.java">
124.           <classpath refid="classpath"/>
125.        </javac>
```

```
126.
127.    </target>
128.
129.    <!— Execute the GWT compiler for client-side code —>
130.    <target name="gwt-compile" depends="init"
131.        description="Execute the GWT compiler">
132.
133.        <!— Invoke GWT compile script —>
134.        <exec executable="${app.dir}/${app}-compile"/>
135.
136.    </target>
137.
138.    <!— Create the GWT Solutions component's JAR file —>
139.    <target name="package-components" depends="init"
140.        description="Create GWT Solutions components JAR">
141.
142.      <ant dir="Components"
143.        antfile="Components.ant.xml"
144.          target="package"/>
145.
146.    </target>
147.
148.    <!— Deploy the specified application —>
149.    <target name="deploy"
150.          depends="package-components, compile, gwt-compile"
151.      description="Deploy the application">
152.
153.    </target>
154.
155.</project>
```

After processing build.properties, we define three properties: app.dir, src.dir, and www.subdir, starting on line 13 of the preceding listing. Those properties point to the application's directory, the directory that contains the source code for the Rolodex application, and the www subdirectory created by GWT when a user clicks the Compile/Browse button in the Google browser. The app.dir, src.dir, and www.subdir properties are based on the basedir property, which is where we ran the ant command, and the app property, which we specified on the command line with the -D property.

On line 23, we define a property, named using.hibernate, with the Ant available task, which sets using.hibernate to true if a hibernate.cfg.xml file exists in the source directory; otherwise, it sets that property to false. We use that property in the copy-hibernate target on line 84, which executes that target only if using.hibernate is true. That way, our build file can also be used for applications that don't use Hibernate.

Then on line 29, we define the classpath for the Java compiler, which includes the servlet API JAR, the GWT servlet JAR, and all the JAR files in the WEB-INF/lib directory.

After those preliminaries, we get to the targets. Here they are:

```
deploy << package-components, compile, gwt-compile
package-components << init
compile << copy-hibernate << prepare-www-dir << init
gwt-compile << init
```

The << symbol denotes *depends on*. Ant targets can depend on one another; in fact, one target can depend on several others, as is the case for the deploy target, which depends on the package-components, compile, and gwt-compile targets.

When you execute a target that depends on other targets, dependent targets are executed first. That means that when we execute the deploy target, Ant first executes the package-components target, but before it executes that target, it executes the init target, because package-components depends on it. So when we execute the deploy target, Ant executes targets in this order: init, package-components, prepare-www-dir, copy-hibernate, compile, gwt-compile. Notice that the init target, which three other targets depend on, is executed only once, as is the case for targets on which more than one target depends.

The package-components target uses the ant task to execute a build file in the Components directory. That build file creates a JAR file that wraps all GWT components.

Now that we've covered the preliminaries, let's briefly discuss each target in the build file.

deploy—By itself, does nothing. But it depends on three other targets: package-components, compile, and gwt-compile.

package-components—Executes an Ant build file in the Components directory with the ant task, which packages GWT Solutions components in a JAR file.

init—Gets the current time and prints a message that tells the user the date and time. Then it checks to make sure the build file was executed with -Dapp=NAME_OF_APP; if not, the task fails and the build stops with the associated error message.

compile—Compiles server-side Java classes. Note that it excludes Java classes under the client directory.

copy-hibernate—Executes only if a hibernate.cfg.xml file exists in the source directory. This target copies all pertinent Hibernate files to `WEB-INF/lib` or `WEB-INF/classes`, as appropriate.

prepare-www-dir—Creates the `WEB-INF`, `WEB-INF/lib`, and `WEB-INF/classes` directories, and copies appropriate non-Hibernate-related files to those directories.

gwt-compile—Executes the GWT compiler on the client-side Java code.

clean—Removes the www subdirectory and, recursively, all its subdirectories.

Now that we have a good grasp of the build file and how it works, let's see how we can actually run the application that our build file has stitched together.

Development Versus Deployment

Our build file creates directories required for the Rolodex application to run in an external server and puts all the associated files in the correct places. After that's accomplished, we could have added to our build file another target that creates what's known as a WAR file (for **w**eb **a**pplication a**r**chive), and we could have copied that WAR file to a deployment directory known to Tomcat.

But do you know what Tomcat does with such a WAR file? It un-WARs it, meaning that it spills the contents of the WAR file into a subdirectory of the deployment directory and then runs the application. Why should we go to the trouble—and more importantly, take the time—to create a WAR file and transfer it to the deployment directory if Tomcat is just going to un-WAR it? The answer is we should not.

Instead, we effectively extend the deployment directory by telling Tomcat where our application's *document base*, or docBase, is located. That way, Tomcat will just run our application where it resides, and we circumvent the need to create a WAR file for the application and copy it to the deployment directory, only to have Tomcat un-WAR it.

Listing 11.4 lists the Rolodex application's XML file that defines the application's document base.

Listing 11.4   rolodex.xml

```
1.<?xml version='1.0' encoding='utf-8'?>
2.<Context
3.   docBase="/Users/david/Documents/books/gwtsolutions/code/Rolodex/www/com.
âgwtsolutions.Rolodex"
4.      path="/rolodex"
5. reloadable="true">
6.</Context>
```

Now all we have to do is copy that puny XML file to `$TOMCAT_HOME/conf/Catalina/`

localhost and type localhost:8080/rolodex in the browser's address bar and off we go. But more importantly, if we make a change to our application, we do not need to redeploy the application. We make our changes, recompile, and refresh the browser. No deploying, and no waiting for the servlet container to undeploy and reload our application. That gives us Ruby on Rails-like instant turnaround after code changes.

Why Do WAR Files Exist?

 After the preceding discussion about the futility of deploying our application as a WAR file, you may wonder why WAR files even exist. The answer is that WAR files are meant to be used when an application runs on a server other than the one on which it was developed.

For example, if you implement an application at home, but you want it to run on a publicly accessible server, then you would create a WAR file and upload it to the server. But *deployment* is not meant for *development*. That fact is often lost on developers who repeatedly create and recreate WAR files that the server subsequently un-WARs. If your external server is your development machine, then instead use an XML file that extends the Tomcat deployment directory to point to your development directory.

One more thing. XML files that extend Tomcat's webapps directory, like the one in Listing 11.4, are server dependent. If you are using a servlet container other than Tomcat, check the documentation for your server to see how you can effectively extend your server's deployment directory.

Debugging Deployed Applications

In both hosted mode and web mode, server-side code is compiled into the exact same bytecode whether you're running in hosted mode in the Google browser or whether you've deployed your application to an external server. Once you've got server-side code working in hosted mode, you're set.

But recall that client-side code is compiled into JavaScript when you deploy to an external server. Wouldn't it be great if you could still debug that code by stepping through the corresponding Java code in an IDE like Eclipse or IDEA? Well, you can, and it's all thanks to the -noserver option. Here's how it works: When you run your application, you specify the -noserver option, as shown in Figure 11.6.

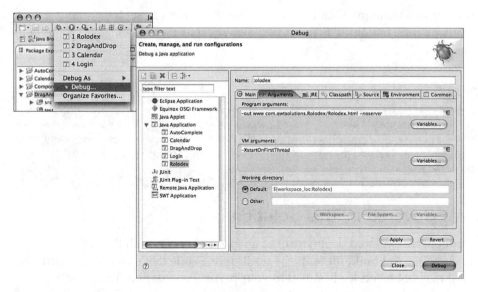

Figure 11.6   Setting the -noserver option

Then you run the application as you normally would from Eclipse or the IDE of your choice, as shown in Figure 11.7.

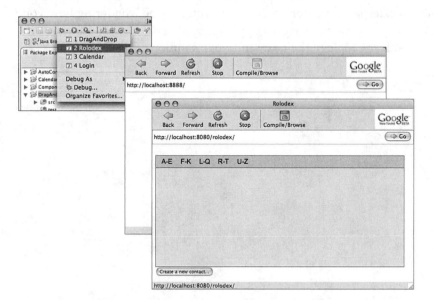

Figure 11.7   Running the Rolodex application with the -noserver option

Notice the middle picture in Figure 11.7. When the Google browser comes up, all that's in the address bar is localhost:8888. It's up to you to type the URL of your application, such as localhost:8080/rolodex, in the browser's address bar, as shown in the bottom picture.

Once you're up and running with the -noserver option, you can set breakpoints in your client-side code in your IDE and debug away, just as though you were running in hosted mode.

 Don't Forget About the -noserver Option

If you debug your application running in *an external server* with the -noserver option and then go on vacation, when you come back, you may be puzzled that all you see in the address bar of the Google browser when you run in *hosted mode* is localhost:8888. If that's the case, then you are running in -noserver mode, and you must type the URL of the application in the browser's address bar.

Stuff We Covered in This Solution

In this solution, we explored deployment to an external server with the aid of Apache's Ant. Our Ant build file suits the needs of the code that's distributed with this book, but it may not be perfectly suited to your particular situation. That's okay because you can take our build file and modify it to suit your needs. We're quite certain that you'll find the core of that build file to be very useful, even if you need to tweak some of the fringes.

Now that you know how to move your application from the internal server provided by GWT and into an external server for deployment, you may be wondering how you can integrate GWT widgets into your legacy applications that are already running on external servers. That is the topic of the next, and final, solution of this book.

GWT and Legacy Code

GWT is arguably the most exciting development for Java-based web development in a long time. As we've seen throughout this book, you can use GWT to easily develop compelling, rich user interfaces that rival the best UIs in the desktop world.

But what if you have legacy code that was implemented with another Java-based web application framework, such as Struts, Tapestry, or JavaServer Faces? In many cases, it's not feasible just to throw out that legacy code and rewrite your entire application with GWT, no matter how compelling you find GWT's impressive capabilities.

You can instead integrate GWT into your legacy applications, in two ways. You can add GWT widgets to your HTML or JavaServer Pages (JSP) pages to create oases of Ajax-goodness in the midst of a desert of user interface mediocrity, or you can out-right replace your HTML and JSP pages with full-fledged GWT views. This solution shows you how to do both.

Stuff You're Going to Learn

This solution explores the following aspects of GWT:

- Creating a GWT/Struts hybrid application (page 353)
- Using Ant to deploy a hybrid application to an external server (page 356)
- Using the root panel to plug GWT widgets into a JSP page (page 348)
- Using the GWT's HttpRequest class for Ajax requests (page 361)
- Using JSON to configure a GWT widget with data from the server (page 361)
- Coordinating legacy code with GWT widgets (page 367)
- Replacing HTML/JSP legacy views with GWT widgets (page 368)

We've got a lot of good stuff to explore in this solution, so let's start by looking at a real-world example of incorporating GWT widgets into an existing Struts-based application.

A Real-World Struts/GWT Hybrid Application

This solution is inspired by the aftermath of a GWT presentation made by David Geary at the Boulder Java Users Group in Colorado in January 2007. After the presentation, David was approached by one of the attendees who had integrated a GWT widget into a Struts-based website. That website is shown in Figure 12.1.

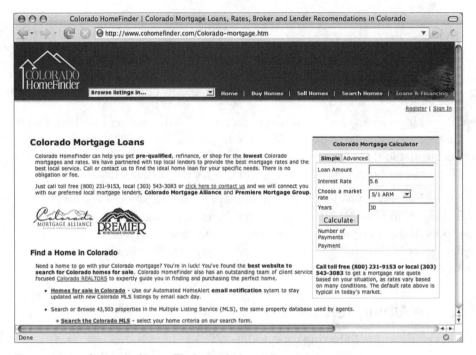

Figure 12.1   Colorado Home Finder website

The HTML page that you see in Figure 12.1 is a Struts application, and the mortgage calculator on the right is a GWT widget. The calculator lets you calculate monthly payments, given the value of your home, the term of the mortgage, and the term's associated mortgage rate. Of course, the interest rate and term are related; for example, if you take out a 30-year mortgage, you will most likely have a different interest rate than for a 15-year mortgage.

The Colorado Home Finder website not only embeds a GWT widget in an HTML page in a Struts application but it also dynamically configures the calculator's interest rate when a user selects a term from the drop-down list. It does that by *invoking a servlet that returns JavaScript Object Notation (JSON) to the client*, which then parses the JSON response to configure the calculator. If that isn't cool, we don't know what is.

We obtained permission from the folks at Colorado Home Finder to use the mortgage calculator for our book and to show you the code, but to be honest, it's not the mortgage calculator widget itself that is the most interesting part of the website. In fact, we don't even list all the code for the calculator (see Listing 12.9 on page 20 for a severely truncated listing of the calculator). The interesting part is the integration between Struts and GWT.

Also, it isn't practical to show you all of the code for Colorado Home Finder, so instead, we developed a simple Struts application and embedded the mortgage calculator into our application to distill the essentials of integrating GWT widgets into a Struts-based application.

 You Can Integrate GWT with Other Legacy Applications, Too

Although we use Struts exclusively to demonstrate integrating GWT with legacy code in this solution, you can apply the principles we discuss no matter what your Java-based web application framework is, as long as you use HTML or JSP for your views. So, for example, if you have legacy applications written in Tapestry or JavaServer Faces, you can apply what you learn in this solution to your applications.

Two Levels of Integration

In this solution, we discuss integrating self-contained Ajax functionality in an existing Struts application. If you want Ajax functionality that's integrated into legacy code[md]for example, GWT widgets that invoke Struts action methods using GWT RPC—then that's a deeper level of integration than what we explore in this solution.

Fortunately, GWT has enough mindshare that there are already integration projects for Struts and other frameworks, such as JavaServer Faces (JSF). See http://swik.net/ GWT-Plugin for Struts integration and https://ajax4jsf.dev.java.net/nonav/ajax/gwt/ gwt-cdk.html for JSF integration.

A Simple Struts Application

We start with a simple Struts login application, shown in Figure 12.2, and then we incorporate the GWT mortgage calculator into that application.

Figure 12.2 shows a successful login, and although this is a simple Struts application, it is, nevertheless, fairly robust. For example, we use the Struts validator to perform client-side validation of the name and password fields. If either of those fields is not filled in when the form is submitted, the application presents a JavaScript alert to the user, as shown in Figure 12.3.

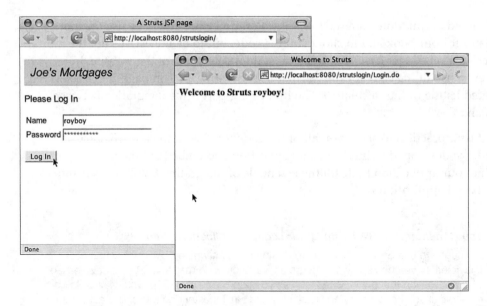

Figure 12.2   A simple Struts login application

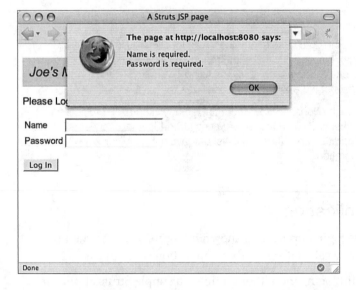

Figure 12.3   Struts validator in action

In addition to client-side validation, our application also features server-side validation of the name and password fields, as shown in Figure 12.4.

To give you a feel for the big picture of this Struts application, we show the application's files and directories in Figure 12.5.

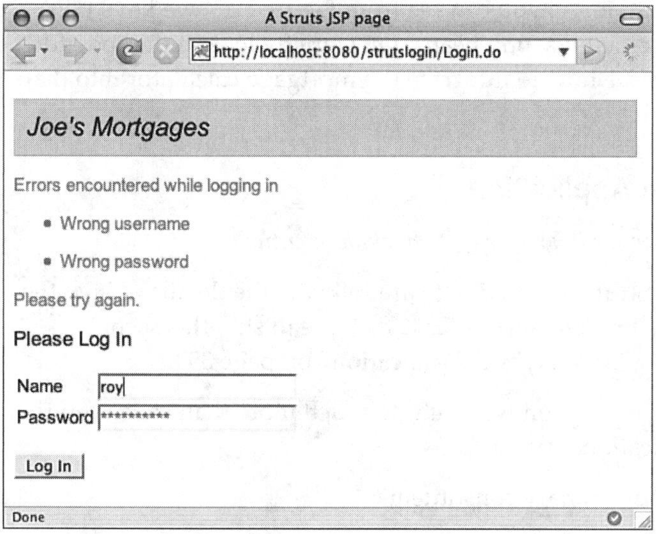

Figure 12.4 Backing up JavaScript validation with server-side validation

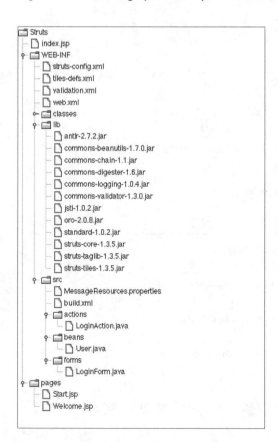

Figure 12.5 The files and directories for the Struts application

This is a standard Struts application. As you can see from Figure 12.5, we have JSP pages, backing beans, form beans, and action beans. Let's briefly look at the code for our Struts application and then see how to integrate the mortgage calculator into that application.

Code for the Struts Login Application

This section is meant to be skimmed, or if you prefer, to be skipped entirely.

If you're already familiar with Struts or you don't care to know the details of how the Struts part of our application is implemented, please feel free to skip this section entirely and move on to "GWT/Struts Hybrid Application" on page 353.

This is not a Struts book, so in this section we don't do much more than show you the main pieces of our Struts application.

Struts applications comprise four primary constituents:

- JSP pages
- Backing beans
- Form beans
- Action beans

Let's look at those pieces for our login application.

JSP Pages

We have two JSP pages, one for the login page and another for the welcome page. Both are shown in Figure 12.2 on page 346.

Listing 12.1 lists `Start.jsp`, which is the login page.

Listing 12.1   Start.jsp

```
1.<%@ page contentType="text/html;charset=UTF-8"
2.         language="java" %>
3.<%@ taglib uri="http://struts.apache.org/tags-bean"
4.           prefix="bean" %>
5.<%@ taglib uri="http://struts.apache.org/tags-html"
6.           prefix="html" %>
7.<%@ taglib uri="http://struts.apache.org/tags-logic"
8.           prefix="logic" %>
9.
10.<%@ taglib uri='http://java.sun.com/jstl/fmt' prefix='fmt' %>
11.
```

```
12.<html>
13.  <head>
14.    <title>
15.      <fmt:message key="login.windowTitle"/>
16.    </title>
17.  </head>
18.
19.  <body>
20.    <p>
21.      <div class="loginTitle">
22.        <fmt:message key='login.title'/>
23.      </div>
24.    </p>
25.
26.    <logic:messagesPresent>
27.      <font color='red'>
28.        <fmt:message key='login.errors.header'/>
29.        <html:errors property='login.name.prompt'/>
30.        <html:errors property='login.password.prompt'/>
31.        <fmt:message key='login.errors.footer'/>
32.      </font>
33.    </logic:messagesPresent>
34.
35.    <p><font size='4'>
36.      <fmt:message key='login.heading'/>
37.    </font>
38.
39.    <p>
40.
41.    <html:form action='/Login' focus='username'
42.        onsubmit="return validateLoginForm(this);">
43.    <table>
44.      <tr>
45.        <td>
46.          <fmt:message key='login.name.prompt'/>
47.        </td>
48.
49.        <td>
50.          <html:text property='username'/>
51.        </td>
52.      </tr>
53.
54.      <tr>
```

Listing 12.1   Start.jsp   *continues*

```
55.          <td>
56.            <fmt:message key='login.password.prompt'/>
57.          </td>
58.
59.          <td>
60.            <html:password property='password'/>
61.          </td>
62.        </tr>
63.      </table>
64.
65.      <p>
66.        <html:submit>
67.          <fmt:message key='login.submitButton.prompt'/>
68.        </html:submit>
69.      </html:form>
70.      <html:javascript formName='loginForm'/>
71.    </body>
72.</html>
```

The preceding JSP page uses JSP tags from the Struts tag libraries to create the login page. We use the Struts validator to perform client-side validation for the name and password fields. We also use tags from the JSP Standard Tag Library (JSTL) to localize text.

Listing 12.2 shows the JSP page for the welcome view.

Listing 12.2   Welcome.jsp

```
1.<%@ taglib uri="http://struts.apache.org/tags-bean"
2.            prefix="bean" %>
3.<%@ taglib uri="http://struts.apache.org/tags-html"
4.            prefix="html" %>
5.
6.<%@ taglib uri='http://java.sun.com/jstl/core' prefix='c' %>
7.<%@ taglib uri='http://java.sun.com/jstl/fmt' prefix='fmt' %>
8.
9.<html:html>
10.    <head>
11.      <title>
12.        <bean:message key="welcome.title"/>
13.      </title>
14.      <html:base/>
```

```
15.  </head>
16.
17.  <body>
18.    <h3>
19.      <fmt:message key='welcome.title'/>
20.      <c:out value='${user.name}'/>!
21.    </h3>
22.
23.  </body>
24.</html:html>
```

Once again, we use Struts and JSTL tags to create a view.

That's it for the JSP pages; now let's look at the Java classes.

The Backing Bean, the Form Bean, and the Action Bean

Our application has one backing bean, so named because it *backs* a JSP page, meaning that it stores bean properties that can be manipulated in the corresponding JSP page. That bean is listed in Listing 12.3.

Listing 12.3   beans.User

```
1.package beans;
2.
3.public class User {
4.   private String name;
5.
6.   public User(String name) {
7.     this.name = name;
8.   }
9.   public String getName() {
10.     return name;
11.   }
12.   public void setName(String name) {
13.     this.name = name;
14.   }
15.}
```

The User class is a simple implementation of a bean that stores the name and password entered in the login page.

Listing 12.4 lists the application's form bean.

Listing 12.4   forms.LoginForm

```
1.package forms;
2.
3.import org.apache.struts.action.*;
4.import org.apache.struts.validator.DynaValidatorForm;
5.
6.import javax.servlet.http.HttpServletRequest;
7.
8.public class LoginForm extends DynaValidatorForm {
9.   public ActionErrors validate(ActionMapping mapping,
10.       HttpServletRequest request) {
11.     String name = (String) get("username");
12.     String pwd = (String) get("password");
13.     ActionErrors errors = new ActionErrors();
14.
15.     if (!name.equals("royboy"))
16.       errors.add("login.name.prompt", new ActionMessage(
17.           "bad.username"));
18.
19.     if (!pwd.equals("ilovestruts"))
20.       errors.add("login.password.prompt", new ActionMessage(
21.           "bad.password"));
22.     return errors;
23.   }
24.}
```

The form bean validates the name and password. If those values are valid, the bean returns an empty error object; if not, it returns an error object with error messages. Struts knows what to do with that error object and moves on to the action bean, listed in Listing 12.5, if there are no errors. Otherwise, in the case of a bad name/password combination, Struts returns to the login page and shows the errors to the user.

Listing 12.5   actions.LoginAction

```
1. package actions;
2.
3. import org.apache.struts.action.*;
4.
5. import javax.servlet.http.HttpServletRequest;
6. import javax.servlet.http.HttpServletResponse;
7.
```

```
8. import beans.User;
9.
10.public class LoginAction extends Action {
11.   public ActionForward execute(ActionMapping mapping,
12.       ActionForm form, HttpServletRequest request,
13.       HttpServletResponse response)
14.       throws java.io.IOException,
15.       javax.servlet.ServletException {
16.
17.     String name =
18.         (String) ((DynaActionForm) form).get("username");
19.     User user = new User(name);
20.     request.getSession().setAttribute("user", user);
21.     return mapping.findForward("success");
22.
23.   }
24.}
```

If the action bean is invoked by Struts, that means validation passed on both the client and the server, so the action bean creates an instance of our backing bean and stores the name and password in the backing bean. Then the action bean forwards the request to the view associated with login success. That view is the welcome JSP page, which subsequently accesses those properties of the backing bean to generate a warm welcome.

We should mention that we've omitted some of our Struts application, mostly XML configuration files. We spare you those details here, but if you're interested, you can find them in the code that accompanies this book.

GWT/Struts Hybrid Application

Now that we've seen an overview of our Struts application, let's see how we can integrate the mortgage calculator into our application. We create a GWT/Struts *hybrid* application, which is half Struts and half GWT.

Figure 12.6 shows the login page for our hybrid application. Visually, that login page is nearly identical to the login page for our plain-vanilla Struts application, except for the Try Our Mortgage Calculator[1] button. In the code for the login page, we've made a handful of changes to integrate our mortgage calculator. We get to that code listing in short order, but if you are curious now, look at Listing 12.6 on page 357.

---

[1] For readability, we capitalize this and other button names even though they're not capitalized onscreen.

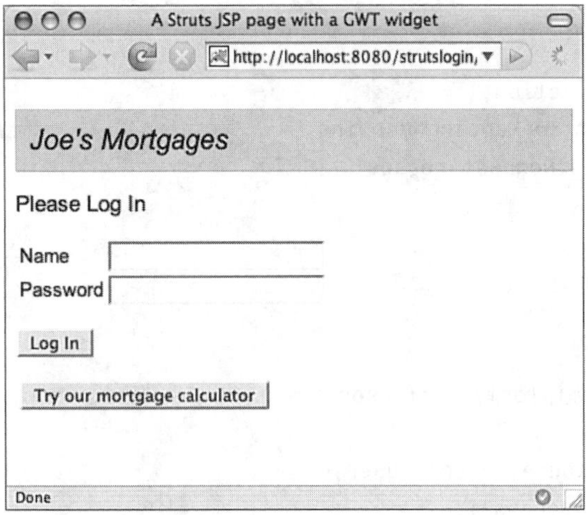

Figure 12.6   Hybrid login page

When you click the Try Our Mortgage Calculator button, the calculator appears as an Ajax update. Thanks to the magic of GWT, the JSP page is not redrawn, but rather the mortgage calculator just suddenly appears beneath the button, as shown in the left picture in Figure 12.7.

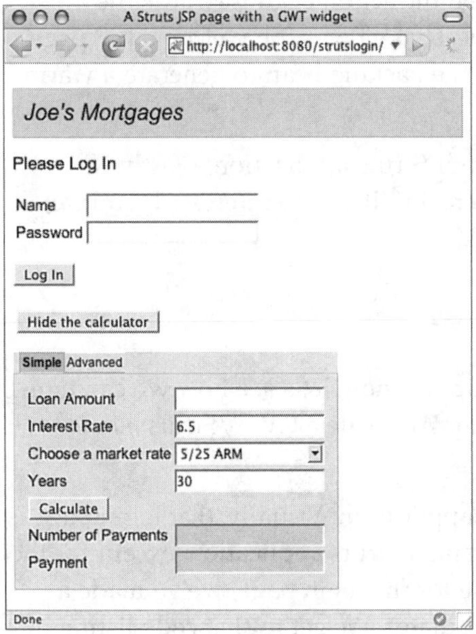

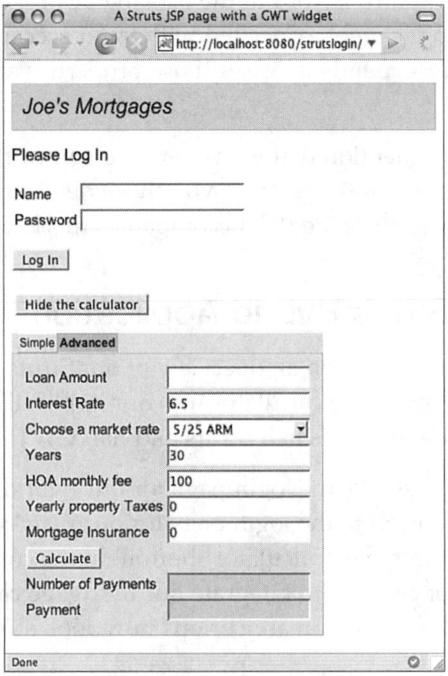

Figure 12.7   Mortgage calculator at work

Notice that after the calculator appears in the page, the text of our Try Our Mortgage Calculator button changes to Hide The Calculator. Actually, that's not entirely accurate; instead, we replace the Try Our Mortgage Calculator button with a Hide The Calculator button. We show you how we did that in "Hybrid Application's Code" on page 357. Regardless, that sleight of hand is also attributable to GWT.

The calculator itself also contributes some Ajaxian goodness by delivering both a simple and advanced version of the calculator, as illustrated in Figure 12.7. Users can switch between the two versions of the calculator by clicking on the tabs in the calculator's tab panel widget.

If a user clicks the Hide The Calculator button, we perform another Ajaxian update to return the login page to its original state, shown in Figure 12.6.

Hybrid Application's Files and Directories

Before we discuss the code for our hybrid application, let's look at Figure 12.8 to find out what files and directories the application contains.

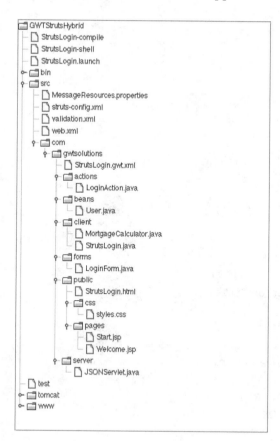

Figure 12.8   Files and directories for the hybrid application

Figure 12.8 shows the hybrid nature of our application. As you can see, we have a standard GWT directory structure and associated files, and we also have Struts-related files, such as JSP pages, beans, and XML files, in the mix. To run our hybrid application in an external server, such as Tomcat, we use Apache's Ant.

Ant Build File, Modified to Incorporate Struts

In Solution 11, we showed you how to deploy GWT applications to an external server, so we don't cover that ground again. Given the Ant build file that we discuss in that solution, we only had to make a small addition to account for Struts. That addition is shown in the following truncated listing of our Ant build file:

```
<project default="deploy">
   ...
   <available property="using.struts"
                  file="${src.dir}/struts-config.xml"/>
   ...
   <!— Copy pertinent files for Struts —>
   <target name="copy-struts" depends="prepare-www-dir"
              if="using.struts"
     description="Copy Struts files">

      <!— Copy Struts config file —>
      <copy todir="${www.subdir}/WEB-INF/classes"
            file="${src.dir}/MessageResources.properties"/>

      <!— Copy Validation config file —>
      <copy todir="${www.subdir}/WEB-INF"
            file="${src.dir}/validation.xml"/>

      <!— Copy Tiles config file —>
      <copy todir="${www.subdir}/WEB-INF"
            file="${src.dir}/tiles-defs.xml"
                            failonerror="false"/>

      <!— Copy Struts config file —>
      <copy todir="${www.subdir}/WEB-INF"
            file="${src.dir}/struts-config.xml"/>

      <!— Copy all Struts JARs to WEB-INF/lib —>
      <copy todir="${www.subdir}/WEB-INF/lib">
         <fileset dir="${struts.dir}/lib"
            includes="*.jar"/>
```

```
        </copy>
      </target>
    ...
</project>
```

Our updated build file adds one new target that is executed only if a Struts configuration file, named struts-config.xml, exists in the src directory. That target copies the relevant XML configuration files, a properties file for internationalization, and the Struts JAR files to their appropriate locations so that the external server can find them. Our Ant build file's targets that are unrelated to Struts handle all the other files in our hybrid application. See Solution 11 for information about those other targets.

Hybrid Application's Code

Now that we've seen the files and directories in our hybrid application and the Ant target that makes them available to an external server, it's time to look at the integration of GWT and Struts at the code level.

We modify our login JSP page (Start.jsp) to incorporate the mortgage calculator. In general, three steps integrate GWT into a JSP or HTML page:

- Add a meta tag to the HTML or JSP file that refers to your GWT module.

- Add a JavaScript script tag to the HTML or JSP file that includes gwt.js.

- Add HTML elements to the HTML or JSP page to act as *slots*.

The preceding steps make perfect sense when you realize that a pure GWT application (meaning one that is not a hybrid of GWT and legacy code) is, in the final analysis, just an HTML file with some GWT additions. All we need to do is incorporate those additions to our Struts JSP page. That JSP page is listed in Listing 12.6.

Listing 12.6   start.jsp for the Hybrid Application

```
1. <%@ page contentType="text/html;charset=UTF-8"
2.          language="java" %>
3. <%@ taglib uri="http://struts.apache.org/tags-bean"
4.          prefix="bean" %>
5. <%@ taglib uri="http://struts.apache.org/tags-html"
6.          prefix="html" %>
7. <%@ taglib uri="http://struts.apache.org/tags-logic"
8.          prefix="logic" %>
9.
10.<%@ taglib uri='http://java.sun.com/jstl/fmt' prefix='fmt' %>
11.
12.<html>
```

continues

Listing 12.6   start.jsp for the Hybrid Application   *continued*

```
13.    <head>
14.      <title>
15.         <fmt:message key="login.windowTitle"/>
16.      </title>
17.    </head>
18.
19.    <meta name='gwt:module'
20.        content='com.gwtsolutions.StrutsLogin'>
21.
22.    <body>
23.      <p>
24.        <div class="loginTitle">
25.           <fmt:message key='login.title'/>
26.        </div>
27.      </p>
28.
29.      <script language="javascript" src="gwt.js"></script>
30.
31.      <logic:messagesPresent>
32.        <font color='red'>
33.           <fmt:message key='login.errors.header'/>
34.           <html:errors property='login.name.prompt'/>
35.           <html:errors property='login.password.prompt'/>
36.           <fmt:message key='login.errors.footer'/>
37.        </font>
38.      </logic:messagesPresent>
39.
40.      <p><font size='4'>
41.         <fmt:message key='login.heading'/>
42.      </font>
43.
44.      <p>
45.
46.      <html:form action='/Login' focus='username'
47.          onsubmit="return validateLoginForm(this);">
48.      <table>
49.        <tr>
50.          <td>
51.             <fmt:message key='login.name.prompt'/>
52.          </td>
53.
54.          <td>
```

```
55.                <html:text property='username'/>
56.            </td>
57.        </tr>
58.
59.        <tr>
60.          <td>
61.            <fmt:message key='login.password.prompt'/>
62.          </td>
63.
64.          <td>
65.              <html:password property='password'/>
66.          </td>
67.        </tr>
68.      </table>
69.
70.      <p>
71.        <html:submit>
72.            <fmt:message key='login.submitButton.prompt'/>
73.        </html:submit>
74.      </html:form>
75.      <html:javascript formName='loginForm'/>
76.
77.      <p>
78.        <table>
79.        <tr><td><div id="showButton"/></td></tr>
80.        <tr><td><div id="hideButton"/></td></tr>
81.        </table>
82.      </p>
83.
84.      <p>
85.        <div id="calculator"/>
86.      </p>
87.
88.    </body>
89.</html>
```

Just like the HTML page for a pure GWT application, we add to our JSP page a `meta` tag that specifies our GWT module. Then we include the standard GWT JavaScript contained in `gwt.js`.

We also add some DIVs to act as slots for three GWT widgets: the Try Our Mortgage Calculator button, the Hide The Calculator button, and the calculator itself.

When GWT processes the meta tag, it invokes our module's entry point, by virtue of the JavaScript code contained in gwt.js. The module's entry point class, listed in Listing 12.7, creates the appropriate widgets and places them in the showButton, hideButton, and calculator slots.

Listing 12.7   com.gwtsolutions.client.StrutsLogin.java

```java
1.package com.gwtsolutions.client;
2.
3.import com.google.gwt.core.client.EntryPoint;
4.import com.google.gwt.user.client.ui.*;
5.
6.public class StrutsLogin implements EntryPoint {
7.
8.   public void onModuleLoad() {
9.      final MortgageCalculator mc = new MortgageCalculator();
10.     final Button showButton =
11.         new Button("Try our mortgage calculator");
12.     final Button hideButton =
13.         new Button("Hide the calculator");
14.
15.     RootPanel.get("showButton").add(showButton);
16.     RootPanel.get("calculator").add(mc);
17.     RootPanel.get("hideButton").add(hideButton);
18.
19.     mc.setVisible(false);
20.     hideButton.setVisible(false);
21.
22.     showButton.addClickListener(new ClickListener() {
23.       public void onClick(Widget sender) {
24.         mc.setVisible(true);
25.         showButton.setVisible(false);
26.         hideButton.setVisible(true);
27.       }
28.     });
29.     hideButton.addClickListener(new ClickListener() {
30.       public void onClick(Widget sender) {
31.         mc.setVisible(false);
32.         showButton.setVisible(true);
33.         hideButton.setVisible(false);
34.       }
35.     });
36.   }
37.}
```

The preceding listing is straightforward GWT code. We create the mortgage calculator and the two buttons and place them in their respective slots, starting on line 9.

Then we hide the calculator and the Hide The Calculator button (showButton) and add a click listener to the Try Our Mortgage Calculator button. That click listener shows the calculator, hides the Try Our Mortgage Calculator button, and shows the Hide The Calculator button.

Finally, we add a click listener to the Hide The Calculator button (hideButton) that hides the calculator and the Hide The Calculator button and shows the Try Our Mortgage Calculator button.

Fundamentally, this is pretty simple. We add some GWT-related directives to a JSP page, which invokes our module's entry point. That entry point creates widgets, places them in the appropriate slots, and provides some event handling.

 Two Levels of Integration

In this solution, we discuss integrating self-contained Ajax functionality in an existing Struts application. If you want Ajax functionality that's integrated into legacy code—for example, GWT widgets that invoke Struts action methods using GWT RPC—then that's a deeper level of integration than what we explore in this solution.

Fortunately, GWT has enough mindshare that there are already integration projects for Struts and other frameworks, such as JavaServer Faces (JSF). See http://swik.net/GWT-Plugin for Struts integration and https://ajax4jsf.dev.java.net/nonav/ajax/gwt/gwt-cdk.html for JSF integration.

Use of JSON to Configure a GWT Widget

So now the secret's out: You know how to create a hybrid GWT/Struts application, and you know how to incorporate a GWT widget into a JSP page to add some Ajax sizzle to your Struts application. And you also know that you can apply the underlying principles to other Java-based web application frameworks, such as JavaServer Faces, that use HTML or JSP for their views.

To wrap up this solution, we visit a few peripheral topics: using the GWT's HttpRequest class to make an Ajax call to the server; using JSON to configure the mortgage calculator; and using Struts tags to influence the calculator. Finally, we touch on how you can replace your HTML or JSP views outright with GWT widgets.

Figure 12.9 shows a feature of the mortgage calculator that we've yet to discuss: synchronizing interest rates to the terms of a loan. Notice that the interest rate is different in the two pictures in Figure 12.9.

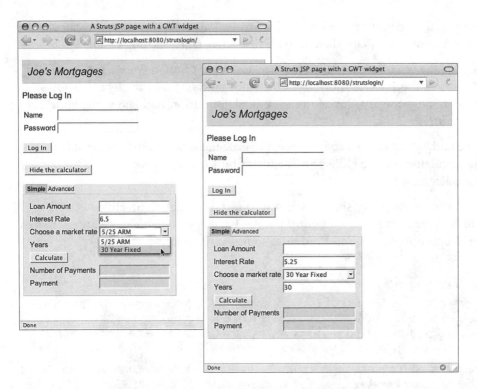

Figure 12.9   Using JSON to change interest rates depending on market rates

When you select the terms of your loan, either an 5/25 adjustable rate mortgage or a 30-year fixed rate, the mortgage calculator modifies the interest rate accordingly. Those interest rates are stored on the server and are returned to the client by a servlet in JSON format. Listing 12.8 lists the servlet.

Listing 12.8   com.gwtsolutions.server.JSONServlet.java

```
1.package com.gwtsolutions.server;
2.
3.import java.io.IOException;
4.import javax.servlet.ServletException;
5.import javax.servlet.http.HttpServlet;
6.import javax.servlet.http.HttpServletRequest;
7.import javax.servlet.http.HttpServletResponse;
8.
9.public class JSONServlet extends HttpServlet {
10.   // return interest rates.
11.   public void doGet(HttpServletRequest req,
12.       HttpServletResponse response) throws ServletException,
13.       IOException {
```

```
14.    response.getWriter().print(
15.        "{thirtyfixed: 6.50, fivearm: 5.25}");
16.  }
17.}
```

The preceding servlet simply writes the string `"{thirtyfixed: 6.50, fivearm: 5.25}"` to the HTTP response. That string is in JavaScript Object Notation (JSON) format. We chose JSON because we want to return multiple values from our servlet. Moreover, GWT provides classes that know how to parse JSON and turn them into objects we can use on the client.

Finally, we come to the mortgage calculator itself. As you might imagine from the screenshots of the calculator in this solution, its implementation is fairly long-winded. So in Listing 12.9, we list a severely truncated version of the calculator that highlights how it handles the JSON that's returned from the servlet listed in Listing 12.8. To learn how the rest of the calculator is implemented, see the code that accompanies this book.

Listing 12.9   com.gwtsolutions.client.MortgageCalculator (truncated)

```
1.package com.gwtsolutions.client;
2....
3.public class MortgageCalculator extends TabPanel {
4.  public MortgageCalculator() {
5.
6.    final Label simpleErrorLabel = new Label("");
7.    final TextBox simpleInterest = new TextBox();
8.    final ListBox simpleRateChoice = new ListBox();
9.    final Label advancedErrorLabel = new Label("");
10.    final TextBox advancedInterest = new TextBox();
11.    final ListBox advancedRateChoice = new ListBox();
12.
13.    final FlexTable simpleft =
14.        generateSimpleUI(simpleInterest, simpleRateChoice,
15.            simpleErrorLabel);
16.    ...
17.    VerticalPanel svp = new VerticalPanel();
18.    svp.add(simpleft);
19.    svp.add(simpleErrorLabel);
20.    ...
21.    add(svp, "Simple");
22.    ...
23.    selectTab(0);
24.  }
```

continues

Listing 12.9   com.gwtsolutions.client.MortgageCalculator (truncated)   *continued*

```
25.  ...
26.  private static final String RATES_URL =
27.      GWT.getModuleBaseURL() + "getRates";
28.  ...
29.  private FlexTable generateSimpleUI(final TextBox interest,
30.      final ListBox rateChoiceBox, final Label errorLabel) {
31.      ...
32.      rateChoiceBox.addChangeListener(new ChangeListener() {
33.        public void onChange(Widget sender) {
34.          HTTPRequest.asyncGet(RATES_URL, rrh);
35.        }
36.      });
37.  ...
38.  private class RatesResponseHandler implements
39.      ResponseTextHandler {
40.      private ListBox rateChoiceBox;
41.      private TextBox interest;
42.
43.      public RatesResponseHandler(ListBox rateChoiceBox,
44.          TextBox interest) {
45.        this.rateChoiceBox = rateChoiceBox;
46.        this.interest = interest;
47.      }
48.      public void onCompletion(String responseText) {
49.        boolean keepGoing = true;
50.        JSONObject jso = null;
51.        JSONValue jsv = null;
52.        try {
53.          jsv = JSONParser.parse(responseText);
54.          jso = jsv.isObject();
55.        }
56.        catch (JSONException je) {
57.          keepGoing = false;
58.          je.printStackTrace();
59.        }
60.        if (keepGoing && jso != null) {
61.          int selected = rateChoiceBox.getSelectedIndex();
62.          Set keySet = jso.keySet();
63.          Object[] keys = keySet.toArray();
64.
65.          if (keys.length == 2) { // expected
```

```
66.          JSONValue v = jso.get((String) keys[selected]);
67.          JSONNumber rate = v.isNumber();
68.          if (rate != null) {
69.              interest.setText(rate.toString());
70.          }
71.        }
72.      }
73.    }
74.  }
75.}
```

When a user selects a value from the Choose A Market Rate pull-down menu, the mortgage calculator issues an Ajax request with GWT's HTTPRequest.asyncGet static method. The URL that the asynchronous call accesses is the module base plus getRates. When that Ajax call is finished, an implementation of GWT's ResponseTextHandler receives the JSON from our servlet and uses GWT's JSON API to extract the rates and store them in the interest widget.

There's one more piece to the JSON/Ajax puzzle, and that's our servlet mapping that maps the getRates URL to our JSONServlet class. Listing 12.10 lists the deployment descriptor for our hybrid application.

Listing 12.10   web.xml

```
1.<?xml version="1.0" encoding="ISO-8859-1"?>
2.
3.<!DOCTYPE web-app PUBLIC
4.    "-//Sun Microsystems, Inc.//DTD Web Application 2.3//EN"
5.    "http://java.sun.com/dtd/web-app_2_3.dtd">
6.
7.<web-app>
8.  <display-name>Struts Blank Application</display-name>
9.  <!— Define the basename for a resource bundle for I18N —>
10.  <context-param>
11.    <param-name>
12.      javax.servlet.jsp.jstl.fmt.localizationContext
13.    </param-name>
14.
15.    <param-value>
16.      MessageResources
17.    </param-value>
18.  </context-param>
19.
```

continues

Listing 12.10   web.xml   *continued*

```
20.   <!— Standard Action Servlet Configuration —>
21.   <servlet>
22.     <servlet-name>action</servlet-name>
23.     <servlet-class>org.apache.struts.action.ActionServlet
24.     </servlet-class>
25.     <init-param>
26.       <param-name>config</param-name>
27.       <param-value>/WEB-INF/struts-config.xml</param-value>
28.     </init-param>
29.     <load-on-startup>2</load-on-startup>
30.   </servlet>
31.
32.   <!— Standard Action Servlet Mapping —>
33.   <servlet-mapping>
34.     <servlet-name>action</servlet-name>
35.     <url-pattern>*.do</url-pattern>
36.   </servlet-mapping>
37.
38.   <servlet>
39.     <servlet-name>json servlet</servlet-name>
40.     <servlet-class>com.gwtsolutions.server.JSONServlet
41.     </servlet-class>
42.     <load-on-startup>3</load-on-startup>
43.   </servlet>
44.
45.   <servlet-mapping>
46.     <servlet-name>json servlet</servlet-name>
47.     <url-pattern>/getRates</url-pattern>
48.   </servlet-mapping>
49.
50.
51.   <!— The Welcome File List —>
52.   <welcome-file-list>
53.     <welcome-file>pages/Start.jsp</welcome-file>
54.   </welcome-file-list>
55.
56. </web-app>
```

com.google.gwt.user.client.HttpRequest

* `static boolean asyncGet(String url, ResponseTextHandler handler)`

Makes an asynchronous Ajax call to the server using the HTTP GET method. After the call is finished, GWT invokes the `onCompletion` method on the specified response text handler. This method returns `true` if the Ajax call was successfully transmitted to the server, and `false` otherwise.

The `HTTPRequest` class provides another `asyncGet` method that takes a username and password. Additionally, the `HTTPRequest` class provides two analogous methods for making Ajax calls with the HTTP `POST` method. Both of those methods are named `asyncPost`. All four methods take an instance of `ResponseTextHandler` that handles the response of the Ajax request.

com.google.gwt.user.client.ResponseTextHandler

* `void onCompletion(String responseText)`

Is called by GWT after an Ajax call, invoked by one of the `HttpRequest` static methods. The string passed to the method is the HTTP response.

Legacy Code and GWT Widget Coordination

Before we wrap up this solution, and for this edition, this book, let's look at one final aspect of our hybrid application, illustrated in Figure 12.10.

Figure 12.10 shows the hybrid application after an unsuccessful login. Notice that the Try Our Mortgage Calculator button has disappeared. We decided that users shouldn't be distracted by the mortgage calculator when dealing with login errors, so we don't show the button when the application has errors. Here's the relevant code from the login JSP page:

```
...
    <logic:messagesNotPresent>
        <p>
          <table>
          <tr><td><div id="showButton"/></td></tr>
          <tr><td><div id="hideButton"/></td></tr>
          </table>
        </p>
```

```
    <p>
        <div id="calculator"/>
    </p>
  </logic:messagesNotPresent>
 </body>
</html>
```

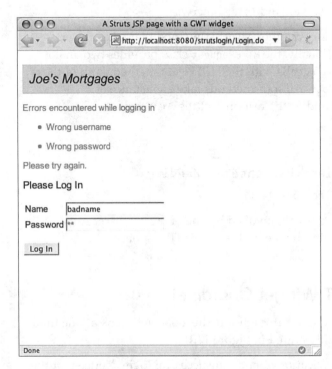

Figure 12.10   Hybrid login page after an unsuccessful login

In the preceding listing, we use the Struts `logic:messageNotPresent` tag to conditionally display our DIVs that correspond to slots for our widgets. If there are no errors, we include the DIVs; otherwise, we omit them. In effect, this is the inverse of what we do in our GWT entry point, which is to inject, if you will, GWT widgets into slots. In that case, GWT controls what widgets get displayed in the JSP page, but here Struts tags control that feature. So this hybrid business can cut both ways.

Replacement of HTML and JSP Views with GWT Views

We learned one important lesson in this solution: GWT views are just HTML pages with some special sauce that hooks up the HTML to a GWT entry point that can inject GWT widgets into the HTML. We took advantage of that fact by injecting the mortgage calculator into a JSP page.

Realize, however, that our JSP page *didn't have to have any Struts tags at all. We could have replaced the JSP in its entirety with GWT widgets.* That means you can take a legacy Struts application and selectively swap out crufty old JSP for sparkling GWT widgets. And the granularity of that swapping is entirely up to you. You could, for instance, replace one JSP page with one GWT view, or you could replace a set of JSP pages with a GWT view. Because GWT widgets are so powerful, it is perfectly reasonable to assume that one GWT view can take on the work of more than one JSP page.

> **i Note**
>
> If you swap out your legacy views entirely with GWT widgets and keep your legacy backend, then you will require deeper integration than the integration we covered in this solution. Typically, for request-based frameworks such as Struts, you will need some server-side software that can translate GWT RPCs to Struts actions. For component based frameworks such as JSF and Tapestry, you can wrap GWT widgets inside custom components. As discussed in the "Two Levels of Integration" note (page 345), there are projects to just that for Struts and JSF.

Because you can mix in self-contained Ajax functionality and integrate GWT widgets into your legacy back end, *you can incrementally move your legacy application from HTML or JSP views to GWT views replete with Ajax-powered widgets.* We think that's very enticing.

Deeper Framework Integration

The integration of GWT widgets into existing web pages, as illustrated in this solution, is simple and powerful, but it only lets you add self-contained GWT widgets to your web pages. If you want deeper integration with your framework's backend, for example by using GWT widgets to access Struts functionality on the back end, then the simplistic strategy discussed in this solution needs some additional functionality.

GWT has gained a lot of mindshare, as evidenced by the open-source support projects that have been built around GWT; in fact, there are several projects that provide the necessary glue between GWT and your framework of choice on the back end. Figure 12.11 shows the homepages for three projects that provide integration with Struts, JavaServer Faces, and Spring.

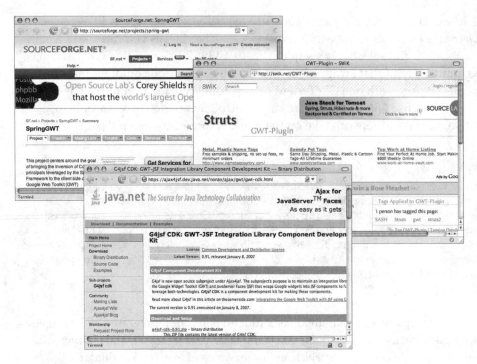

Figure 12.11   Open-source projects that integrate GWT with popular web application frameworks

Here are the homepages for those projects:

- Spring: http://sourceforge.net/projects/spring-gwt

- Struts: http://swik.net/GWT-Plugin

- JavaServer Faces: https://ajax4jsf.dev.java.net/nonav/ajax/gwt/gwt-cdk.html

The SpringGWT project lets you use Spring dependency injection with GWT, the GWT-Plugin lets you invoke methods on Struts actions using GWT widgets, and G4JSF lets you wrap GWT components in JSF components.

Stuff We Covered in This Solution

Do you have a legacy application that your manager or your clients would like to Ajaxify? In this solution, we've given you the tools to do just that. You can add GWT widgets to your HTML or JSP pages, or you can go crazy and outright replace those HTML or JSP pages entirely with GWT widgets.

It's no accident that with GWT, you can incrementally change your old-school, form-based application into a modern UI that rivals the rich interactivity provided by desktop applications while retaining legacy server-side functionality. Once again, we find that GWT is an incredibly well-thought-out framework that can accommodate your every need, provided, that is, that you've purchased the right book.

Index

Symbols